The Macroeconomics of Decarbonisation

Decarbonisation is the reduction of CO_2 emissions using low-carbon technologies, thereby lowering the output of greenhouse gasses into the atmosphere. This is essential to meet global temperature standards set by international climate agreements. To limit global warming to 1.5°C, hence avoiding the worst-case scenarios predicted by climate science, the world economy must rapidly reduce its emissions and reach climate neutrality within the next three decades. This will not be an easy journey. Shifting away from carbon-intensive production will require a historic transformation of the structure of our economies. Written by a team of academics linked to the European think tank Bruegel, *The Macroeconomics of Decarbonisation* provides a guide to the macroeconomic fundamentals of decarbonisation. It identifies the major economic transformations, both over the long and short run, and the roadblocks requiring policy intervention. It proposes a macroeconomic policy agenda for decarbonisation to achieve the climate goals of the international community.

GRÉGORY CLAEYS is a senior fellow at the Brussels-based economic think tank Bruegel, where he has been working since 2014, and an associate professor at the Conservatoire National des Arts et Métiers in Paris (LIRSA EA4603), where he has been teaching macroeconomics since 2015. His research interests include international macroeconomics and finance, central banking and European economic governance.

MARIE LE MOUEL is an affiliate fellow at Bruegel and a lecturer at Tilburg University, where she has been teaching economic growth since 2018. Her research interests include the macroeconomics of decarbonisation, green industrial policy, drivers of productivity growth and dispersion, and intangible assets.

SIMONE TAGLIAPIETRA is a senior fellow at Bruegel. He is also Professor of Energy and Climate Policy at The Johns Hopkins University – School of Advanced International Studies in Bologna and at the

Catholic University of the Sacred Heart in Milan. He is the author of *Global Energy Fundamentals* (Cambridge University Press, 2020).

GUNTRAM B. WOLFF has been the Chief Executive Officer of the German Council on Foreign Relations (DGAP) since 2022. He is also Professor of Political Economy and Public Policy at the Willy-Brandt-School of the University of Erfurt. He is a widely cited academic working on European political economy, climate, macroeconomic policy and geopolitics. From 2013 to 2022, he developed Bruegel into a globally leading institute and regularly testified at informal meetings of European Union finance ministers.

GEORG ZACHMANN is a senior fellow at Bruegel. Over the past decade, his empirical works on European energy and emission markets, regional industrial strength and the distributional effects of energy and climate policies informed policymaking. In the energy crisis Zachmann's assessments of Europe's supply situation gained prominence in the media.

The authors provide a unique insight into the short and long-term economic implications of decarbonisation, applying a rigorous and thorough approach to assessing the multidimensional facets of the transition. A "must read" for policymakers and the private sector whose combined mobilisation will be essential to achieve climate neutrality by 2050.

Alexandra Dimitrijevic – Managing Director, Global Head of Research, S&P Global Ratings

Climate action carries risks. In contrast to the devastating consequences of climate change, however, they remain manageable. "The Macroeconomics of Decarbonization", authored by distinguished thought leaders, unravels intricate dynamics underpinning the shift toward climate neutrality. If you are eager to explore advanced climate economics in a clear, accessible language, this guide is an essential read.

Ottmar Edenhofer – Director and Chief Economist, Potsdam Institute for Climate Impact Research

An important book on one of the defining challenges of our time. Getting the green transition right requires understanding the various macroeconomic implications of decarbonization on industries, jobs and budgets, and putting in place ambitious policies to drive it forward. This book sheds light on how it can be done.

Paolo Gentiloni – Commissioner for the Economy, European Commission and Former Prime Minister of Italy

If you ever dreamed to understand what economists think and know about climate policies without the technicalities, here is the book you absolutely need to read! It is clear, comprehensive and powerful.

Christian Gollier – Managing Director, Toulouse School of Economics

Achieving net zero will have profound macroeconomic implications from distributional consequences and debt sustainability concerns necessitating fiscal adjustments to stranded assets impacting financial stability. These are just some of the topics covered in this excellent and comprehensive textbook. A must read for all who want to meaningfully participate in the public debate on green transition!

Beata Javorcik – Chief Economist, European Bank for Reconstruction and Development

The *Macroeconomics of Decarbonization* is a rare, solutions-oriented look at the intersection of the clean energy transition and the systemic change that underpins it. From fostering large-scale innovation and spurring green market creation to accelerating sustainable finance, it lifts the curtain on the critical policy interventions necessary to pursue a clean, future-oriented and resilient growth model.

Ann Mettler – Vice-President Europe, Breakthrough Energy

Covering all the macroeconomic implications of climate policy in just one book seems impossible but the authors come very close. Comprehensive and well-grounded, yet accessible to a broader audience, this book takes the reader on a journey through the various economic effects of decarbonisation. With this thorough account, the authors fill an important gap!

Sabine Mauderer – Member of the Executive Board, Deutsche Bundesbank

Some may wonder whether there's a need another book about climate change, given the hundreds that have now been produced. The answer in this case is "yes," because this new work by a set of talented researchers at Bruegel, the highly-regarded Brussels think tank, and others, provides a perspective which is decidedly macroeconomic, and thus complements rather than duplicates the vast majority of the existing literature. Faculty, students, policy makers, and the broader public will find useful insights about the great challenges we face.

Robert N. Stavins – A. J. Meyer Professor of Energy and Economic Development, John F. Kennedy School of Government, Harvard University

Meeting the objectives of the Paris Agreement will involve an unprecedented mobilization of resources and a fundamental rewiring of our economies. Designing effective and fair policies to make this possible requires deep theoretical understanding, which this excellent book provides. It is an essential guide for policymakers and climate campaigners everywhere.

Laurence Tubiana – CEO, European Climate Foundation

The climate transition is the first policy induced industrial revolution, impacting all segments of the economy and raising as many policy issues. The book offers a broad and accessible overview of the current state of the question in a way that is relevant to both experts and people looking for a good introduction on the macroeconomics of decarbonisation.

Pierre Wunsch – Governor of the National Bank of Belgium

The Macroeconomics of Decarbonisation
Implications and Policies

GRÉGORY CLAEYS
Bruegel and Conservatoire National des Arts et Métiers

MARIE LE MOUEL
Bruegel

SIMONE TAGLIAPIETRA
Bruegel

GUNTRAM B. WOLFF
German Council on Foreign Relations

GEORG ZACHMANN
Bruegel

CAMBRIDGE
UNIVERSITY PRESS

Shaftesbury Road, Cambridge CB2 8EA, United Kingdom

One Liberty Plaza, 20th Floor, New York, NY 10006, USA

477 Williamstown Road, Port Melbourne, VIC 3207, Australia

314–321, 3rd Floor, Plot 3, Splendor Forum, Jasola District Centre, New Delhi – 110025, India

103 Penang Road, #05–06/07, Visioncrest Commercial, Singapore 238467

Cambridge University Press is part of Cambridge University Press & Assessment, a department of the University of Cambridge.

We share the University's mission to contribute to society through the pursuit of education, learning and research at the highest international levels of excellence.

www.cambridge.org
Information on this title: www.cambridge.org/9781009438360

DOI: 10.1017/9781009438353

First published 2024

A catalogue record for this publication is available from the British Library

Library of Congress Cataloging-in-Publication Data
Names: Claeys, Grégory, 1980– author | Le Mouel, Marie, 1988– author | Tagliapietra, Simone, 1988– author | Wolff, Guntram B., 1974– author | Zachmann Georg, 1979– author
Title: The macroeconomics of decarbonisation : implications and policies / Grégory Claeys, Bruegel and Conservatoire National des Arts et Métiers, Marie Le Mouel, Bruegel, Simone Tagliapietra, Bruegel, Guntram B. Wolff, German Council on Foreign Relations, Georg Zachmann, Bruegel.
Description: Cambridge, United Kingdom ; New York, NY : Cambridge University Press, 2024. | Includes bibliographical references and index.
Identifiers: LCCN 2023033299 | ISBN 9781009438360 (hardback) | ISBN 9781009438353 (ebook)
Subjects: LCSH: Carbon dioxide mitigation – Economic aspects. | Carbon offsetting – Economic aspects. | Environmental policy – Economic aspects. | Environmental economics. | Macroeconomics.
Classification: LCC HC79.P55 L4195 2024 |
DDC 363.738/746–dc23/eng/20230726
LC record available at https://lccn.loc.gov/2023033299

ISBN 978-1-009-43836-0 Hardback
ISBN 978-1-009-43839-1 Paperback

Contents

Figures

Tables

Boxes

Introduction

.

Scientific evidence is clear: human activities have released enough greenhouse gases (GHG) into the atmosphere to have already altered the climate, with already strong effects on ecosystems, societies and economies. On current emissions paths, climate change is set to become dramatically worse. To limit global warming, and hence avoid the worst-case scenarios predicted by climate science, the world economy must rapidly reduce its GHG emissions and reach climate neutrality within the next three decades.

This will not be an easy journey. Shifting away from carbon-intensive production will require a historic transformation of the structure of our economies. Capital and labour will have to be reallocated from brown to green activities. Many needed technologies are still under development and cannot yet be deployed. Some of the major changes that will need to take place are already clear: electricity production will need to be fully decarbonised, most economic activities will need to be electrified and energy will need to be used with much higher efficiency. But these changes will have major ramifications throughout the economy, which are less well understood.

In particular, as the time horizon of these adjustments has shrunk significantly, the decarbonisation path will impact the workings of the economy and even the business cycle in ways previously unaccounted for. In short, achieving climate neutrality by mid-century will have significant macroeconomic implications that need to be understood and adequately managed by policymakers.

Economic growth has so far driven emissions: higher levels of economic activity require more consumption of energy, of which 80 per cent globally is still produced by burning fossil fuels

(IEA, 2021b). In 2019, annual global GHG emissions stood at 37 billion tons of CO_2, 62 per cent higher than in 1990, the year of the first Intergovernmental Panel on Climate Change report, and 4 per cent higher than in 2015 when the Paris Agreement was signed (Friedlingstein et al., 2020). Even unprecedented circumstances such as the massive restrictions introduced to contain COVID-19 led only to a 6 per cent drop in emissions in 2020, from which a quick rebound to pre-pandemic levels promptly followed (IEA, 2021b).

In order to restrict global warming to 1.5°C and mitigate severe climate impacts, the global economy must swiftly cut greenhouse gas emissions and achieve climate neutrality by 2050. At current emissions levels, the global carbon budget that would still be compatible with the 1.5°C goal would be exhausted by 2030. Annual global GHG emissions currently show no sign of peaking. A far-reaching transformation of the global economy to reduce emissions is still needed.

One of the most fascinating ways to appreciate this problem is to look at the identity formulated by Kaya and Yokoburi (1998), which decomposes total CO_2 emissions into various components,[1] clearly illustrating the trade-offs implied in reducing emissions.

$$CO_2 \text{ emissions} = \text{population} \star \frac{GDP}{\text{population}} \star \frac{\text{energy demand}}{GDP} \star \frac{CO_2 \text{ emissions}}{\text{energy demand}}$$

The identity illustrates how total CO_2 emissions are the product of population, gross domestic product (GDP) per capita, the energy intensity of GDP and the CO_2 intensity of energy. Acting on any of these levers would contribute to decreasing total emissions in this model.

What this identity also shows is that if improvements in energy efficiency (third component) or in the CO_2 emissions from energy

---

[1] For conceptual simplicity, we focus here only on CO_2 emissions and not other GHGs such as methane. To effectively limit climate change, all relevant GHG emissions need to be reduced.

(fourth component) are too slow, then drastic reductions in emissions can come only from drastic reductions in economic activity or population. In practice, the main discussion centres around the emissions intensity of production (third and fourth components) and the level of GDP per capita (second component). This tension is at the heart of the macroeconomic impacts of decarbonisation. Population growth is usually set aside for good reasons. Much of population growth happens in parts of the world where per capita emissions are very low. Meanwhile population growth has stagnated in the regions of the world where emissions per capita are high.

In practice, improving the third component of the Kaya identity, energy use per unit of GDP, can be achieved through improvements in energy efficiency from using better technologies for production, transport or insulation; by behavioural change towards less energy-intensive consumption (e.g. increased use of public transport, a larger sharing economy and more re-use of durable goods); and by a changing economic structure towards a more 'immaterial' service-oriented economy. Improvements in the last component of the Kaya identity, CO_2 emissions per unit of energy demand, are mostly achieved by shifting away from fossil fuels to renewable energy sources, which might imply electrifying certain uses, notably transport.

If the decline in these two factors outpaces economic growth, absolute decoupling of GDP and emissions will take place. This is a situation in which emissions go down while real GDP continues to grow. This is already happening, albeit modestly, in Europe and the United States. Globally however, there is no sign of absolute decoupling, but only of relative decoupling (CO_2 emissions grow less than proportionately to real GDP). Explained in terms of the Kaya identity, while CO_2 emissions per unit of GDP are falling (the third and fourth factors combined), the fall is slower than the increase in real GDP (the first and second factors) so that overall emissions continue to rise. Figure I.1 shows that in the last hundred years, annual CO_2 emissions have risen tenfold, even though emissions per unit of GDP have been slashed by almost two thirds.

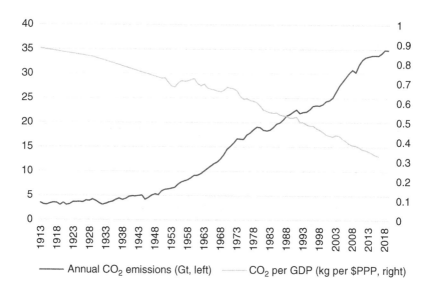

— Annual CO_2 emissions (Gt, left)   ---- CO_2 per GDP (kg per \$PPP, right)

FIGURE 1.1 Global annual CO_2 emissions from the burning of fossil
fuels for energy production (in gigatonnes) and CO_2 emissions per unit
of GDP (in kilograms per \$PPP)
Source: Author's elaboration based on IEA (2021a) and OECD (2021a).

To understand how much the world still falls short of the
required speed of decoupling, we use historical and projected data
from the Organisation for Economic Co-operation and Development
(OECD) on population and GPD per capita as well as historical
International Energy Agency (IEA) data on energy and emissions to
compare recent average rates of change of each factor of the Kaya
identity to estimate what it would take to reach net zero emissions by 2050 (Table 1.1). We assume that the reduction of energy
use to produce GDP will continue its current downward trend. We
make this assumption not because energy efficiency does not play
an important role in reducing emissions – on the contrary. Here,
we want to illustrate the speed at which decarbonising the production of energy itself would have to accelerate if all else is assumed
constant.

    This simulation suggests that the global decoupling rate between
emissions and GDP (bottom row) needs to accelerate by a factor of six

Table I.1 *Factors of the Kaya identity, CO_2 and CO_2/GDP, average yearly rates of change (%) in 1995–2018 (historical data) and in net zero emission scenario 2019–50*

	World	
	Historical 1995–2018	Scenario 2019–50
CO_2	2.0	–6.9
Population	1.2	0.8
Real GDPpc	2.6	2.3
Energy/GDP	–1.7	–1.7
CO_2/energy	0.0	–8.2
CO_2/GDP	–1.6	–9.7

Source: Authors' elaboration based on data from IEA (2021a) for CO_2 emissions, CO_2/real GDP and CO_2/energy demand, OECD (2018) for GDP per capita, OECD (2021a) for population and OECD (2021b) for energy demand/real GDP.

to reach net zero by 2050.[2] Annual emissions per unit of energy would have to fall by 8.2 per cent per year, compared with the current 0 per cent (Lenaerts et al., 2022, provide more details).

The Kaya identity thus shows that achieving decarbonisation by mid-century would be a historic endeavour. Shifting away from carbon-intensive production will require a historic transformation of the structure of our economies. Electricity production will need to be

[2] If the reduction in energy use continues its current path, the decarbonisation of the energy system has to proceed at around 8.2 per cent per year – a huge acceleration compared to the previous decades. The simulation exercise of Table I.1 applied at the country level shows that for the European Union and the United States, the decoupling challenge is somewhat less daunting: only a threefold acceleration is needed. This is partly because their economies are expected to grow more slowly than the global average. But it is also because the European Union and the United States both have higher decoupling rates of –2.5 per cent, as they are already visibly reducing the carbon intensity of their energy production. Meanwhile, China has seen even faster decoupling of CO_2 and real GDP. However, its very strong catch-up growth in GDP per capita still drives up total emissions.

fully decarbonised, most economic activities will need to be electrified and energy will need to be used with much higher efficiency (IEA, 2021b; IRENA, 2021). But these will have ramifications throughout the economy, which are less well understood (Pisani-Ferry, 2021).

One example in the energy system is that the transition from burning fossil fuels to using renewable sources will have implications for the location of energy production, with knock-on effects on international trade and competitiveness (McWilliams & Zachmann, 2021). Put together, achieving climate neutrality will likely have implications of macroeconomic importance.

The public policy debate on addressing climate change is shifting rapidly for at least three reasons. First, evidence from the climate science shows that non-linear climate developments are becoming more likely with even small changes in temperature.[3] Slow and long-term responses are simply inadequate as the costs of climate change may well explode much earlier than previous policymaking assumed. Second, there is an increasing public sense of urgency, also resulting from the very tangible extreme weather events that are being felt.[4] Many people in our societies increasingly want to act on climate change. Third, policy commitments to tackle climate change are becoming more credible. These factors are rapidly pushing the frontier of the debate among economists as well. While much previous research focussed on questions of the 'optimal speed of decarbonisation', weighing costs against benefits, economic research is increasingly focusing on the need to rapidly decarbonise to net zero in the next twenty-five years. How to successfully reach net zero emissions rapidly and what the economic consequences and policy requirements for such change are the new frontiers of research.

The acceleration of climate action (necessary to still avoid catastrophic climate pathways) means that the macroeconomic implications of climate action become bigger. Rapidly adjusting the energy

---

[3] See for example National Research Council (2013), Franzke (2014) and Zickfeld et al. (2021).
[4] See for example Bartusek et al. (2022).

system requires major upfront investments in green infrastructure such as solar panels and wind parks, the electricity grid, storage facilities and new heating and cooling systems. The green energy system will likely be more capital intensive than the brown energy system, and the more rapid the transition is happening the faster brown assets, that are still functioning, will have to be depreciated. A macroeconomically relevant reduction of the capital stock will be combined with a major increase in investments into green, amounting to as much as 2 per cent of GDP per year over decades. How will these investments impact the cost of credit? And how will the ongoing tightening of monetary policy impact the cost of renewable investments? Since fossil fuel-based power plants have comparably low upfront costs, a rise in the cost of capital may discourage efforts to decarbonise our economies rapidly.[5] For example Monnin (2015) finds that low interest rates increase the competitiveness of green energy technology relative to brown. On the other hand, green energy has relatively low variable costs. How will a macroeconomy look like when the cost of energy consumption significantly falls? The energy crisis of 2022 and the oil price shocks of the 1970s give some indication as to the macroeconomic implications of rapidly changing energy consumption costs.

Accelerating the transition to a climate-neutral economy and society requires major public policy interventions of macroeconomic relevance. Greenhouse gas emissions need to be penalised, for example by taxing them. How big are the government revenues generated from such taxes and what are the macroeconomic implications of such taxes? If new technologies need to be developed, what is the role for government in that process? What are the distributional implications of climate policies? Is our financial system structured appropriately to ensure the funding of green investments? Will green firms be able to hire the qualified staff they need? How can displaced workers successfully find new employment?

[5] For a detailed discussion, see for example Schnabel's speech on monetary policy tightening and the green transition on 10 January 2023, www.ecb.europa.eu/press/key/date/2023/html/ecb.sp230110~21c89bef1b.en.html

The purpose of this book is to advance the understanding on the macroeconomic fundamentals of decarbonisation. It identifies the major economic transformations and roadblocks requiring policy intervention. It develops a macroeconomic policy agenda for decarbonisation that would achieve the climate goals of the international community. While the book takes a global prospect on the issue, it provides specific insights into the European Green Deal, as one of the most ambitious decarbonisation agendas in the world.

Getting global decarbonisation right means that the macroeconomic implications of the process have to be understood and taken into account when designing climate policies. A costly and inefficiently done decarbonisation strategy will not be economically and socially viable while a wrong set of macroeconomic and structural policies may raise the cost of decarbonisation to unacceptable levels. The book seeks to shed light at this crucial intersection, reviewing systematically the existing evidence and reflecting on the key policy trade-offs and potential ways forward.

The book is written in the form of a textbook so as to be accessible to a wide readership. It adopts a simple language, avoiding the jargon that often characterises the debate in the field. In order not to compromise on rigour, it not only utilises the most authoritative data sources in the field but also has made plenty of references to primary literature for those who might wish to delve more deeply into the topics discussed. Each chapter has a set of review questions and key takeaways.

Chapter 1, 'Understanding Deep Decarbonisation over the Long Run', illustrates how economists have traditionally thought about decarbonisation. It notably provides an overview of the structure and key assumptions of Integrated Assessment Models, the main tool used by economists to model climate–economic interactions, with the aim of discussing their main policy lessons with regard to the macroeconomic implications of decarbonisation.

Chapter 2, 'Understanding Decarbonisation's Short-Term Disruptions to Economic Activity', discusses a different analytical framework used by economists to understand the short-run effects of climate policy: Dynamic Stochastic General Equilibrium models. It presents recent empirical findings in this area and describes the main lessons learned from these models.

Chapter 3, 'The Distributional Effects of Climate Policy', first illustrates the risk of decarbonisation impacting low-income households more than high-income ones, as they devote a larger share of their income to energy consumption and as they face more difficulties in switching to green alternatives. It then discusses which kind of policies can be adopted in order to avoid such risks and to ensure a fair transition with no social and political backlash.

Chapter 4, 'Public Finances and Decarbonisation', discusses the role that fiscal policy can play in the transition to a carbon-neutral economy. In other words, it discusses how to design fiscal policy, both on the revenue and on the expenditure side, to reach net zero emissions by mid-century in a credible growth- and distribution-friendly way. Furthermore, the chapter discusses how decarbonisation is likely to impact public finances, shedding light on what change might be required in tax revenues/expenditures, and if debt sustainability risks might arise from the green transition.

Chapter 5, 'Greening Innovation, Industrial and Competition Policies', discusses the importance of technological progress for achieving climate goals and how innovation, industrial and competition policies can work as powerful engines to spur decarbonisation and what it would take to ensure that the decoupling of economic growth from GHG emissions occurs at the speed necessary to reach climate neutrality by 2050.

Chapter 6, 'Mobilising the Financial System for Decarbonisation', discusses how decarbonisation will affect capital markets and how capital markets can support decarbonisation. One notable focus is on the risk of 'stranded assets', that is assets that lose value because of decarbonisation, and the potential implications for financial stability. The chapter also analyses how capital markets can become a key enabler of decarbonisation, also thanks to new sustainable finance instruments such as green bonds.

Chapter 7, 'Decarbonisation and Labour Markets', explains the consequences on the labour market of the structural changes induced by decarbonisation policies. These policies are likely going to have consequences on labour income distribution given existing rigidities in the labour markets and their different impacts on sectors and job categories. The chapter notably discusses whether decarbonisation can be a net job creator or destroyer, illustrating how job losses can be managed in a fair manner and how green jobs creation can be incentivised.

Chapter 8, 'Greening Central Banks', illustrates how decarbonisation is likely to have implications for the business cycle. In this context, it discusses how decarbonisation can change the effectiveness of monetary policy. It also discusses what the scope is for monetary policy to be more actively engaged in decarbonisation efforts, both from an economic and from an institutional perspective.

The authors hope that this book will help the present and next generation of teachers, students, policymakers and citizens with an interest in economic and climate issues to develop a clearer understanding of the macroeconomic implications of decarbonisation, so that they may be better able to contribute to the resolution of the complex issues associated with this aspect of the historical climate challenge we all face. In conclusion, the authors would like to thank Bruegel's research assistants Giulia Gotti, Catarina Martins, Kamil Sekut, Cecilia Trasi and Lennard Welslau for their excellent research support. They would also like to thank Bruegel's data scientist Michal Krystyanczuk for his support in the preparation of the Index. Finally, the authors would like to sincerely thank the European Climate Foundation for providing the financial support that made this work possible.

REFERENCES

Bartusek, S., K. Kornhuber, and M. Ting (2022) 'North American Heatwave Amplified by Climate Change-Driven Nonlinear Interactions', *Nature Climate Change*, 12, 1143–50, https://doi.org/10.1038/s41558-022-01520-4

Franzke, C. L. E. (2014) 'Nonlinear Climate Change', *Nature Climate Change*, 4:6, 423–24, https://doi.org/10.1038/nclimate2245

Friedlingstein, P., M. O'Sullivan, M. W. Jones, R. M. Andrew, J. Hauck, A. Olsen, et al. (2020) 'Global Carbon Budget 2020', *Earth System Science Data*, 12:4, 3269–40, https://doi.org/10.5194/essd-12-3269-2020

IEA (2021a) *World Energy Outlook 2021 – Analysis* (Paris: International Energy Agency), www.iea.org/reports/world-energy-outlook-2021

(2021b) 'Net Zero by 2050 – Analysis', www.iea.org/reports/net-zero-by-2050

IRENA (2021) 'Renewable Energy Statistics 2021', www.irena.org/publications/2021/Aug/Renewable-energy-statistics-2021

Kaya, Y., and K. Yokoburi (1998) *Environment, Energy, and Economy: Strategies for Sustainability* (Tokyo: United Nations University Press).

Lenaerts, K., S. Tagliapietra, and G. Wolff (2022) 'How Can the European Union Adapt to Climate Change while Avoiding a New Fault Line?', Policy Contribution 11/2022, Bruegel, www.bruegel.org/policy-brief/how-can-european-union-adapt-climate-change

McWilliams, B., and G. Zachmann (2021) 'A New Economic Geography of Decarbonisation?', Bruegel, www.bruegel.org/blog-post/new-economic-geography-decarbonisation

Monnin, P. (2015) 'The Impact of Interest Rates on Electricity Production Costs', CEP Discussion Note 2015/3, June 2015, www.oecd.org/ukraine-hub/policy-responses/why-governments-should-target-support-amidst-high-energy-prices-40f44f78/#section-d1e298

National Research Council (2013) *Abrupt Impacts of Climate Change: Anticipating Surprises* (Washington, DC: The National Academies Press), https://doi.org/10.17226/18373

OECD (2018) Economic Outlook No 103 – Long term baseline projections, www.oecd-ilibrary.org/economics/data/oecdeconomic-outlook-statistics-and-projections/long-term-baseline-projections-no-103_68465614-en

(2021a) Population Statistics, https://stats.oecd.org/index.aspx?lang=en

(2021b) Primary Energy Supply, https://data.oecd.org/energy/primary-energy-supply.htm

Pisani-Ferry, J. (2021) 'Climate Policy Is Macroeconomic Policy, and the Implications Will Be Significant', Policy Brief PB21-20, Peterson Institute for International Economics, https://ideas.repec.org/p/iie/pbrief/pb21-20.html

Zickfeld, K., D. Azevedo, S. Mathesius, and H. D. Matthews (2021) 'Asymmetry in the Climate–Carbon Cycle Response to Positive and Negative CO_2 Emissions', *Nature Climate Change*, 11:7, 613–17, https://doi.org/10.1038/s41558-021-01061-2

I Understanding Deep Decarbonisation over the Long Run

I.I INTRODUCTION

Economists use theoretical models to understand which mechanisms drive an economy. Models, be they economic or otherwise, are simplified representations of the world. The art of modelling consists in deciding which aspects of the world can be ignored in order to focus on the main mechanisms of interest. With the exception of a specific subfield, most economic models have assumed that the interaction between the economy and the broader natural environment is of secondary importance. One notable exception stands out. A specific field of large computational models, so-called Integrated Assessment Models (IAMs), emerged in the 1990s to challenge the view that the greenhouse gas (GHG) emissions resulting from economic activity do not matter (Nordhaus, 1992). The researchers in this field set out to quantify the trade-off between economic activity and environmental degradation, in particular global warming resulting from GHG emissions.

This chapter presents the main structure of IAMs and discusses the lessons that have emerged from this literature. These models have been used to address two broad types of questions. The first consists in describing an optimal path of GHG emissions over multiple decades. The second seeks to quantify the impact of achieving a given path of emissions on economic activity. This second exercise has given rise to some clear recommendations concerning which policy options deliver on emissions targets at the lowest possible cost to the economy.

Finally, we present the main theoretical limitations of this field of research. They highlight important economic trade-offs and call for additional analytical tools found in other branches of economics. First, we argue that the nature of the climate change crisis has considerably shrunk the timescale left to address the problem of GHG emissions. Hence, in addition to considerations around a smooth long-term transition to a carbon-free economy, a number of short-run transitory effects are likely to become more relevant. Second, we argue that IAMs make unsatisfactory assumptions about the nature of technological progress and about the ability of economies to allocate resources. Finally, these models completely abstract away issues of policy credibility and fairness considerations, which are nevertheless key components of the success of a decarbonisation strategy.

1.2 HOW ECONOMISTS HAVE THOUGHT ABOUT DECARBONISATION

Starting with the seminal Dynamic Integrated Climate Economy model of William Nordhaus (1992), a prolific field of economics has emerged to link economic activity to the resulting GHG emissions and the feedback of climate conditions on the economy. This class of models adds three elements to a standard model of the economy.

1. **An emissions module** describes how economic activity generates GHG emissions, often offering a very detailed breakdown of which sectors are responsible for emissions. For example, they can separate fossil fuel-based electricity production from renewables, or carbon-intensive manufacturing, such as steel, cement and paper, from the rest of the manufacturing sector. They make use of databases that measure the flows of goods and services between sectors of the economy, so-called Input–Output Tables. These models can also easily integrate trade considerations. They are particularly useful to identify the extent of sectoral reallocation implied by decarbonisation and its distributional consequences.

2. **A climate module** draws on climate science to map how the level of emissions translates into environmental damage, especially global temperature increases.

3. **A damage module** describes the feedback mechanism whereby climate change will impose costs on economic activity through, for example, the destruction of economic assets from extreme weather events or the loss of productivity from heatwaves. This damage module builds on a diverse literature quantifying the costs of climate and weather events on economic activity (see Box 1.1 for a detailed overview).

BOX 1.1 **The impact of climate change on economic activity**

Developments in empirical studies documenting the effect of climate change on the economy are well summarised in Carleton and Hsiang (2016) and Dell et al. (2014). Some studies focus on the whole economy, while others focus on specific dimensions of the economic system. In either case, temperature is by far the most used metric to represent climate change across studies. Other less used metrics include precipitation, used in the literature analysing the impacts on agriculture, and extreme weather events, used in the studies focusing on the impact on the financial sector.

Regarding economic output, consensus seems to emerge regarding the negative effect of temperature on output and the uneven impact of climate change on different regions across the globe. For example, Dell et al. (2012) find that temperature rises have a negative effect on economic growth for poor countries – namely a 1°C rise in temperature in a given year reduces economic growth by 1.3 percentage points on average – while the results for rich countries are not statistically significant. Using a larger sample, Acevedo Mejia et al. (2018) estimate that for the median low-income country a 1°C increase from a temperature of 25°C lowers growth in the same year by 1.2 percentage points.

Burke et al. (2015) argue that higher temperatures affect both poor and rich countries, especially because the evidence does not seem to suggest any significant differences in adaptation between the two groups of countries. Nonetheless, given that poorer countries are predominantly located in regions with warmer climate, they are still the ones most affected by increases in temperature. Kahn et al. (2021) support the view that both poor and rich countries are affected by increases in temperature and argue that by 2100 gross domestic product (GDP) per capita of all countries will suffer in the absence of climate change mitigation policies. This is mainly because both persistent increases in temperatures and the degree of climate variability affect economic growth. Kahn et al. provide estimates for the global economy by 2100 under three different scenarios: (i) the absence of mitigation policies and an average increase in global temperature; (ii) the absence of mitigation policies combined with country-specific variability of climate conditions; and (iii) compliance with the 2015 Paris Agreement objective. For the three scenarios, the reduction in world GDP per capita would be 7 per cent, 13 per cent and 1 per cent, respectively, highlighting the crucial role of climate action in reducing the negative long-run economic effects.

Labour productivity is frequently analysed alongside other key economic variables. Evidence of reduced productivity as a result of temperature increases also highlights the importance of climate adaptation. Kjellstrom et al. (2009) quantify the impact of climate warming on labour productivity, for several regions, assuming a trend towards less labour-intense work but no adaptation to climate change under two scenarios: (a) a moderately high emissions scenario and (b) a scenario that assumes reduced GHG emissions. By the 2080s, the increase in the percentage of workdays lost could be as high as 27 per cent for Central America under scenario (a) and 16 per cent under scenario (b). There would be regions, however, experiencing productivity increases under scenario (b), for example, Oceania and Central and South Sub-Saharan Africa. Under the mitigation scenario (b), Europe would barely experience any changes in productivity (in a range between –0.1 per cent and 0 per cent), while North America could experience productivity losses of up to 5 per cent.

The size of this last figure can somewhat explain the findings of Deryugina and Hsiang (2014). When considering several forms of adaptation, they estimate a negative impact of temperature on productivity for the United States. These findings emphasise that, although the country is an advanced economy, adaptation there is still sub-optimal and insufficient to cancel out the negative effects of high temperatures. In China, high-temperature subsidies are granted to employees who work under extreme heat conditions, which means that an increase in the frequency of high-heat events will lead to a rise in labour costs (Zhao et al., 2016).

Furthermore, there are research efforts dedicated to understanding the mechanisms through which climate change impacts different economic sectors, human health and natural systems (Auffhammer, 2018). Agriculture, forestry and fishery are highly dependent on climatic conditions and hence are among the sectors most affected by climate change. Thiault et al. (2019) analyse the effect of climate change on the agriculture and fishery sectors for countries around the globe in a comprehensive manner. They consider a country's dependency on each sector for food, economic output and employment and also the respective adaptive capacity. The results are striking: by 2100, under a high emissions scenario, around 90 per cent of the world population would be in countries estimated to have productivity losses in agriculture and fisheries. When considering a strong mitigation scenario, this figure could be reduced to 60 per cent of the population.[1]

Climate change is also changing energy consumption patterns (Auffhammer & Mansur, 2014) and could have negative impacts on the supply side (Ciscar & Dowling, 2014). For example, lower water availability due to reduced rainfall could force power plants to reduce production capacity given the essential role of water for power plant cooling. Financial institutions are also greatly affected by climate change and its consequences (Financial Stability Board, 2020). For instance, natural disasters can have a significant impact on the value of certain assets, such as real estate (Ouazad & Kahn, 2019). The transition to a low-carbon economy can lead to necessary, sometimes sudden, value adjustments of assets and liabilities, potentially creating stranded assets (Shimbar, 2021). Accounting for climate risk has become crucial to ensure the resilience and stability

---

[1] Thiault et al. (2019) compare different Representative Concentration Pathway (RCP) scenarios, which are reference scenarios adopted by the Intergovernmental Panel on Climate Change. The RCPs – originally RCP 2.6, RCP 4.5, RCP 6 and RCP 8.5 – are labelled after a possible range of radiative forcing values in the year 2100 (2.6, 4.5, 6 and 8.5 W/m^2, respectively). Thiault et al. (2019) use RCP 8.5 as their high emissions scenario and RCP 2.6 as the strong mitigation scenario.

of the financial system (Brunetti et al., 2021; European Central Bank, 2021). The impacts of climate change are not limited to economic activity; there is also evidence of its negative impact on population health and mortality (Carleton et al., 2020; Romanello et al., 2021). The increased intensity of heat waves and the heightened risk of infectious disease transmission are just two examples of climate change consequences that can have serious health implications.

I.3 EMPIRICAL LESSONS FROM IAMS

Integrated Assessment Models are designed to simulate the steady state of an economy according to given emissions targets and to map its evolution to this steady state over the long run, for example up to 100 years ahead. This framework has been used to answer two types of questions. The first approach is to use this modelling infrastructure to determine what is the socially optimal quantity of emissions, given different characteristics of the model, such as the value of economic activity and people's impatience. The main concept that is associated with this approach is the social cost of carbon (SCC).

The second approach is the reverse: these simulations can tell us how specific paths of emissions lead to changes in economic activity. This is the approach used by policy institutions to estimate how many points of GDP will be lost or gained from achieving specific emissions targets. The relevant concept in this second approach is the 'shadow price of carbon', which tells us by how much could output increase if an additional tonne was added to the carbon budget.

This shift in the debate happened following the Paris Agreement in 2015 (Weder di Mauro, 2021). The expert debate moved away from a Pigouvian internalisation approach to carbon pricing, namely one that estimates the present value of the flow of marginal damages of one tonne of CO_2. Instead, the focus has increasingly shifted to a maximum quantity approach, which consists in estimating the optimal dynamic path for the shadow carbon price compatible with the carbon budget that would limit warming to 1.5 or 2°C (Gollier, 2021).

1.3.1 Social cost of carbon

Most of the academically oriented research using IAMs has focused on estimating the SCC. This is the net marginal economic loss coming from an additional tonne of atmospheric carbon. In other words, it measures the trade-off between an extra unit of GDP and the additional climate damage associated with emitting an additional tonne of carbon. This number is used to assess the urgency needed to reduce emissions: a higher SCC implies larger damages from emissions and hence suggests that faster mitigation action is economically desirable. It also corresponds to the optimal value of a carbon tax, which is the preferred policy tool to address GHG emissions.

There is little consensus over the actual value of the SCC, and there are rising concerns about its usefulness as a concept, precisely because of its sensitivity to particular assumptions and to modelling shortcomings. Golosov et al. (2014) find that the SCC depends on only three quantities: the discount rate, the damage function and the rate at which carbon depreciates in the atmosphere. Researchers such as Pindyck (2013) and Heal (2017) argue that this simplification weakens the framework, because the assumptions that economists make on the first two dimensions are particularly arbitrary.

Choosing the right discount rate has sparked a vivid debate. On the one hand, researchers such as Nordhaus argue for using a discount rate close to the market interest rate, around 1.5 per cent (Nordhaus & Boyer, 2003). On the other hand, researchers such as Nicholas Stern (2007) argue for using a much more conservative interest rate, as low as 0.1 per cent. Golosov et al. (2014) estimate the SCC using these two discount rates to illustrate this sensitivity. In their baseline model, the SCC is equal to $57/ton of coal when using a discount rate of 1.5 per cent and $500/ton of coal when using the more conservative discount rate of 0.1 per cent. They also provide estimates calculated over a range of possible damages. For a discount rate of 1.5 per cent, the SCC ranges from $25/ton for moderate damages to $489/ton in the case of catastrophic damages. For a discount rate of 0.1 per cent, these estimates

Table 1.1 *Estimates of the SCC from Golosov et al. (2014), in $/ton of coal*

Discount rate	Low damages	Baseline	Catastrophic damages
1.5%	25	57	489
0.1%	221	500	4,263

range from $221/ton to $4,263/ton. The range of estimates is summarised in Table 1.1. The work of Gerlagh and Liski (2018a) shows that the value of the SCC is also sensitive to the shape of the discount rate and to the ability of decision-makers to commit to a given path of emissions. Comparing various approaches, Gerlagh and Liski estimate values of the SCC that differ from each other by an order of 20.[1]

The strongest criticism addressed to the IAM framework concerns its inability to take into account the possibility of catastrophic climate events (Wagner & Weitzman, 2016). This is not a specificity of climate models. In fact, all economic models are notoriously ill-suited to include non-linearities and threshold effects, therefore ruling out the possibility of extreme scenarios. However, in the field of climate economics this is a major shortcoming, given that not only the damages but also the response of the economy are very likely to have these characteristics.

Cai and Lontzek (2019) address this concern by allowing for both threshold effects in the damage function, that is, climate tipping points, and uncertainty around the response of the economy to productivity shocks. They circumvent the theoretical limitations by exploiting the opportunity offered by massive computational power and estimate these effects numerically. They argue that including both economic and climate risks in an IAM leads to higher estimates of the SCC than are common in the literature. Gerlagh and Liski (2018b) additionally test how sensitive the estimate of the SCC is to society's ability to learn

---

[1] Gerlagh and Liski (2018a) assume hyperbolic, as opposed to exponential, discounting. This assumption introduces a discontinuity between the discount rate used for the near future and that used for the distant future.

about future damages. They find that if past events are poor predictors of future damages then the optimal SCC should rise faster than GDP.

The SCC remains a controversial concept and has been superseded in the policy debate, at least in European policy circles. Climate policy is increasingly being seen as an insurance mechanism against catastrophic damage (Wagner & Weitzman, 2016). Along with companies, cities and financial institutions, more than 130 countries have now set or are considering a target of reducing emissions to net zero by mid-century (United Nations, 2022). In the rest of this book, we take these commitments as given and credible and focus on understanding how reaching these commitments will affect economic structures.

1.3.2 Long-Term Impacts of Decarbonisation

Policy institutions such as the European Commission, the International Monetary Fund (IMF) and the European Bank of Reconstruction and Development (EBRD) also make use of IAMs to answer a different question. These institutions seek to evaluate the economic impact of reaching specific emissions targets or adopting specific climate policy packages. In this section, we discuss how IAMs are used to quantify the net effect on the economy of reaching net zero emissions within the next three decades. In practical terms, this involves simulating the evolution of the economy in a reference scenario and in an emissions reduction scenario and comparing the level of GDP and associated employment between these two scenarios in 2050.

Comparing the different estimates produced by the literature is difficult, because different exercises use different assumptions, focus on different geographic areas and assume different reference scenarios. Most point estimates are often reported with margins of error that increase with the time horizon of the exercise, to warn the reader of the amount of uncertainty.

The choice of reference scenario is particularly important. It can range from a business-as-usual scenario – which would imply global warming beyond 3°C – to relatively ambitious targets, such as the Nationally Determined Contributions (NDCs) submitted under the Paris Agreement – which would imply global warming of around 2°C (Climate Action Tracker, 2021). Studies that use an ambitious reference scenario, such as the NDCs, lead to smaller estimates of the costs associated with an additional tightening of emissions targets.

It is also worth noting that many reference scenarios do not fully account for the benefits of avoiding climate change, as these are difficult to estimate. This is a reasonable assumption given the time lag involved between emissions and realised climate damage. The climate consequences felt within the next decades will depend on the accumulation of past emissions more than on current emissions. Although unrealistic, this omission does not alter the nature of the conclusions: including these averted damages in the analysis only strengthens the case for climate action, by lowering the total burden of mitigation especially over long time horizons.

Köberle et al. (2021) argue that reports estimating mitigation costs tend to misrepresent their results, to the detriment of the policy dialogue. A key assumption of the reference scenario that is rarely emphasised is that there is a constant rate of technological progress that drives GDP growth in the background. Hence, reporting a 1 percentage point drop in GDP compared to a growing baseline means that the economy in 2050 will nevertheless be larger than it is today, although not quite as large as it would be without climate policies. It is often mistaken to mean that the economy in 2050 will be 1 percentage point smaller than it is today. The correct interpretation puts the mitigation costs in the appropriate perspective and suggests that mitigation costs can be manageable.

Finally, Köberle et al. (2021) make a methodological proposal to use the IAM framework in a more policy-relevant manner. They suggest using this modelling infrastructure to compare various policy scenarios that achieve the same path of emissions or of temperature.[2] This would reduce the sensitivity of the results to the choice of reference scenario and circumvent the need to estimate averted climate damages.

---

[2] The former exercise allows for temperature overshooting, while the latter is the stricter target.

Despite the difficulty in comparing these different results, a consensus seems to emerge. Decarbonisation appears achievable and affordable given the present state of technology, projections for technological improvement and realistic strengthening of existing policy instruments. This conclusion crucially depends on assuming that full decarbonisation is indeed technically possible given existing technologies and some form of exogeneous technological progress that improves energy efficiency. In particular, the models allow for a wide array of substitution options,[3] which ensures a lot of flexibility in the economy and means that estimated costs will be on the lower end of those proposed by the literature.

For example, estimates for the European Union suggest that achieving net zero emissions by 2050 will come at moderate costs in terms of GDP. Vrontisi et al. (2020) compare the effect on the EU-28 of achieving the NDCs submitted to the Paris Agreement (namely reducing emissions by 40 per cent by 2030 compared with 1990 levels) with a pre-Paris Agreement scenario. They find that GDP will be 0.2 percentage points lower than the baseline scenario in 2030 and between –0.6 and +0.4 percentage points different by 2050. This difference between a positive and a negative effect depends on whether there is international coordination on emissions reductions. Additionally, when, in 2020, the European Commission proposed to tighten the European Union's emissions reduction target for 2030 from at least 40 per cent to at least 55 per cent, it published a thorough impact assessment based on the conclusions of three IAMs. The results suggest that there would be an additional loss of 0.3 percentage points of GDP compared to the targets set in the Paris Agreement (European Commission, 2020; Varga et al., 2021).

---

[3] For example, in the more fine-grained models, firms can substitute between fossil fuel and carbon-free energy, and they can substitute energy for other factors of production, such as labour and capital. Another dimension that allows for flexibility is the sectoral breakdown available in the model. In general, the more margins of response are present in the model, the quicker the transition and the lower the estimated impact on the economy.

At the global level, an IMF report paints a similar picture (IMF, 2020). Using a combination of a green investment push, carbon pricing and redistributive transfers delivers a net positive effect on global growth in the initial years. But in the medium run, after fifteen years, GDP is lower by up to 1 per cent compared to the reference scenario and does not fully recover to the baseline level by 2050. The report argues that this is in line with other estimates, which range between 1 and 6 percentage points of GDP lost by 2050. In a sensitivity analysis that allows for faster technological progress, world GDP goes back to baseline by 2050, suggesting no loss of output in the long run.

These recent results stand in contrast to those reported in the 2010s, when renewable energy, especially wind and solar photovoltaic, was still very inefficient and expensive compared to existing sources of energy. For example, the EBRD reported in 2011 average global GDP losses of around 1.5 per cent compared to a business-as-usual scenario and losses of up to 5 percentage points of GDP for the EBRD's region of interest (Bowen & Albertin, 2011). In these scenarios, nuclear energy makes a much larger contribution to the final energy mix and the switch to decarbonised electricity creates more significant productivity losses than would be predicted in 2020. Indeed, during the 2010s, the levelised cost of energy of onshore wind declined by 70 per cent while that of utility-scale solar photovoltaic costs declined by 90 per cent (Lazard, 2021), as shown in Figure 1.1.

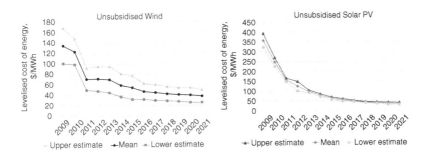

FIGURE 1.1 Evolution of the levelised cost of energy from onshore wind and solar photovoltaic
Source: Authors' calculations, from Lazard (2021).

1.4 POLICY LESSONS FROM IAMS

Beyond the general conclusion that a transition to a decarbonised economy by 2050 is achievable with manageable shifts in the economy, the main value of the exercises reported in the previous section is in identifying the conditions under which the economic costs of the transition can be minimised, and even turned into net gains. Using economic models, even with limitations, helps us to understand the transmission channels and reallocations that are predicted to take place. Three policy lessons emerge from simulations run using IAMs:

1. Carbon pricing is a necessary policy tool to spur the transition.
2. The ways in which carbon revenues are redistributed make the most difference in the total economic impact.
3. Global coordination is necessary to achieve ambitious emissions reduction at the lowest possible cost.

1.4.1 Carbon Pricing Is Necessary

The reduction in global GHG emissions necessary to limit global warming to 1.5°C, which we take as our starting point, will not be achieved without making all actors in the economy take into account the societal damage caused by their GHG emissions. Policies need to be introduced for this externality to be internalised.

Charging a price for carbon emissions is widely recognised as the single most important policy tool to align incentives with this objective. By directly addressing the externality to be tackled, it creates a clear signal concerning which harmful behaviour needs to be corrected. But it also leaves enough flexibility for the market to determine which margin of adjustment is most efficient (e.g. demand switching, energy efficiency, investment in abatement technology). In practice, the design of the carbon pricing mechanism matters for how effective emissions reduction will be. See Box 1.2 for an overview of the main carbon pricing schemes.

BOX 1.2 **Implementation of carbon pricing**

Carbon pricing is the preferred instrument of economists to tackle climate change because it directly addresses the main externality at the heart of this problem. Setting a price on carbon requires emitters to pay for the GHG emissions they release into our collective atmosphere, which affect our collective climate system. This forces them to take into account the consequences of their action on everyone else. However, it does not prescribe how this is to be done. This flexibility ensures that firms and consumers who can lower their emissions at the lowest cost will do so first. In practice there are two mechanisms to introduce a price on carbon: through the creation of a market or through taxation.

Creating a market for carbon requires assigning emissions certificates to companies and allowing them to exchange these among each other. The reduction in emissions is obtained by reducing the number of certificates through time. The efficiency of reductions is achieved by letting firms decide whether they would rather reduce emissions, for example through changing practices or investing in abatement technology, or rather purchase certificates at the going market price. The clear advantage of this mechanism is that it ensures certainty regarding emissions, as these are fixed, but it leaves firms to bear the risk in terms of price volatility.

The other mechanism is the imposition of a carbon tax, whereby governments require firms to pay a fixed monetary amount per quantity of emissions. This is often referred to in economic theory as a Pigouvian tax. For this tax to achieve the promised result efficiently, its level needs to be calculated precisely. It needs to reflect the trade-off between the societal benefits of reducing emissions and the additional abatement costs borne by firms. In other words, the level of the tax should equal the SCC. In contrast to market-based mechanisms, carbon taxes provide firms with certainty regarding the price they have to pay for emissions and leave society to bear the risk in terms of the quantity of GHG being emitted.

As the discussion on the SCC suggests, the optimal carbon price is difficult to estimate. The High-Level Commission on Carbon

Prices (2017) provides a useful focal point. It suggests that a carbon price level consistent with achieving the Paris Agreement is $40–$80/tonne of CO_2 by 2020, rising to $50–$100/tonne of CO_2 by 2030. The number of countries implementing carbon pricing instruments has been steadily increasing, from seven in 2000 to nineteen in 2010, fifty-eight in 2020 and sixty-four in 2021 (World Bank, 2021). The share of global emissions covered by these instruments reached 5 per cent in 2005 with the introduction of the European Union's Emissions Trading System (EU ETS), rose to 10 per cent in 2014, rising steadily to 15 per cent by 2020. In 2021, the launch of an ETS in China, which covers the energy sector, meant that an additional 7.5 per cent of world GHG emissions were covered by a carbon pricing instrument. However, the level of the carbon price in these schemes remains much below the $40–$80/ tCO_2 recommended by the High-Level Commission on Carbon Pricing. Figure B1.2.1 shows the share of emissions from the energy sector covered by various effective levels of carbon price. Figure 4.2 shows the cumulative amount of emissions covered by a carbon price (tax and certificates) in 2022.

Market-based and taxation-based systems also differ in terms of administration costs and political feasibility. Whereas both systems require monitoring the emissions of the firms subject to the carbon price, the cap-and-trade system additionally requires setting up a well-functioning market for emission permits. However, these schemes tend to be more politically feasible, as they are perceived as better reflecting the 'polluter-payer' principle. On the other hand, carbon taxes tend to be more acutely felt by final consumers and may meet more resistance.

Finally, fossil fuel subsidies act as a negative price on carbon, incentivising consumers to emit more. The rapid elimination of fossil fuel subsidies is therefore an important climate policy. The distributional and poverty alleviation goals of these subsidies can be achieved with other tools less detrimental to the climate.

Figure B1.2.1 should be read as follows. In Finland, 6 per cent of emissions are priced at a rate between €0 and €5/tonne of CO_2, 39 per cent of emissions between €5 and €30, 5 per cent of emissions

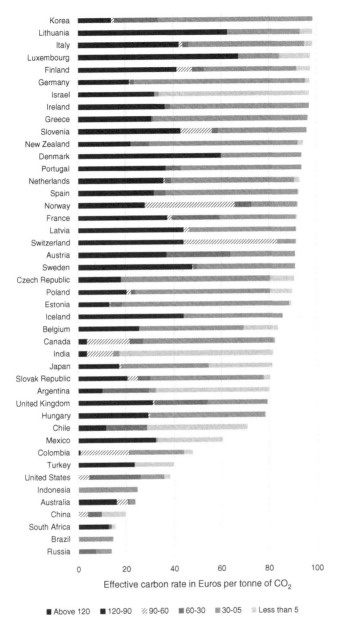

FIGURE BI.2.I Share of emissions from the energy sector priced at an effective carbon rate, in €/tonne of CO$_2$, 2018
Source: Authors' calculations based on the OECD effective carbon rates (OECD, 2021).

between €30 and €60, 6 per cent of emissions between €60 and €90, 17 per cent of emissions between €90 and €120, and finally 24 per cent of emissions are taxed above €120/tonne of CO_2. This sums to 97 per cent of emissions from the energy sector being subject to a carbon pricing scheme.

In the context of IAMs, the optimal level of emissions and the optimal price of carbon are two sides of the same coin and are often used interchangeably. When modelling the evolution of the economy along a fixed path of emissions (e.g. reaching net zero by 2050), IAMs assume the existence of a carbon price even if it operates mostly in the background (Bowen & Albertin, 2011; European Commission, 2020; IMF, 2020). Understanding the economic effects of decarbonisation cannot be separated from an analysis of the transmission channels of the climate policies used to change behaviour.[4]

1.4.2   Redistributing Carbon Revenue

The introduction of a price on carbon can yield substantial revenues and how this revenue is redistributed can make large differences for the overall macroeconomic effects of the transition.

In an empirical analysis, the European Commission's impact assessment of the revised emissions reduction target predicts that energy taxes and carbon prices combined would raise, by 2030, between €55 billion and €75 billion annually, representing between 1.8 per cent and 2.25 per cent of GDP (European Commission, 2020). The impact assessment presents different options for recycling these revenues and finds contrasting results between lump-sum redistribution and redistribution aimed at reducing other distortionary taxes. Using a hybrid model that mixes IAM elements with a more standard model of the macroeconomy, Estrada García and Santabárbara García

---

[4] As will be discussed in Chapter 2, Dynamic Stochastic General Equilibrium models, which look at the short-term effects of decarbonisation, tend to focus on the carbon price itself and discuss its effect on the demand side of the economy and on variables such as inflation and consumption.

(2021) analyse the effect of introducing a carbon tax in Spain and find that the total costs on the economy depend on how carbon revenues are recycled.

There are four main avenues through which carbon revenues can be recycled. First, carbon revenues can be distributed back to households in a lump-sum manner, with varying degrees of universality. The purpose of this alternative is to focus on redistributive justice and alleviate the burden of a higher carbon price for low-income households. The second option is to reduce public deficits and debt levels. These first two alternatives do not change the relative prices in the economy and hence have a limited impact on economic activity and emissions but pursue other policy objectives. The third option is to use the carbon revenues to improve the carbon efficiency of energy and production, by investing in research and development (R&D). Finally, the revenues can be used to reduce other distorting taxes in the economy, such as capital taxes, consumption taxes and social security contributions. Research shows that these last two alternatives have a strong potential to lower the overall cost of the transition. R&D subsidies hasten technological progress and the availability of low-carbon alternatives (Acemoglu et al., 2012; Aghion et al., 2009). Decreasing social contributions lowers the cost of hiring labour and has positive effects on employment, especially of low-wage workers most likely to bear the burden of increased energy prices. These considerations will be discussed in more detail in Chapter 4, which focuses on carbon pricing in the context of fiscal policy.

1.4.3 International Coordination

The final policy lesson is that international coordination lowers the cost of reducing GHG emissions for every individual country. IAM-based analyses point to the importance of international coordination of emissions reductions. GHG emissions create a global externality, and a consistent result across all models, including approaches other than IAM, is that the emissions reductions are more pronounced and the economic losses are dampened under scenarios with effective international coordination compared to unilateral efforts, for example by the European Union (Vrontisi et al., 2020). This is because in a world with trade openness, carbon-intensive industries that are subject to a domestic carbon price are vulnerable to international competition. Carbon leakage refers to the situation where domestic demand for goods subject to carbon pricing is substituted by imports coming either from foreign producers or relocated domestic producers. This will imply important losses of economic activity domestically, as activity decreases, but results in limited reductions in global GHG emissions, which happen in regions where carbon is not priced. In particular, Estrada García and Santabárbara García (2021) and Ferrari and Pagliari (2021) find that double dividends, that is net GDP gains, are feasible only in a scenario with international coordination.

I.5 MAIN SHORTCOMINGS OF IAMs

In practice, the carbon price is not a sufficient tool to achieve decarbonisation. For the carbon price to create the right incentives, the rest of the economy needs to operate perfectly. However, on the issue of climate change, additional market failures compound with the externality of GHG emissions, which necessitate additional policy responses (Köberle et al., 2021; Krogstrup & Oman, 2019). However, these market failures are assumed away in IAMs. This means that we need to look to other fields of economic analysis for evidence in these areas. IAMs abstract away from the following considerations:

1. Nominal variables, agents' expectations and business cycle dynamics
2. Distributional effects
3. Knowledge spillovers in the innovation system
4. Policy uncertainty and instability
5. Imperfect information and market frictions

I.5.1   *Looking at the Short Run*

Integrated Assessment Models were developed to analyse the conditions under which an optimal transition to a low-carbon economy could take place. In this framework, the time horizon of the transition is not of concern because it is assumed that long-run adjustment processes can take place without inherent frictions. However, climate science shows that there is an increasingly pressing need for reducing GHG emissions to mitigate climate change. IAMs are ill-adapted to provide guidance at this much shorter time horizon, because they do not include nominal variables (namely prices and wages), rigidities and inflation in these nominal variables, a central bank with a monetary policy rule, financial instruments for lending and borrowing (i.e. bonds), imperfect information, agent's preferences and the formation of expectations. All of these elements are necessary to explain how economies respond to shocks and the presence of risk. Some IAMs do have dynamic (e.g. capital accumulation, intertemporal consumption) and stochastic (productivity shocks) elements, but they are at heart designed to look at the evolution of the steady state of the economy, rather than its deviations from trend.

Chapter 2 will describe in detail how Dynamic Stochastic General Equilibrium models can provide insights on the short-run disruptions created by an accelerated transition. These models are designed precisely to look at the transmission of shocks and the resulting business cycle dynamics. This allows for an understanding of how the introduction of climate policies themselves can affect the economy, for example how the carbon price can have inflationary consequences that effect aggregate demand. These models can also tell us how this will affect the volatility of variables of interest and the transmission mechanisms of other policies, such as monetary policy.

1.5.2 Technological Progress, Innovation and Knowledge Spillovers

At the heart of the decarbonisation challenge is the issue of the technological feasibility of decoupling economic activity from emissions. When faced with a carbon price, the availability and cost of various alternatives determine the scope that firms and households have to reduce emissions and the resulting macroeconomic impact.

As IAMs tend to adopt a static view of innovation and technological progress, the number and productivity improvements of various technologies is fixed in the premises of the model. On the one hand, by including enough alternatives in the assumptions, the models can predict a realistic and flexible response of the economy. On the other hand, this oversimplification can lead to overestimating the cost of the transition, because both the rate of technological progress and the number of alternatives are economic choices that can be influenced by policy.

First, the amount of innovation and hence the rate of technological progress can be incentivised. Because of the knowledge spillovers inherent in the innovation process, the private sector will not invest sufficiently in innovation. The rate of progress will be too slow, which means that for a given level of technology, reducing emissions will have to come from reducing output. This type of market failure justifies public support for innovation to increase the speed of improvements in emissions efficiency (Aghion et al., 2009).

Second, the relative efficiency of green versus brown technologies itself can be influenced. The models of Acemoglu et al. (2012, 2016) and Aghion et al. (2009) have a more sophisticated view of innovation, disaggregating innovation into different fields and allowing firms to switch between technologies. This view of technical change as a process with a direction implies that support to innovation can and should be targeted towards 'green' technologies. This line of research shows that targeted R&D subsidies can significantly lower the transition costs. In the extreme case where green technologies are very inefficient, this sector attracts little innovation because of its reduced market potential. If a carbon price is introduced to disincentivise carbon emissions, this will be achieved mostly through reductions in output and will require a very high carbon price. Generous research subsidies for green technologies can help this sector catch up to carbon-intensive technologies. Once this catch-up has taken place and green technologies become competitive unaided, a lower carbon price can be sufficient.

However, a number of questions remain regarding the role of technological progress in achieving decarbonisation at the smallest possible cost. Within the field of green technologies, policymakers can decide whether to incentivise technological paths or seek to remain technologically neutral. Furthermore, the economic tools at our disposal do not provide much guidance in terms of allowing for and supporting the emergence of radical innovations. On the one hand, these tools represent risky gambles with low probability of very high payoffs. On the other hand, these might lead to the sudden depreciation of investment efforts in previous vintages of technologies. Finally, the path of productivity growth in an economy on the transition path to decarbonisation is unclear. While switching to less efficient green technologies might lead to a drop of productivity in the short run, this could be compensated by higher productivity growth once green technologies have caught up. These questions will be discussed in further detail in Chapter 5.

1.5.3 Policy Uncertainty and Instability

Economic models assume that policies are credibly adopted and perfectly implemented. However, the policy process itself is subject to capture, renegotiation and error. In particular, the time inconsistency inherent in setting a carbon tax is likely to create uncertainty for economic actors. It may thus be rational to undertake less mitigation measures than in a world without uncertainty given that the policy measures that will be implemented may be smaller because of the credibility issue. Most models do not explicitly consider this policy uncertainty.

Moreover, the carbon price is not introduced in a vacuum but in the presence of other distortionary policies, which are likely to interact and possibly counteract the effectiveness of the carbon price. The models that look at the carbon price in isolation will tend to underestimate the total disruption caused by this transition. In Chapter 4, we will discuss how carbon taxation fits into a broader fiscal framework, where other taxes, such as capital or labour taxes, might dampen its effectiveness. In Chapter 8, we will discuss the role of monetary policy in a world with climate change and climate policies, in particular how it should respond to energy-driven inflation.

1.5.4 Imperfect Information and Market Frictions

Even with an efficient innovation system that provides the optimal amount of low-carbon alternatives, the cost of the transition will also depend on the ability of firms and households to adopt and deploy these alternatives. In other words, markets need to function smoothly for resources – goods, capital, workers – to relocate to these new uses. IAMs typically assume that markets function perfectly and allocate resources to their most efficient use. This assumption can be relaxed in two directions, with differing implications for the macroeconomy.

On the one hand, if there are unused resources in the economy, for example excess savings looking for returns or high unemployment, then these will tend to decrease the cost of the transition, because resources will not have to be taken out of otherwise productive uses. On the other hand, if there are frictions on other markets, then the reallocation will be more protracted, leading to a longer transition. This can happen for example if capital markets lack information to identify green projects and to price their risks correctly or if new green activities require a different set of skills that take time for workers to acquire. Finally, other issues concerning market design might also affect the efficient allocation of resources. For example, the potential of digital technologies to increase market concentration and the scope of competition policy in ensuring the emergence and deployment of green technologies are likely to matter.

The issue of information failures in financial markets is a particularly important market friction for achieving decarbonisation. Installing green technologies requires capital investments, but at present there is a lack of credible information as to which projects are green. This information failure hampers the ability of financial markets to direct funding correctly and highlights the importance of developing reporting tools such as disclosure standards and investment taxonomies to avoid greenwashing. Additionally, renewable energies have a different cost structure compared to fossil fuel-based electricity production. The former implies high capital expenditures in the installation phase but require much lower operating expenses once in operation. This is likely to have an impact on financial markets. Chapter 6 will discuss how decarbonisation is likely to affect financial markets and macroeconomic stability, highlighting the importance of macro- and micro-prudential policies to ensure an efficient transition.

Chapter 7 will explore the effect of decarbonisation on labour markets, which creates a double challenge. On the one hand, workers currently employed in emitting activities will see their jobs transformed or altogether disappear. These workers will need to be accompanied as they find new opportunities in the labour market. On the other hand, the rise of green activities will create demand for 'green jobs' and much uncertainty remains regarding the ease with which firms will be able to find workers with the desired skill set.

1.5.5 Fairness and Redistributive Justice

Finally, in addition to efficiency concerns, the optimal design of climate policy needs to consider fairness and distributive justice. The costs of the transition will be concentrated sectorally, geographically, in low productivity firms and in low-income households (Zachmann et al., 2018). Designing compensatory policies is thus crucial to ensure the social acceptability and hence political viability of climate policies. Distributive considerations also matter across countries. This can be seen by the important weight given to funding for 'loss and damage' or 'climate reparations' in international climate negotiations, especially the yearly United Nations Conference of Parties. These issues will be discussed in further detail in Chapter 3.

1.6 CONCLUSION

The field of climate economics has developed a very sophisticated modelling framework capable of simulating the response of an economy to climate objectives over multiple decades. This framework has been used to determine the optimal rate at which GHG emissions should be reduced. However, these results remain inconclusive, while those coming from climate science have created a new sense of urgency. It has become clear that GHG emissions need to stop as fast as possible, with the middle of the twenty-first century being the ultimate deadline to avoid the most catastrophic impacts of climate change.

The models developed by climate economists tell us that in 2050, a decarbonised economy will differ from one that continues to use fossil fuels by only a few percentage points, in either direction. An important caveat to this statement is that both scenarios ignore the averted climate change damages. The key to achieving decarbonisation is to introduce a carbon price, which forces economic agents to integrate in their decision-making the externality they create by emitting. These models emphasise two policy choices that make the difference between having a smaller or a larger economy. First, a smart use of the revenues raised from pricing carbon, one which decreases other distortionary taxes, can lead to double dividends. Second, limiting economic losses requires concerted efforts from all emitters, in order to avoid displacing emissions and economic activity.

However, IAMs, like all models, need to ignore certain workings of the economy. In the case of climate change mitigation, some of these abstractions hide important aspects of the economic response to decarbonisation and thus the policy response. The purpose of this book is thus to bring together lessons from different fields of economics to obtain a broad-ranging view of this topic.

1.7 KEY TAKEAWAYS

1.7.1 How Economists Have Thought about Decarbonisation

- Integrated Assessment Models are the main economic tool through which environmental considerations have been included in economic thinking.
- They make three major additions to standard models of the economy: an emissions module, a climate module and a damage function.

1.7.2 Empirical Lessons from IAMs

- IAMs have been used to investigate two types of questions: What is the socially optimal quantity of emissions? How do specific emissions pathways lead to changes in economic activity?
- The SCC has been used to explore questions regarding the socially optimal quantity of carbon and is defined as the marginal economic loss coming from an additional tonne of atmospheric carbon.
- The SCC has been superseded in the climate policy debate due to its sensitivity to heavily debated modelling assumptions, such as the appropriate discount rate.
- Using IAMs to understand possible changes in economic activity along various emissions pathways has led to a consensus: decarbonisation appears to be achievable and affordable.
- But the achievability and affordability of decarbonisation is highly dependent on existing technologies meeting their expected potential and additional technological progress.

1.7.3 Policy Lessons from IAMs

- To achieve climate change mitigation, the global externality caused by carbon emissions should be directly addressed through carbon pricing.
- The approach taken to redistribute the revenues from carbon pricing has a significant impact on the total economic cost of the transition.
- Global coordination is necessary to achieve ambitious emissions reduction at the lowest possible cost. In a world with trade openness, the risk of carbon leakage needs to be acknowledged.

1.7.4 Main Shortcomings of IAMs

- In practice, the carbon price is not a sufficient tool to achieve decarbonisation, because the presence of market failures throughout the economy creates inefficiencies and obstructions to the transition.
- Moreover, IAMs do not account for many of the market failures present in real-world economies.
- They are silent on the impact of nominal variables and short-run rigidities, especially of prices and wages, and hence on the resulting short-term economic instability.

- They ignore the fact that the speed and direction of innovative effort can be steered towards the decarbonisation objective, which would reduce the overall welfare loss of the transition.
- They assume that policy decisions are perfectly calibrated and credible and are taken as given by all economic agents.
- They ignore the lack of information and market frictions that might slow down the reallocation of capital and labour out of emitting and into low-carbon activities.
- Finally, they ignore the distributional consequences of the transition, which is nevertheless vital for its social and political acceptability.

REFERENCES

Acemoglu, D., P. Aghion, L. Bursztyn, and D. Hemous (2012) 'The Environment and Directed Technical Change', *American Economic Review*, 102:1, 131–66, https://doi.org/10.1257/aer.102.1.131

Acemoglu, D., U. Akcigit, D. Hanley, and W. Kerr (2016) 'Transition to Clean Technology', *Journal of Political Economy*, 124:1, 52–104, https://doi.org/10.1086/684511

Acevedo Mejia, S., M. Mrkaic, N. Novta, E. Pugacheva, and P. B. Topalova (2018) *The Effects of Weather Shocks on Economic Activity: What Are the Channels of Impact?* (Rochester, NY: Social Science Research Network), https://doi.org/10.2139/ssrn.3221232

Aghion, P., R. Veugelers, and D. Hemous (2009) '*No Green Growth without Innovation*', Bruegel, November 23, www.bruegel.org/2009/11/no-green-growth-without-innovation/

Auffhammer, M. (2018) 'Quantifying Economic Damages from Climate Change', *Journal of Economic Perspectives*, 32:4, 33–52, https://doi.org/10.1257/jep.32.4.33

Auffhammer, M., and E. T. Mansur (2014) 'Measuring Climatic Impacts on Energy Consumption: A Review of the Empirical Literature', *Energy Economics*, 46, 522–30, https://doi.org/10.1016/j.eneco.2014.04.017

Battiston, S., I. Monasterolo, K. Riahi, and B. J. van Ruijven (2021) 'Accounting for Finance Is Key for Climate Mitigation Pathways', *Science*, 372:6545, 918–20, https://doi.org/10.1126/science.abf3877

Bowen, A., and G. Albertin (2011) *The Economic Impacts of Climate Change Mitigation Policy* (London, UK: European Bank for Reconstruction and Development), pp. 20–37, www.ebrd.com/pages/homepage.shtml

Brunetti, C., B. Dennis, D. Gates, D. Hancock, D. Ignell, E. K. Kiser, et al. (2021) 'Climate Change and Financial Stability', *FEDS Notes*, www

.federalreserve.gov/econres/notes/feds-notes/climate-change-and-financial-stability-20210319.htm

Burke, M., S. M. Hsiang, and E. Miguel (2015) 'Global Non-linear Effect of Temperature on Economic Production', *Nature*, 527:7577, 235–39, https://doi.org/10.1038/nature15725

Cai, Y., and T. S. Lontzek (2019) 'The Social Cost of Carbon with Economic and Climate Risks', *Journal of Political Economy*, 127:6, 2684–734, https://doi.org/10.1086/701890

Carleton, T. A., and S. M. Hsiang (2016) 'Social and Economic Impacts of Climate', *Science*, 353:6304, https://doi.org/10.1126/science.aad9837

Carleton, T. A., A. Jina, M. T. Delgado, M. Greenstone, T. Houser, S. M. Hsiang, et al. (2020) 'Valuing the Global Mortality Consequences of Climate Change Accounting for Adaptation Costs and Benefits', NBER Working Paper No. 27599, p. 57.

Ciscar, J.-C., and P. Dowling (2014) 'Integrated Assessment of Climate Impacts and Adaptation in the Energy Sector', *Energy Economics*, 46, 531–38, https://doi.org/10.1016/j.eneco.2014.07.003

Climate Action Tracker (2021) 'Glasgow's 2030 Credibility Gap: Net Zero's Lip Service to Climate Action', https://climateactiontracker.org/publications/glasgows-2030-credibility-gap-net-zeros-lip-service-to-climate-action/

Dell, M., B. F. Jones, and B. A. Olken (2012) 'Temperature Shocks and Economic Growth: Evidence from the Last Half Century', *American Economic Journal: Macroeconomics*, 4:3, 66–95, https://doi.org/10.1257/mac.4.3.66

——— (2014) 'What Do We Learn from the Weather? The New Climate-Economy Literature', *Journal of Economic Literature*, 52:3, 740–98, https://doi.org/10.1257/jel.52.3.740

Deryugina, T., and S. Hsiang (2014) 'Does the Environment Still Matter? Daily Temperature and Income in the United States', NBER Working Paper No. 20750, https://doi.org/10.3386/w20750

Estrada García, A., and D. Santabárbara García (2021) *Recycling Carbon Tax Revenues in Spain: Environmental and Economic Assessment of Selected Green Reforms* (Madrid: Banco de Espana), https://repositorio.bde.es/handle/123456789/16552

European Central Bank (2021) *Climate-Related Risk and Financial Stability: ECB/ESRB Project Team on Climate Risk Monitoring* (Brussels: Publications Office of the European Union), https://data.europa.eu/doi/10.2866/913118

European Commission (2020) *Stepping up Europe's 2030 Climate Ambition: Investing in a Climate-Neutral Future for the Benefit of Our People* (Brussels: European Commission).

Ferrari, M. M., and M. S. Pagliari (2021) *No Country Is an Island: International Cooperation and Climate Change* (Frankfurt: European Central Bank), https://doi.org/10.2139/ssrn.3870019

Financial Stability Board (2020) *The Implications of Climate Change for Financial Stability* (Basel: Financial Stability Board), p. 35.

Gerlagh, R., and M. Liski (2018a) 'Consistent Climate Policies', *Journal of the European Economic Association*, 16:1, 1–44, https://doi.org/10.1093/jeea/jvx010

(2018b) 'Carbon Prices for the Next Hundred Years', *The Economic Journal*, 128:609, 728–57, https://doi.org/10.1111/ecoj.12436

Gollier, C. (2021) 'Efficient Carbon Pricing under Uncertainty'(London: Centre for Economic Policy Research), https://cepr.org/voxeu/columns/efficient-carbon-pricing-under-uncertainty

Golosov, M., J. Hassler, P. Krusell, and A. Tsyvinski (2014) 'Optimal Taxes on Fossil Fuel in General Equilibrium', *Econometrica*, 82:1, 41–88, https://doi.org/10.3982/ECTA10217

Heal, G. (2017) 'The Economics of the Climate', *Journal of Economic Literature*, 55:3, 1046–63, https://doi.org/10.1257/jel.20151335

High-Level Commission on Carbon Prices (2017). Report of the High-Level Commission on Carbon Prices. World Bank, Washington, D.C, https://doi.org/10.7916/d8-w2nc-4103

IMF (2020) 'Mitigating Climate Change – Growth- and Distribution-Friendly Strategies', World Economic Outlook 2020, A Long and Difficult Ascent (Washington, DC: International Monetary Fund), www.researchgate.net/publication/349346129_Mitigating_Climate_Change-Growth_and_Distribution_Friendly_Strategies

Kahn, M. E., K. Mohaddes, R. N. C. Ng, M. H. Pesaran, M. Raissi, and J.-C. Yang (2021) 'Long-Term Macroeconomic Effects of Climate Change: A Cross-Country Analysis', *Energy Economics*, 104, 105624, https://doi.org/10.1016/j.eneco.2021.105624

Kjellstrom, T., R. S. Kovats, S. J. Lloyd, T. Holt, and R. S. J. Tol (2009) 'The Direct Impact of Climate Change on Regional Labor Productivity', *Archives of Environmental and Occupational Health*, 64:4, 217–27, https://doi.org/10.1080/19338240903352776

Köberle, A. C., T. Vandyck, C. Guivarch, N. Macaluso, V. Bosetti, A. Gambhir, et al. (2021) 'The Cost of Mitigation Revisited', *Nature Climate Change*, 11:12, 1035–45, https://doi.org/10.1038/s41558-021-01203-6

Krogstrup, W., and S. Oman (2019) '*Macroeconomic and Financial Policies for Climate Change Mitigation: A Review of the Literature*', IMF Working

Paper No. 2019/185, www.imf.org/en/Publications/WP/Issues/2019/09/04/ Macroeconomic-and-Financial-Policies-for-Climate-Change-Mitigation-A-Review-of-the-Literature-48612

Lazard (2021) 'Levelized Cost of Energy, Levelized Cost of Storage, and Levelized Cost of Hydrogen', Lazard.com, www.lazard.com/perspective/levelized-cost-of-energy-levelized-cost-of-storage-and-levelized-cost-of-hydrogen/

Nordhaus, W. D. (1992) 'An Optimal Transition Path for Controlling Greenhouse Gases', *Science*, 258:5086, 1315–19, https://doi.org/10.1126/science.258.5086.1315

Nordhaus, W. D., and J. Boyer (2003) *Warming the World: Economic Models of Global Warming* (Cambridge, MA: MIT Press).

OECD (2021) *Effective Carbon Rates 2021: Pricing Carbon Emissions through Taxes and Emissions Trading* (Paris: OECD), https://doi.org/10.1787/0e8e24f5-en

Ouazad, A., and M. E. Kahn (2019) 'Mortgage Finance and Climate Change: Securitization Dynamics in the Aftermath of Natural Disasters', NBER Working Paper No. 26322, https://doi.org/10.3386/w26322

Pindyck, R. S. (2013) 'Climate Change Policy: What Do the Models Tell Us?', *Journal of Economic Literature*, 51:3, 860–72, https://doi.org/10.1257/jel.51.3.860

Romanello, M., K. van Daalen, J. M. Anto, N. Dasandi, P. Drummond, I. G. Hamilton, et al. (2021) 'Tracking Progress on Health and Climate Change in Europe', *The Lancet Public Health*, 6:11, e858–65, https://doi.org/10.1016/S2468-2667(21)00207-3

Shimbar, A. (2021) 'Environment-Related Stranded Assets: An Agenda for Research into Value Destruction within Carbon-Intensive Sectors in Response to Environmental Concerns', *Renewable and Sustainable Energy Reviews*, 144, 111010, https://doi.org/10.1016/j.rser.2021.111010

Stern, N. (2007) *The Economics of Climate Change: The Stern Review* (Cambridge University Press).

Thiault, L., C. Mora, J. E. Cinner, W. W. L. Cheung, N. A. J. Graham, F. A. Januchowski-Hartley, et al. (2019) 'Escaping the Perfect Storm of Simultaneous Climate Change Impacts on Agriculture and Marine Fisheries', *Science Advances*, 5:11, eaaw9976, https://doi.org/10.1126/sciadv.aaw9976

United Nations (2022) 'Net Zero Coalition', United Nations, www.un.org/en/climatechange/net-zero-coalition

Varga, J., W. Roeger, and J. in 't Veld (2021) '*E-QUEST – A Multi-region Sectoral Dynamic General Equilibrium Model with Energy Model Description and Applications to Reach the EU Climate Targets*, European

Economy – Discussion Papers 2015', Directorate General Economic and Financial Affairs (DG ECFIN), European Commission, September, https:// ideas.repec.org/p/euf/dispap/146.html

Vrontisi, Z., K. Fragkiadakis, M. Kannavou, and P. Capros (2020) 'Energy System Transition and Macroeconomic Impacts of a European Decarbonization Action towards a Below 2 °C Climate Stabilization', *Climatic Change*, 162:4, 1857–75, https://doi.org/10.1007/s10584-019-02440-7

Wagner, G., and M. L. Weitzman (2016) *Climate Shock: The Economic Consequences of a Hotter Planet, Climate Shock* (Princeton University Press), https://doi.org/10.1515/9781400880768

Weder di Mauro, B. (2021) *Combating Climate Change: A CEPR Collection* (London: CEPR Press), https://cepr.org/system/files/publication-files/Combating%20 Climate%20Change%3A%20A%20CEPR%20Collection.pdf

World Bank (2021) *State and Trends of Carbon Pricing 2021* (Washington, DC: World Bank), https://doi.org/10.1596/978-1-4648-1728-1

Zachmann, G., G. Fredriksson, and G. Claeys (2018) 'Distributional Effects of Climate Policies', Bruegel. www.bruegel.org/sites/default/files/wp_ attachments/Bruegel_Blueprint_28_final1.pdf

Zhao, Y., B. Sultan, R. Vautard, P. Braconnot, H. J. Wang, and A. Ducharne (2016) 'Potential Escalation of Heat-Related Working Costs with Climate and Socioeconomic Changes in China', *Proceedings of the National Academy of Sciences*, 113:17, 4640–45, https://doi.org/10.1073/pnas.1521828113

2 Understanding Decarbonisation's Short-Term Disruptions to Economic Activity

2.1 INTRODUCTION

Prominent policymakers have acknowledged that the time horizon for ambitious climate action has shrunk significantly and that it will have implications at the time scale of the business cycle. In particular, they have become more conscious of the potential inflationary effect of the transition and how it can affect the ability of central banks to carry out their price stability mandates (Schnabel, 2022).

This chapter aims to understand whether the optimistic conclusions derived from the long-run analyses presented in Chapter 1 still hold when looking at this shorter time horizon. In the short run, three main challenges arise that might slowdown the efficient reallocation of resources out of carbon-intensive activities and that could generate economic instability.

First, economies face nominal rigidities – that is the prices of goods and the wages of workers take time to adjust to changing conditions. This limits the economy's ability to respond to shocks optimally and amplifies business cycle fluctuations. Hence, the response to climate policy will also be affected by the presence of these nominal rigidities and will likely be accompanied by economic instability. Second, in the short run, firms can respond to climate policy using only existing technologies, because the development of low-carbon substitutes is driven by innovation cycles that are longer than business cycles. This means that in the short run, there is a fixed relationship between the amount of emissions and economic output. Reductions in emissions can be achieved only through spending on expensive abatement technology (i.e. on technologies that lower emissions for a given level of output) or reductions in output. Finally, at the time scale of the business cycle, climate action yields only negligeable benefits in terms of prevented damages. This stems from the fact that these damages from climate change depend on the accumulated stock of global emissions, rather than current flows.

Hence, in the short run, decarbonisation efforts will happen in a context riddled with frictions. This means that it is likely to lead to important distortions in economic activity, which will appear, at least within this timeframe, uncompensated by the benefits of climate change mitigation.

This chapter will address two types of question. First, it will discuss how the economy responds to the introduction of climate policy at the time horizon of the business cycle. In general, climate policy is understood as the introduction of a price on carbon emissions,[1] which leads to higher energy costs and represents a negative supply shock for the economy. However, the overall effect on the macroeconomic variables of interest, such as output, employment and inflation, depends on the response of demand. This chapter will therefore discuss some of the main transmission mechanisms of climate policy into aggregate demand, such as the presence of behavioural biases, of difference in the ability of households to smooth consumption and of constraints on the ability of banks to extend credit.

The second section of this chapter will discuss how climate policy interacts with business cycle fluctuations and with macroeconomic stabilisation tools. During the transition, economies will continue to be hit by shocks (productivity, monetary or fiscal policy, extraordinary shocks). Does climate policy exacerbate or dampen these

---

[1] In practice, this simplification can also cover other policies such as standards or bans with an equivalent effect on production prices and therefore overall macroeconomic consequences.

economic fluctuations, and is there a trade-off between volatility in output and volatility in prices? Does it change the effectiveness of the other macroeconomic stabilisation tools? Can these macroeconomic tools be used as a substitute for carbon pricing or should their role be limited to dampening fluctuations coming from decarbonisation?

The answers to these questions is found in a different branch of economic research than the one presented in Chapter 1 – Dynamic Stochastic General Equilibrium (DSGE) models. This is the work-horse model that researchers and policymakers, especially central banks, use to understand business cycle fluctuations, the underlying frictions and shocks that drive these cycles and the potential of different policies (monetary, fiscal and macro-prudential) to stabilise them.

This class of models differs in many respects from the Integrated Assessment Models (IAMs) presented in Chapter 1. IAMs were developed to analyse the conditions under which an optimal transition to a low-carbon economy could take place.[2] They focus on determining the new steady state of a decarbonised economy and on the trajectory that will lead there.

In contrast, DSGE models are designed to explain business cycles and focus on deviations from the economy's steady state. They include many elements that are entirely absent from IAMs. These are nominal variables (namely prices and wages), rigidities and inflation in these nominal variables, a central bank with a monetary policy rule, financial instruments for lending and borrowing (i.e. bonds), imperfect information, agent's preferences and the formation of expectations. The policy conclusions emerging from this type of analysis are most applicable to managing the instability arising from climate action, rather than to understand how to achieve decarbonisation. The main differences between IAMs and DSGE models are shown in Table 2.1. More details on the main elements of DSGE models and how they are used to address research questions relating to climate policy are provided in Box 2.1.

---

[2] Some IAMs do have dynamic (e.g. capital accumulation, intertemporal consumption) and stochastic (productivity shocks) elements though.

Table 2.1 *Characteristics of IAMs and DSGE models*

	IAM	DSGE
Focus of the model	Climate	Economy
Time horizon	Long run (100 years)	Business cycle (5–10 years)
Nominal variables	No	Yes
Monetary policy	No	Yes
Degree of granularity	Sectoral breakdown	Whole economy
Markets	Perfect	Frictions

Source: Authors

BOX 2.1   **History of how New Keynesian macroeconomic models included climate considerations**

The purpose of New Keynesian macroeconomic models has been to explain what drives business cycles. Early DSGE models, in the tradition of real business cycle (RBC) theory, have focused on productivity shocks as the main driver of economic fluctuations. These models have a simple economic structure, where households participate in perfectly competitive markets for goods, labour and capital. These early models crucially do not include nominal variables and hence have no scope for price rigidities and for monetary policy. They assume perfect markets, which means that there are no inefficiencies in the economy. The main shock that can create volatility is thus shocks to the productivity of firms. The models of the RBC tradition that include climate policy have focused on determining the optimal design of carbon pricing. In practice, this research compares how much economic volatility follows productivity shocks in the presence of cap and trade, carbon taxes and intensity targets.

This parsimonious structure, while easily tractable, means that these models have been unable to match a number of empirical trends. In particular, they are unable to predict the behaviour on the labour market, especially the fluctuation in hours worked and its correlation with wages. Furthermore, many of the underlying microeconomic assumptions, notably perfect credit markets or frictionless labour markets, are not supported by empirical evidence. Finally, they assume away the possibility of monetary policy to support the economy. New Keynesian models have built on the RBC structure to address these limitations.

At their core these models consist of three relationships.

1. an equation that represents aggregate demand: this relationship is determined by consumers' decisions about consumption, savings and investment and by government spending;
2. the Phillips curve, which relates inflation and economic output, as the result of the firms' price-setting and production decisions;
3. an equation that describes the central bank's monetary policy and how it reacts to deviations of inflation from target.

A crucial element of New Keynesian models is the inclusion of market power, which allows firms to set prices but also creates frictions in this process that hinder the ability of firms to adapt optimally. The most prominently used price rigidity is the so-called Calvo pricing, whereby in a given year only a fraction of firms can update their prices in response to changes in the economic situation. This means that firms respond by changing the quantity of goods they produce. This gives aggregate demand a prominent role in driving economic activity. It is these nominal rigidities that allow different sorts of shocks to drive economic fluctuations.

In the context of climate policy, research using New Keynesian models has looked at how the presence of climate policy changes the response of the economy to these various sorts of shocks. In particular, this class of models allows for climate policy shocks, namely the abrupt introduction of a high carbon price, to disturb the functioning of the economy. They have also focused on determining the optimal interaction between climate policy and other macroeconomic policies.

The inability of macroeconomic researchers to predict the financial crisis of 2008 led to a thorough evaluation of the shortcomings of DSGE models. Hence, macroeconomic research since the financial crisis has incorporated a number of refinements that relax some of the fundamental assumptions of these models.

Before the financial crisis, DSGE models did not include a financial sector and hence ruled out the possibility of financial crises transmitting to the real economy. Subsequent research therefore included a financial sector, where frictions such as moral hazard and borrowing constraints can generate a financial crisis.

Another development has been to relax the assumption of the representative household and allow for different types of consumers. A common approach has been to split households between those that can save and borrow freely and smooth their consumption and those that are financially constrained and that need to consume all their income in each period.

Finally, the assumption of perfect rationality has also been relaxed by allowing certain actors to form expectations that are not perfectly forward-looking.

All these developments in the standard macroeconomic literature have been applied in the context of climate policy to answer two types of questions. First, the introduction of financial frictions in the models is used to understand whether climate policy can lead to the sudden devaluation of fossil fuel assets, negatively impacting the balance sheets of banks, and therefore to a financial crisis. Second, allowing for more realistic assumptions on the formation of expectations or on the financial constraints faced by households exacerbates the economic disruption caused by climate policy.

2.2 THE EFFECT OF CLIMATE POLICY ON MACROECONOMIC VARIABLES

2.2.1 *Climate Policy Is a Negative Supply Shock*

In the short term, the introduction of climate policy is a negative supply shock for the economy (Annichiarico et al., 2022; Fischer & Heutel, 2013; McKibbin et al., 2020). In practice, climate policy can be conceptualised as the introduction of a carbon pricing instrument,[3] which results in higher energy prices.

Empirical analyses confirm the transmission of carbon pricing into higher energy prices. Two prominent examples are the European Union's Emissions Trading System (EU ETS), analysed by Känzig (2021), and the carbon tax introduced in British Columbia, analysed by Konradt and Weder di Mauro (2021). Känzig (2021) finds that regulatory announcements regarding the EU ETS led to a strong and immediate increase in the energy component of the Consumer Price Index (CPI). Konradt and Weder di Mauro (2021) similarly find that the energy component of the CPI increased in British Columbia, compared to other Canadian provinces, following the introduction of a carbon tax.

These higher energy prices translate into higher production costs for firms, who respond by producing less and spending more on abatement, which allows them to emit less for the same level of production. The drop in aggregate supply creates inflationary pressure, for the given level of aggregate demand.

However, the overall response of the economy depends on the response of aggregate demand. Carbon prices can also create a negative demand shock. The expected future increases in the carbon price leads households to anticipate lower incomes and firms to anticipate lower profits. This depresses current demand and puts downward pressure on prices. Ferrari and Nispi Landi (2022) find that empirically this negative demand shock is larger than the inflationary pressure created through the higher costs faced by firms.

---

[3] There are multiple instruments to introduce carbon pricing. The main distinction is between quantity restrictions, such as a cap-and-trade system, and carbon taxes. Intensity targets, which place a restriction on emissions per quantity of output, have also been discussed but in practice have yet to be implemented.

Climate policy instruments can go much beyond introducing a price on carbon. For example, regulations on the energy use of appliances or subsidies for investment in solar panels also contribute to decarbonisation. The insights from the models presented in this chapter will apply to these measures only to the extent that they increase the price of energy.

Four additional transmission channels can affect the relative importance of the supply and the demand shocks arising from climate policy.

The first transmission channel goes through the expectations of households and firms. The extent to which economic agents find the policy credible will affect the speed at which they adjust their behaviour.

The second transmission channel is household heterogeneity. Households differ in their exposure to increases in energy prices and in their ability to respond. If the share of exposed households is large enough, a fall in their consumption can have an aggregate impact.

The third transmission channel is the 'financial accelerator'. Climate policy can also create instability through its impact on financial markets. A sudden depreciation of carbon-intensive assets can spill over into the real economy and create a recession.

The fourth transmission channel is the response of macroeconomic policy itself, in particular monetary policy, to economic conditions. Depending on the relative sensitivity of monetary policy to inflation and output, it will react more or less strongly to the inflationary pressure.

2.2.1.1 Difference between Climate Policy and Oil Price Shocks

The analysis of the effect of climate policy on macroeconomic volatility builds on the tools developed to understand the effect of energy price shocks, especially oil price shocks. The initial response, in particular the negative supply shock, transmits to the economy in a similar fashion. However, climate policy shocks and oil price shocks differ in two important dimensions that matter for the second-round general equilibrium effects.

First, oil price shocks are assumed to be transitory and therefore not to affect the economy's steady state. Firms and households adapt to weather the shock, for example through borrowing. Importantly, they assume that the economy will get back to its pre-shock conditions.

On the contrary, for climate policy to be effective, it requires the introduction of a permanent carbon price. In addition, for emissions to continue decreasing at a steady rate and reach their target, the carbon price needs to be steadily increasing. This sets the economy on a path towards a new steady state. Reaction to climate policy therefore depends on the credibility of the commitment and of the policies introduced. Furthermore, it will be affected by the extent of uncertainty on what the new steady state will be.

Second, an oil price shock represents a negative terms-of-trade shock for oil-importing countries. This means that collectively the importing country is poorer while the exporting country benefits from the higher price. While the shock is temporary, the loss in purchasing power is real. Carbon pricing, however, increases the cost of using fossil fuels. At the same time and as we will discuss in Chapter 4, the carbon tax results in government revenues that can be used elsewhere. This should lead to different economic effects between the temporary oil price shock and the permanent carbon price rise.

Finally, this difference between the two types of shocks also translates into different incentives for innovation (Barrage, 2020; Känzig, 2021). Oil price shocks create incentives to innovate in energy-saving measures, whereas climate policy creates incentives to innovate in technologies that use no fossil fuels.

2.2.2 The Importance of Expectations

In standard macroeconomic theory, consumers are generally assumed to be rational and to maximise their utility (consumption and leisure) and policy decisions to be credible. This means that consumers should expect climate policy to be permanent. In this case, they will anticipate a fall in their future income and immediately reduce consumption and increase savings to smooth consumption over their lifetime. This will create a negative demand shock, which will dampen the inflationary consequences of the carbon price.

2.2.2.1 Rapid Reaction of Forward-Looking Households and Firms

The importance of anticipation is highlighted by the results of Diluiso et al. (2021): they simulate a decrease of emissions by 24 per cent over a ten-year period, which requires a steadily increasing carbon price. By allowing for capital investment in this economy, this analysis amplifies the importance of the forward-looking behaviour of firms and of households.

The simulation predicts a small initial increase in output in the first years, arising from both the supply and demand sides. Because firms anticipate the cost of energy to go up in the future, they will bring forward production and initially boost output. Consumers also anticipate higher energy prices, so they immediately lower consumption and increase labour supply, which further contributes to higher output in the short term. The combination of higher output and lower demand has a deflationary effect.

However, eventually, as energy prices rise, output starts to decline. In this later part of the transition, the reaction of monetary policy plays a crucial role in ensuring that inflation remains close to the target of the central bank. Achieving the emissions reduction target comes at the cost of permanently lower output. Although the model allows for some amount of substitution out of fossil fuel energy into low-carbon energy, this substitution is assumed to be imperfect: firms cannot entirely exit fossil fuels. As the carbon tax makes fossil fuel energy relatively more expensive compared to low-carbon energy, firms will reduce their use of fossil fuel energy to a large extent. Yet, they will continue to use a small but now more expensive quantity of it. This results, at the end of the simulation, in a decrease of overall energy demand and consequently of output.

2.2.2.2 Delayed Response through Backward-Looking Expectations or Lack of Policy Credibility

However, in practice, the assumption of rational expectations can fail in many ways. In reality, economic agents are often backward looking, for example when they use observed past inflation to predict future inflation. In addition, if firms and households do not believe in the credibility of the policy, or if there is uncertainty over which new steady state the economy is converging to, then agents will postpone their action. This dampens the immediate response but amplifies the subsequent adjustment, leading to a sharper drop in output and higher inflation for a longer period.

Annicchiarico et al. (2022) provide an illustration of this result by relaxing the assumption of rational expectations in two dimensions. First, they allow for bias in the formation of normal economic expectations. This concerns beliefs about the determinants of inflation and about the credibility of the central bank. Second, they allow agents to doubt the credibility of the climate policy itself.

Annicchiarico et al. (2022: 31) conclude: 'The presence of behavioural agents with cognitive limitations amplifies business cycle fluctuations and allows for the emergence of waves of optimism and pessimism along the mitigation path, injecting further uncertainty regarding the impact and effectiveness of climate policies.'

In practice, Annicchiarico et al. (2022) simulate the effect of reducing emissions by 1 per cent. Under perfect rationality, this would lead to a 2.9 per cent increase in the carbon price, a permanent fall in output of 0.15 per cent and an initial increase of inflation by 0.005 percentage points, which would recover its initial level after five quarters.

Next, they simulate the response of the economy if consumers are backward looking and believe that the carbon price will be temporary rather than permanent. This results in a belated change of behaviour and a delay in the negative demand shock. The initial negative supply shock is therefore less counter-balanced, leading to inflationary pressure.

Allowing for these backward-looking expectations doubles the time needed to reach an emissions reduction target of 1 per cent from four quarters to nine quarters. It also leads to a much higher increase in inflation, to 0.001 percentage points above its initial value that is resorbed only after ten quarters.

2.2.3 Household Heterogeneity

In addition to rational expectations, standard macroeconomic theory has long been formulated in terms of the 'representative agent', whereby one household and one firm suffice to represent the average behaviour of all households and of all firms. Recent research has highlighted how relaxing this assumption reveals an additional channel through which climate policy can result in a negative demand shock.

In particular, the work of Känzig (2021) highlights the importance of 'hand-to-mouth' households in the response of aggregate consumption. Hand-to-mouth households differ from the representative household in that they consume all their income and have no access to financial markets to save and borrow to smooth out shocks. More than access to borrowing, what matters in this context is their inability to save, due to low income, that makes their consumption very sensitive to shocks.

Using survey data for the United Kingdom, Känzig (2021) confirms that low-income households devote a larger fraction of their budget to energy expenses and are thus more sensitive to increases in energy prices. He also documents that these households tend to be employed in sectors that are strongly correlated with aggregate demand (construction, wholesale and retail, hotels and restaurants, and other social and personal services). This means that their income is also exposed to economic conditions. Climate policy thus leads to a second-round indirect effect, where lower economic activity disproportionally decreases the income of these vulnerable households. Therefore, the higher the share of hand-to-mouth households in the economy, the more pronounced will be the drop in demand arising from increased energy prices. Measures to support the income of these households, for example from recycling carbon revenues, can attenuate the drop in aggregate demand.

Känzig (2021) empirically measures the response of macroeconomic variables in the euro area to climate policy shocks. The methodology uses surprise announcements on the functioning of the EU ETS, as a driver of exogenous shocks to the carbon price. An increase in the carbon price leads to an immediate positive increase in energy prices, an immediate decrease in emissions, an increase in inflation and unemployment and a decrease in output. Output recovers its initial level after around forty months, while emissions remain permanently lower, implying an improvement in emissions efficiency. However, the unemployment rate and inflation both remain above their starting point even beyond fifty months.

Känzig (2021) analyses the effect of climate policy on the expenditure and income levels of three groups of households: the bottom 25 per cent, the middle 50 per cent and the top 25 per cent. He finds that low-income households reduce their expenditure significantly and persistently. In contrast, the expenditure response of higher-income households is short-lived and barely statistically significant. Regarding income, low-income households experience the largest and most persistent drop in income. Higher-income households also experience a non-negligible drop in income, but it is not persistent. The fact that this drop in income for higher-income households does not translate into a significant drop in expenditure highlights the importance of savings in smoothing temporary drops in income.

Finally, disaggregating by the type of expenditure, Känzig (2021) finds that energy expenditure is inelastic and that households in all income groups increase their spending on energy. The drop in consumption is driven by spending on non-durable goods, especially for low-income households.

2.2.4 The Bank Lending Channel and the Financial Accelerator

2.2.4.1 The Risk of Financial Instability

Accounting for the presence of the banking sector, especially if it is subject to frictions, introduces an additional channel through which climate policy can accentuate economic volatility. In addition, a shock can also arise within the banking sector, whereby fossil fuel assets face a sudden depreciation, leading to a credit crunch or even a financial crisis that spills over into the real economy. This type of shock could arise from policy changes, but also from technological development or changes in behavioural patterns.

To make it simple, the banking sector gathers the deposits of households and provides loans to companies. But banks can face frictions in their ability to finance the economy. Following prudential regulation that fixes capital ratios, the amount of credit that banks can lend to companies depends on the value of the assets on their balance sheets. This gives rise to the so-called financial accelerator channel. If financial assets lose part of their value, this decreases the net worth of banks and thereby limits their ability to extend credit. In the context of climate policy, it is important to distinguish two types of assets that can be in bank portfolios: assets corresponding to the fossil fuel-intensive industries and low-carbon sectors.

The financial accelerator contributes to amplifying the contractionary effects of climate policy in the following way. As output declines following the introduction of a steadily increasing carbon price, there is a drop in the value of fossil fuel assets. This leads to a decline in the net worth of banks and, as a direct consequence, in lending. This initial deterioration in the banks' balance sheet triggers a fire sale to satisfy the leverage ratios imposed by prudential policy. This leads to a further depreciation of asset prices and ultimately to a drop in credit availability (see e.g. Diluiso et al., 2021).

2.2.4.2 *Investment Reallocation Out of Brown and into Green Activities*

Research focusing on the frictions present in financial markets also helps understand the factors that can slowdown the reallocation of capital from brown to green activities. This is the focus of the analysis of Carattini et al. (2021). They simulate the introduction of a permanent carbon tax of around $30/ton of CO_2 in an economy consisting of a brown and a green sector. The climate policy leads to a drop in both brown and green outputs and in the value of assets linked to these sectors. Production and investment in the brown sector keep declining, as they are disincentivised by the carbon price.

The presence of financial frictions matters for the recovery of production and investment only in the green sector. Without financial frictions, namely, when the amount of credit that banks can provide is not dependent on their net worth, production in the green sector immediately recovers from the initial drop and surpasses its initial level after twenty periods. Investment in the green sector initially decreases slightly and quickly starts growing. This differs significantly in a world where credit is constrained by the net worth of banks (even if this is justified for prudential purposes). The depreciation of brown assets limits the ability of banks to provide credit to both sectors of the economy, thus penalising the green sector.

The research presented here suggests that the financial system can amplify the effects of climate policy. First, the effect of carbon pricing on the real economy can be amplified by the financial accelerator. Second, the sudden stranding of fossil fuel assets, which can arise because of the sudden introduction of carbon pricing but also from technological progress or changes in behaviour,[4] can also cause a fall in output. Finally, the presence of financial frictions can also hinder the reallocation of assets towards the green sector.

However, the empirical importance of this transmission channel is discussed in further detail in Chapter 6. In particular, since the financial crisis of 2008, both the sophistication of models used by policymakers and the prudential framework have been strengthened. It remains an open question whether decarbonisation would represent a shock of the same order of magnitude as the financial crisis. One key difference is the long-term and anticipated nature of

---

[4] As regards technological progress, this can be caused by a climate policy understood in its broader meaning than simply introducing a carbon price. In the absence of carbon pricing, climate policy can be achieved by supporting green technologies through, for example, subsidising innovation or capital investments. In the presence of learning-by-doing, the latter can lead to significant drops in the cost of renewable technology, thereby rendering fossil fuel energy less competitive and triggering a devaluation of assets.

decarbonisation (even if economic agents can have myopic behaviours), which decreases the likelihood of observing a sudden depreciation of assets.

2.2.5 The Response of Monetary Policy to the Introduction of Climate Policies

Climate policy does not happen in an institutional vacuum, and policies introduced to manage or reduce macroeconomic volatility will respond to the instability created by the introduction of climate policy.

Since the 1980s and the advent of inflation targeting, central banks' main mandate has been to ensure price stability. Responding to the economic volatility created by the introduction of climate policy is thus part of their price stability mandate. There is a clear consensus around the fact that a strong reaction of monetary policy to the inflationary pressure of climate policy can be successful at maintaining price stability (Annicchiarico & Di Dio, 2017; Annicchiarico et al., 2022; Diluiso et al., 2021; McKibbin et al., 2020).

Central banks' mandate sometimes also includes the stabilisation of other macroeconomic variables such as employment or output. This multiplicity of objectives (which can sometimes lead to some trade-offs) is often represented through the use of a reaction function of the central bank called the Taylor rule, in which the central bank attributes some weight to the volatility of inflation and output depending on the preference of its decision-makers or on its precise mandate, as explained in Box 2.2.

BOX 2.2   **The Taylor rule**

The Taylor rule is an approximation of how central banks conduct monetary policy through the determination of their main policy rate. It summarises the variables that enter in the decision-making process and expresses the main trade-off faced by monetary policy in response to the introduction of climate policy.

$$i_t = \pi_t + r_t^* + \alpha(\pi_t - \pi_t^*) + \beta(y_t - \bar{y}_t)$$

where

i_t is the target short-term nominal interest rate (e.g. the federal funds rate in the United States, the Bank of England base rate in the United Kingdom),

π_t is the rate of inflation as measured by a CPI,

π_t^* is the target rate of inflation,

r_t^* is the equilibrium real interest rate,

y_t is a measure of real GDP, and

$\bar{y}_t$ is potential output as determined by statistical methods (such as a simple linear trend) or by a method based on production functions.

The parameters α and β represent the relative weight given to the deviation of inflation from its target and the deviation from potential output.

The higher the weight is attributed to price stability, the more contained will be the inflationary pressure. However, this will be achieved at the cost of a sharp drop in output, which itself contributes to reaching the emissions target, through the proportional relationship between output and emissions. On the other hand, placing some weight on maintaining the level of output near its potential leads monetary policy to react less to an increase in the carbon price, which dampens the drop in output and consequently the drop in emissions, but possibly at the expense of a significant deviation of inflation from the central bank's target. An additional advantage of targeting output in the decarbonisation context is that it is better at insulating households from income shocks, which will dampen the negative demand shock (McKibbin et al., 2020).

When climate policy itself creates volatility, it becomes more difficult for the central bank to identify if the economy faces a supply or a demand shock and therefore to respond appropriately. Placing more weight on inflation means that the response of monetary policy will be stronger, irrespective of the source of inflationary pressure.

In the case where the demand shock is large enough compared to the supply shock from climate policy, the economy faces deflationary pressure. An expansionary response of monetary policy in these initial periods can result in lower total output losses over the whole transition.

Finally, a strong reaction of monetary policy can dampen the amplified effect of the introduction of carbon pricing on the economy due to the presence of behavioural biases. This holds irrespective of the relative weights attributed to inflation and output. As Annicchiarico et al. (2022) argue, 'By implementing successful stabilization policies, central banks can highly reduce the uncertainty surrounding the introduction of carbon pricing policies, ensuring better conditions for successful climate actions.'

2.3 STABILISING BUSINESS CYCLE FLUCTUATIONS IN A DECARBONISING ECONOMY

The transition to net zero will take place over multiple decades. During this time, economies will continue to be hit by shocks (productivity shocks, policy shocks, other extraordinary shocks) and to experience business cycle dynamics and volatility. How will economies engaged on an ambitious decarbonisation path respond to these shocks? In other words, does the presence of carbon pricing amplify or dampen economic volatility. Will existing macroeconomic stabilisation policies, notably monetary and fiscal policies, and prudential policy remain effective?

2.3.1 Business Cycles and the Design of Climate Policies

The specific design of climate policy affects the trade-off between output and price volatility, and hence the economy's response to shocks. Two important characteristics of climate policy have been analysed in light of how they affect the transmission of shocks in the economy, and hence the degree of overall macroeconomic volatility. The first concerns the choice between a quantity and a price instrument, and the second concerns the optimal adjustment of climate policy over the business cycle. In practice, the real-world implementation of climate policy is lagging behind these considerations, as many jurisdictions have yet to implement any form of carbon pricing.

2.3.1.1 Quantity versus Price Instruments

The comparison of quantity instruments (cap and trade) and price instruments (carbon tax) looks at their respective ability to dampen economic volatility arising from shocks hitting the economy. The main intuition is that a quantity instrument will restrict fluctuations in output, thus acting as an automatic stabiliser, but lead to higher volatility of prices. A price instrument will have the opposite effect, dampening volatility in prices at the expense of volatility of output (Annicchiarico & Di Dio, 2015). The stabilising effect of a cap on emissions, which increases the volatility of inflation, can complicate the ability of monetary policy to maintain price stability.

Given that emissions are a by-product of production and are thus naturally pro-cyclical, 'a cap on emissions has a built-in dampening effect on the business cycle' (Annicchiarico et al., 2021). Expansionary economic shocks, such as a positive productivity shock or expansionary fiscal or monetary policies, should lead to higher output and emissions. However, in the presence of a carbon cap, this will require firms to invest more in abating emissions and will lead to an increase in the price of emission permits. This higher spending on abatement leaves fewer resources for consumption, which dampens demand and thus output.

Conversely, when the economy is faced with negative shocks, such as cost-push shocks or contractionary fiscal or monetary policy, output decreases, bringing down emissions, which therefore requires less expenditure on abatement to meet the emissions cap, mitigating the fall in demand.

Furthermore, the stabilising properties of the cap on emissions are welfare improving when nominal rigidities are strong. This is because nominal rigidities amplify business cycle fluctuations. If firms cannot fully adjust their prices, they fulfil demand by adapting the quantity of output produced. At the aggregate level, stickier prices imply a more important role for aggregate demand in driving output, accentuating business cycle dynamics. Therefore, a regulation that forces a smoothed response of real variables tends to be preferred. As prices become more flexible, the differences between the different carbon pricing instruments become negligible.

2.3.1.2 Optimal Cyclicality of Carbon Pricing

The welfare effects of imposing a carbon price, especially as a tax instrument, can be improved by ensuring that its stringency is pro-cyclical for its effect to be counter-cyclical on the economic activity (Annicchiarico & Di Dio, 2015; Heutel, 2012; Jaccard et al., 2020). In an expansion, for example driven by a positive productivity shock, output and emissions increase. This means that the tax needs to go up to bring them down. A symmetric reasoning applies in the case of a downturn, for example from contractionary monetary policy that dampens demand.

Annicchiarico and Di Dio (2015) argue that expansionary fiscal policy is an exception to this principle. Because increased fiscal spending is already crowding out consumption, investment and resources available for abatement, the carbon tax should become less stringent.

2.3.1.3 Implementation of Carbon Pricing in Practice

These conclusions concerning the optimal design of carbon pricing omit a number of important practical considerations involved in implementing the pricing. Hence, the overall welfare effects of fine-tuning climate policy, for example to respond to business cycles, might differ from those reported in the earlier sections.

The first omitted element is the administrative or political economy costs involved with the implementation. Estimates of the size of these costs are difficult to come by, but their importance is seen in the fact that the implementation of carbon pricing is lagging behind these theoretical considerations. As Figure 4.2 (in Chapter 4) shows, the proportion of global greenhouse gas (GHG) emissions covered by any form of carbon pricing instrument reached only around 20 per cent of global emissions in 2022.

A second consideration so far omitted from the welfare analysis is the factoring in of the revenues raised and how they are used. The carbon tax introduced in 2008 in the province of British Columbia in Canada came with a progressive redistribution system of the revenues to households. The cyclicality of the revenues and their distributional consequences are yet to be factored into a welfare analysis.

A final consideration that might alter the welfare calculation is the time scale of damages from GHG emissions. In the case of CO_2 emissions, the damages to the climate, and to the economy, depend on the cumulative stock of emissions. This implies that the damages are not sensitive to business cycle considerations. This might differ for other GHG gases, which have a shorter lifespan in the atmosphere, such as methane. Adjusting climate policy for the business cycle has larger welfare gains for flow pollutants than it has for stock pollutants (Annicchiarico et al., 2021).

2.3.2 *Interaction between Climate Policy and Other Policy Tools*

The transmission of shocks in the economy is affected by the design of the climate policy introduced to achieve decarbonisation. This raises the question of which policy mix will ensure the reduction of emissions at the least possible cost in terms of output and inflation volatility.

2.3.2.1 *Optimal Policy Mix*

The main macroeconomic policy studied in this context is monetary policy.[5] It has been shown to play a crucial role in accommodating the negative implications of climate policy (Annicchiarico et al., 2021; Ferrari & Pagliari, 2021). By stabilising economic activity through its effect on demand, monetary policy can avoid excessive expansions and downturns, thus reducing the welfare costs of climate policy. Dampening expansions makes achieving emissions reductions

---

[5] The reason behind this is methodological bias. The literature presented in this chapter relies on DSGEs, which are models traditionally used to analyse the transmission of monetary policy.

achievable with a lower carbon price. Mitigating downturns helps to minimise the social costs of decarbonisation. However, climate policy itself represents a challenge for monetary stability, as it creates additional volatility, adding noise to price signals. The answer to this is to adopt more stringent response to volatility irrespective of its origin.

Other policies can also have a role to play in ensuring a smooth decarbonisation process. For example, if the economy is faced with a positive productivity shock, which leads to an increase in output and hence emissions, the optimal response of fiscal policy is to reduce government spending, in order to leave more resources for abatement (Chan, 2020).

In an open economy setting, where countries trade goods, introducing climate policy unilaterally is welfare reducing (Ferrari & Pagliari, 2021). The country that sets a carbon tax will witness an exchange rate appreciation, which reduces exports. But imports increase, including of carbon-intensive goods from foreign countries. Emissions can therefore increase globally. Hence, climate policy needs to be accompanied by international cooperation and can be aided by a trade policy that would impose tariffs on carbon-intensive goods coming from abroad (see the discussion and Box 4.1 on carbon border adjustment mechanism in Chapter 4).

2.3.2.2 Can Macroeconomic Policy Substitute Carbon Pricing?

In certain countries, the introduction of carbon pricing has proven politically impossible. Some researchers have thus looked at whether significant reductions in emissions could nevertheless be achieved by including a target for emissions in the other policy tools for macroeconomic stabilisation, such as monetary policy, fiscal policy and financial regulation. The main takeaway from these exercises is that using these instruments for reducing emissions comes at the cost of not achieving the original targets, namely it allows more macroeconomic instability.

In general, macroeconomic policy tools can trigger decreases in emissions only by being contractionary. To maintain the level of output while reducing emissions, firms need to invest in abatement. Hence only policies that directly impact the cost of abatement, namely carbon pricing, can achieve that.

Ferrari and Pagliari (2021) explore whether monetary policy on its own could achieve decarbonisation. This would be achieved by including an emissions target (which would be close to an output target) in the objective of the central bank. Ferrari and Pagliari find that this is the least effective option to bring down emissions.

This stems from the mismatch between the role of monetary policy and the nature of CO_2 emissions. Monetary policy aims to address the volatility of macroeconomic variables around the economy's long-run trend but not the steady state itself. CO_2 emissions, on the other hand, because of their persistence in the atmosphere affect the steady state of the economy but are of little relevance for short-term fluctuations. Therefore, policies to achieve decarbonisation need to address the steady state of the economy. Policies to stabilise deviations from this steady state only have the potential to smoothen the transition.

Additionally, researchers have also explored whether including a green bias in policies could help with decarbonisation. However, these seem to offer little scope in this direction. For example, Abiry et al. (2022) analyse the merits of green quantitative easing, which refers to a policy where the central bank changes the composition of its private asset portfolio to include only green bonds (see detailed discussion in Chapter 8). The main effect of green quantitative easing is to make capital in the carbon-intensive sector more expensive, which could even be counterproductive because it could lead firms to substitute capital for labour and energy, thus increasing energy intensity. A carbon price on the other hand directly targets the price of energy and incentives substitution in the other direction. The simulation performed by Abiry et al. (2022) suggests that the maximum reduction in emissions that can be achieved through green quantitative easing could also be achieved with a carbon tax of $3/ton of CO_2. This is much lower than most estimates of the optimal carbon price, suggesting that this reduction is far too small to have a significant effect on emissions. More generally, while green quantitative easing maintains its effectiveness sustaining aggregate demand, it performs barely better than a neutral asset program, because of the small size of the green sector in the overall economy.

2.4 CONCLUSION

In the short and medium run, economies face frictions that limit their ability to respond optimally to shocks, making them subject to volatility. Macroeconomic policy, such as monetary, fiscal and prudential policy, aims at managing this volatility. At this time scale, climate policy, interpreted as the introduction of a carbon price, represents an additional source of volatility. It represents a shock in itself, it amplifies the effects of other shocks and it affects the effectiveness of prudential policy.

When it is introduced, climate policy represents a cost shock. By increasing the cost of energy faced by firms, it will create a negative supply shock. But aggregate demand also drops in response to this shock. The relative response of demand compared to supply, and hence the overall equilibrium response of the economy, depends on four mechanisms.

First, if economic actors delay their response, the supply shock will outweigh the demand shock, leading to inflationary pressure. Once expectations catch up to the situation, and agents do respond, this delay leads to an amplification of the negative demand shock and of the overall volatility. Second, if there is a large share of hand-to-mouth households in the economy, they will be directly impacted by higher energy prices. Their inability to save hampers their capacity to absorb the consumption shock. In addition, as they tend to work in sectors that are responsive to demand, their income is affected by a second-round indirect effect. This means that the demand shock has the potential to be very pronounced, leading to a sharp drop in output and deflationary pressure. Third, the presence of financial frictions in financial markets, which can result from prudential regulation imposing capital requirements, can exacerbate the negative supply shock by limiting the amount of credit available in the economy. Finally, central banks following their price stability mandate have an important role to play in responding to this volatility. They can dampen inflationary pressure when the demand response is delayed or be accommodating in case of an important drop in economic activity.

In addition to these mechanisms, the very presence of carbon pricing affects the response of economic variables to other shocks. The main trade-off concerns the choice between a price and a quantity instrument. What emerges is a trade-off between output and price stability. Setting a target on one dampens volatility in that variable, but at the cost of creating more volatility in the other. Because of the tight relationship between output and emissions at the time scale of the business cycle, introducing a cap on emissions acts as an automatic stabiliser for output. However, this increases price volatility, complicating the ability of central banks to disentangle demand and supply shocks and hence achieving their price stability mandate.

The role and effectiveness of the other tools of macroeconomic policy are also affected by the decarbonisation objective. Achieving decarbonisation will change the steady state of the economy. Therefore, the policies that contribute directly to this goal are those that determine the cost of abatement, namely the amount of emissions generated by economic activity. The tools of macroeconomic policy that address the economy's deviations from its trend have an important role to play in alleviating the negative impacts stemming from increased volatility. But they cannot substitute for climate policies that affect the relative cost of carbon.

2.5   KEY TAKEAWAYS

- Dynamic Stochastic General Equilibrium models are the main analytical framework used to understand the short-run disruptions created by decarbonisation.

2.5.1   The Effect of Climate Policy on Macroeconomic Variables

- In the DSGE framework, the introduction of climate policy is modelled as the introduction of carbon prices. This increases the costs of firms, creating a negative supply shock and inflationary pressure.
- However, the overall impact on macroeconomic variables of interest (output, inflation, interest rates) depends on the relative size of the response of aggregate demand.
- Four transmission channels can affect the relative importance of supply and demand.
- The first transmission channel goes through the expectations of households and firms. The extent to which economic agents find the policy credible will affect the speed at which they adjust their behaviour.
- The second transmission channel is the degree to which households differ in their exposure to increases in energy prices and in their ability to respond. If the share of exposed households is large enough, a fall in their consumption can have aggregate impacts.
- The third transmission channel is the 'financial accelerator'. Climate policy can create instability through a sudden devaluation of carbon-intensive assets that impacts the ability of banks to provide loans.
- The fourth transmission channel is the strength of the monetary policy response to inflationary pressure.

2.5.2   Stabilising Business Cycle Fluctuations in a Decarbonising Economy

- Economies will continue to be hit by shocks throughout the transition to net zero.
- The presence of carbon pricing affects the response of economic variables to other shocks.
- The main trade-off concerns the choice between a price and a quantity instrument. A carbon tax exacerbates output volatility, whereas a cap-and-trade instrument exacerbates price volatility.
- The role and effectiveness of the other tools of macroeconomic policy are also affected by decarbonisation. However, they cannot substitute for climate policies that affect the relative cost of carbon.

REFERENCES

Abiry, R., M. Ferdinandusse, C. Nerlich, and A. Ludwig (2022) 'Climate Change Mitigation: How Effective Is Green Quantitative Easing?', ECB Working Paper Series No. 2701, p. 43, www.ecb.europa.eu/pub/pdf/scpwps/ecb .wp2701~72d8bfaa67.en.pdf

Annicchiarico, B., S. Carattini, C. Fischer, and G. Heutel (2021) 'Business Cycles and Environmental Policy: Literature Review and Policy Implications', NBER Working Paper No. 29032, July, https://doi.org/10.3386/w29032

Annicchiarico, B., and F. Di Dio (2015) 'Environmental Policy and Macroeconomic Dynamics in a New Keynesian Model', *Journal of Environmental Economics and Management*, 69, 1–21, https://doi.org/10.1016/j.jeem.2014.10.002

(2017) 'GHG Emissions Control and Monetary Policy', *Environmental and Resource Economics*, 67:4, 823–51, https://doi.org/10.1007/ s10640-016-0007-5

Annicchiarico, B., F. Di Dio, and F. Diluiso (2022) 'Climate Actions, Market Beliefs and Monetary Policy', CEIS Working Paper No. 535, March, https:// papers.ssrn.com/sol3/papers.cfm?abstract_id=4066585

Barrage, L. (2020) 'Optimal Dynamic Carbon Taxes in a Climate–Economy Model with Distortionary Fiscal Policy', *The Review of Economic Studies*, 87:1, 1–39, https://doi.org/10.1093/restud/rdz055

Carattini, S., G. Heutel, and G. Melkadze (2021) 'Climate Policy, Financial Frictions, and Transition Risk', NBER Working Paper No. 28525, p. 60, www.nber.org/system/files/working_papers/w28525/w28525.pdf

Chan, Y. T. (2020) 'Are Macroeconomic Policies Better in Curbing Air Pollution than Environmental Policies? A DSGE Approach with Carbon-Dependent Fiscal and Monetary Policies', *Energy Policy*, 141, 111454, https://doi .org/10.1016/j.enpol.2020.111454

Diluiso, F., B. Annicchiarico, M. Kalkuhl, and J. C. Minx (2021) 'Climate Actions and Macro-Financial Stability: The Role of Central Banks', *Journal of Environmental Economics and Management*, 110, 102548, https://doi .org/10.1016/j.jeem.2021.102548

Ferrari, A., and V. Nispi Landi (2022) 'Will the Green Transition Be Inflationary? Expectations Matter', www.dropbox.com/s/71agxwh79ykkobh/Ferrari%20 and%20Nispi%20Landi%20QEF%20sito.pdf?dl=0

Ferrari, M. M., and M. S. Pagliari (2021) 'No Country Is an Island: International Cooperation and Climate Change', ECB Working Paper No. 20212568, 1 June, https://doi.org/10.2139/ssrn.3870019

Fischer, C., and G. Heutel (2013) 'Environmental Macroeconomics: Environmental Policy, Business Cycles, and Directed Technical Change', *Annual Review of Resource Economics*, 5:1, 197–210, https://doi.org/10.1146/annurev-resource-091912-151819

Heutel, G. (2012) 'How Should Environmental Policy Respond to Business Cycles? Optimal Policy under Persistent Productivity Shocks', *Review of Economic Dynamics*, 15:2, 244–64, https://doi.org/10.1016/j.red.2011.05.002

Jaccard, I., G. Benmir, and G. Vermandel (2020) 'Green Asset Pricing', *SSRN Electronic Journal*, https://doi.org/10.2139/ssrn.3706133

Känzig, D. R. (2021) 'The Unequal Economic Consequences of Carbon Pricing', https://doi.org/10.2139/ssrn.3786030

Konradt, M., and B. Weder di Mauro (2021) 'Carbon Taxation and Inflation: Evidence from the European and Canadian Experience', https://papers.ssrn.com/abstract=3928675

McKibbin, W. J., A. C. Morris, P. J. Wilcoxen, and A. J. Panton (2020) 'Climate Change and Monetary Policy: Issues for Policy Design and Modelling', *Oxford Review of Economic Policy*, 36:3, 579–603, https://doi.org/10.1093/oxrep/graa040

Schnabel, I. (2022) 'A New Age of Energy Inflation: Climateflation, Fossilflation and Greenflation', www.ecb.europa.eu/press/key/date/2022/html/ecb.sp220317_2~dbb3582f0a.en.html

3 The Distributional Effects of Climate Policy

3.1 INTRODUCTION

The transition to a zero-carbon economy is a crucial step towards addressing the global threat of climate change. However, the distributional consequences of this transition must also be considered. Inequality, or the unequal distribution of economic outcomes such as income and wealth, takes many forms, including disparities within a single country or between countries. Reducing inequality, or at least not exacerbating it, is important for the overall welfare of a population. At a minimum, the climate transition should avoid the deterioration of individuals' access to basic goods and services such as housing, heating, health, and education. Discontent with the distributional consequences of policy can rapidly erode national and international political support for the green transition. The protests in France by the 'Yellow Vests' (*Gilets jaunes*) is just one example of discontent against a planned climate policy. Hence, the potential impact of the green transition on inequality should be carefully considered when designing climate policy. In this chapter, we will examine key channels determining the distributional consequences of the transition to a zero-carbon economy, including the impact of different policies both nationally and globally.

The chapter first covers the concept of inequality and common measures and explains the relevance of distributional impacts for climate policy from a welfare, political and economic perspective. It then covers distributional effects of national climate policies by assessing how various policies may affect the expenditures and incomes of households. The final part of the chapter covers factors that may lead to distributional impacts between different countries.

3.2 WHAT IS INEQUALITY AND WHY DOES IT MATTER FOR THE GREEN TRANSITION?

Inequality comes in many shapes and forms. While inequality of opportunity exists when circumstances early in the life of an individual determine differences in life outcomes, inequality of outcome is commonly concerned with the distribution of economic outcomes like returns from labour and capital, or wealth. Inequality can refer to disparities within a single country or between several countries. Between-country inequality is commonly measured by the difference between countries' gross domestic product (GDP) and has been decreasing because of globalisation and relatively higher rates of economic growth in the developing world. Fast-growing economies in East Asia especially have continued to close the gap with Western economies, whose economic growth has slowed considerably (Alvaredo et al., 2017). Development in China and India in particular have reduced inequality in the global distribution of incomes (Darvas, 2019).

Within-country inequality is commonly measured in terms of relative measures like the share of aggregate income held by the top quantile of society or the Gini coefficient.[1] Disparities in wealth within countries tend to be more enduring and pronounced than income inequality. Overall, within-country inequality has increased considerably over the past decades (Balestra& Tonkin, 2018). While these measures do a good job at capturing varying outcomes of different income groups, one should note that they may not succeed in capturing the distributional effects of climate policies on households with similar income.[2] So-called horizontal inequalities can be attributed to factors like the climate surrounding the household and the commuting distance of its members (Rausch et al., 2011), the

---

[1] The Gini coefficient is a measure of the level of disparity among a population, expressed as a value between 0 and 1, with 0 representing perfect equality and 1 representing perfect inequality.

[2] For empirical studies emphasising horizontal inequality, see for example Poterba (1991), Rausch et al. (2011), Cronin et al. (2019), Pizer and Sexton (2019) and Steckel et al. (2021).

household's energy efficiency (Hänsel et al., 2022) or race of its members (Dogan et al., 2022). These types of inequality are not well captured by Gini coefficients measuring income inequality.

3.2.1 Inequality and Welfare

The level of wealth and/or income inequality has direct implications for the overall welfare of a population. Income and wealth are essential for individual welfare as they enable access to goods and services, including housing, health and education. The welfare of a society is typically defined using a welfare function that aggregates the welfare of its individuals. A common assumption is that welfare functions display 'decreasing marginal returns', meaning that improvements in welfare from additional income gets smaller at higher levels of income. The reasoning behind this assumption is intuitive: a poor individual receiving an increase in income that allows for the satisfaction of basic needs like purchasing food or housing will experience a large welfare gain; a wealthy individual receiving an increase of the same absolute amount will not experience a substantive gain in welfare, since their basic needs are already satisfied. When income and wealth become more concentrated among a small number of individuals at the expense of large parts of the population, the aggregate welfare of a country may decrease due to the lower welfare experienced by the majority of its individuals.

Figure 3.1 shows an example of the income distribution of Australia, Denmark and the Unites States, plotted in the form of a Lorenz curve; this plots the cumulative percentage of the population against the cumulative percentage of income earned by that population. The closer the Lorenz curve is to the main diagonal, the more even is the distribution. In 2021, the three countries had similar per capita income levels.[3] The distribution of income, however, was most equal in Denmark and most unequal in the United States.

---

[3] In constant 2015 US$, GDP per capita in 2021 was $58,780 in Australia, $58,586 in Denmark and $61,280 in the United States, according to World Bank data.

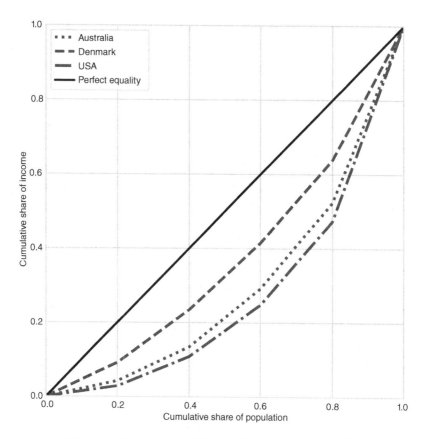

FIGURE 3.1 Lorenz curve of income distribution in Australia, Denmark and the United States, 2021
Source: Authors' calculations based on Australian Bureau of Statistics (2022), Eurostat (2022a), and United States Census Bureau (2022)

The organisation of labour markets, limiting of market power and reducing concentration of wealth all have major implications for the distribution of primary incomes, that is, incomes before the distributional policies of the state. Policies such as taxation and the payment of income transfers can increase the aggregate level of welfare by redistributing income from wealthier individuals to poorer ones. In the same way, a policy that benefits predominantly wealthier households or harms poorer individuals can decrease overall welfare. If, for example, an industrial sector that employs predominantly low-income earners is replaced by a renewable industry that employs high-income earners, this holds implications for overall welfare.

3.2.2 Political Support for Climate Policy

The distributional impact of climate policies significantly affects the political support of said policies. As Dechezlepretre et al. (2022) show based on analysing surveys,[4] public support for climate policies is largely dependent on perceptions of the policies' effectiveness in reducing emissions, their distributional impact on lower-income households and their impact on the respondents' own household. A growing body of literature exploring the drivers of support for climate policies confirms these findings. If policies are regressive, or perceived as such by the public, support erodes (e.g. Brannlund & Persson, 2012; Dietz & Atkinson, 2010; Sommer et al., 2022). Vona (2018) also finds that public perception of, and support for, climate policies is significantly reduced in the presence of negative shocks like job losses. Such losses can either be due to policies themselves or be the consequence of external shocks. This can be particularly problematic in areas and sectors that have been hit hard by economic recession and international competition, as the associated job losses can lead to a feeling of disenfranchisement and disempowerment. Because of the concentration of job losses in specific sectors and regions, negative perceptions and the resulting lack of support for climate policies may persist even if aggregate labour market effects of the policies are positive.

An example for the failure of climate policy based on the unequal effect on different groups and the perception of such disproportionality is the Gilets jaunes (or the 'yellow vest') movement. The movement began in France in October 2018 against a planned increase in fuel taxes. In the context of rising oil prices and a general perception of societal injustice, the disproportionate effect the tax would have on rural households, who are more reliant on cars for transportation, sparked nationwide protests, resulting in the eventual

---

[4] That together cover more than 40,000 respondents in twenty countries that account for 72 per cent of global CO_2 emissions.

cancelation of the fuel tax (Gagnebin et al., 2019; Jetten et al., 2020). Reflecting on the events in France, Gagnebin et al. (2019) find that the regressive nature of similar policies necessitates the compensation of lower-income groups to ensure political stability.

3.2.3 Burden Sharing and Global Political Consensus

The shift towards a low-carbon economy is likely to affect countries differently. Changes in patterns of resource demand, for example, create both risks and opportunities for different countries. Oil-exporting economies may see the value of their resource endowment decline as the demand for fossil fuels declines, while mineral-exporting countries may benefit from increased demand for raw materials used in renewable energy technologies.[5] At the same time, the extraction of these raw materials could pose conflict risks that need to be carefully managed (Hafner & Tagliapietra, 2020).

Hafner and Wochner (2020) argue that effective governance of a green transition hinges on increased ownership of climate policies among countries through a more inclusive and equitable distribution of burdens. Countries are more likely to support a policy if they believe that it will benefit them economically or if the policies help to mitigate problems related to climate change in the region. A country that is disproportionately negatively affected by a given policy may choose to obstruct a global green transition. The international consensus required to find effective policy paths towards the green transition is thus partly contingent on the effect of climate policy on between-country inequality.

Sharing the burden of climate transition has been a prominent issue in all documents and meetings of the United Nations Framework Convention on Climate Change (UNFCCC). In this context, 'common

---

[5] A report published by the International Institute for Sustainable Development identifies twenty-three key minerals that will be critical to the development and deployment of renewable technologies, such as solar panels, wind turbines, electric vehicles and energy storage technologies, many concentrated in politically fragile states (Church & Crawford, 2018).

but differentiated responsibilities' has become a core principle of international environmental law. Also during the implementation of the European Green Deal, the plan to decarbonise the EU economy by 2050, the European Commission provides grants to member states having identified the territories expected to be the most negatively impacted by the green transition to share the burden more equally between its member countries. Leonard et al. (2021) explore the potential ramifications of the European Green Deal on the competitiveness of countries outside of the European Union. They conclude that to mitigate geopolitical fallout and strengthen global climate efforts, the European Union will need to support the renewable transition at home and abroad, work with international partners, set standards and promote coalitions for climate change mitigation.

3.3 ANALYTICAL FRAMEWORK FOR WITHIN-COUNTRY INEQUALITY

The impact of climate policies on households varies based on a range of factors, including geographic location, gender, wealth and other demographic characteristics. For example, a fuel tax may have a disproportionate impact on rural households compared to urban ones. Other factors that could influence the impact of climate policies on households include nationality, income, ethnicity, region, occupation and education (Box 3.1). To understand how climate policies affect households, we can use a stylised model of economic welfare that includes three components: the income side, the expenditure side and the government side.

BOX 3.1   **Inequality and the macroeconomy**

Climate policies that increase inequality may indirectly affect economic growth and the business cycle. In very simplified terms, higher inequality, on the one hand, can induce higher economic growth as richer households save and invest more; on the other hand, it can lead to weaker economic performance as poorer households cannot invest enough in human capital. Ostry et al. (2014) find that in the medium run the negative effects of inequality prevail and hamper economic growth. Increasing inequality can also lead to economic and political instability, which in turn decreases investment levels. Additionally, inequality can contribute to financial instability, leading to declining growth (Coibion et al., 2014).

One of the main mechanisms through which inequality affects growth is by undermining education opportunities for children from poorer socio-economic backgrounds, resulting in reduced social mobility and skills development (Cingano, 2014; Ostry et al., 2014). When those at the bottom of the income distribution are at risk of not reaching their potential, the economy pays a price not only with weaker demand today but also with lower growth in the future. Protectionist policies and declining investments in education, which have both been linked to economic inequality, may exacerbate this problem (Cingano, 2014; Jaumotte & Osorio, 2015).

Beyond medium-term effects on growth, inequality can also worsen economic outcomes through its impact on business cycle fluctuations. The rapidly growing HANK literature models general equilibrium implications of inequality and finds that it may substantially weaken aggregate demand, as those at the bottom spend a larger fraction of their income than those at the top (e.g. Auclert et al., 2020; Gornemann et al., 2016; Kaplan et al., 2018). Bilbiie et al. (2022) find that inequality can theoretically amplify business cycle fluctuations, due to cyclical precautionary saving behaviour. Confronted with the risk of unemployment and low income, households may reduce their consumption in favour of saving. Since the risk of income drops is greater in less equal societies and felt most during recessions, inequality could exacerbate economic downturns.

3.3.1 Income Side

Households generate income when working or because they own capital that gives a return. Climate policies can affect this income in various ways. For example, the owner of a coal mine may see the income they earn from their mine decline because of carbon pricing, while a biotech engineer may see an increase in income due to increased investment in advanced biofuels. Low-income households typically own fewer production factors, such as land or capital, than high-income households. However, skill-based income (i.e. labour) represents a higher share of total income for low-income households, even though the wages they earn with these skills may be lower. Households can use their budget to invest in production factors, such as land, capital assets or education. While high-income households may often find that such investments increase their overall wellbeing, low-income households may need to invest all of their income to pay for basic needs, such as food and rent. Without the means to invest into their education or purchase goods like electric vehicle, low-income households may not be able to adjust to a decarbonised economy as well as high-income households.

3.3.2 Expenditure Side

Households make consumption decisions based on a combination of factors, including the utility they derive from immediate consumption and the welfare they can expect to receive from the acquisition of durable goods, like housing. Additionally, the provision of goods and services by the government, as well as the quality of the environment, play a role in the overall wellbeing of households. Consumption decisions of households can be seen as actions aimed at maximising their individual utility by acquiring the optimal combination of goods and services. Expenditure decisions depend on several factors, including a household's preferences for individual goods and services, its borrowing constraints and the total budget it allocates to consumption. Because of these factors, climate policies may affect low and high-income households in different ways.

(1) Preferences differ between households; low-income individuals, for example, often put a higher value on immediate consumption and might benefit less from climate policies that promote investments in low-carbon technologies and appliances. (2) Given their lower credit scores and lack of collateral, low-income

households also often face stricter borrowing constraints than wealthier households. This can prevent them from investing in technologies that would reduce their monetary and carbon expenditure over time. (3) Differences in the consumption level between lower- and higher-income households are partly explained by the size of their budget allocated to consumption.[6] Because basic goods (such as heating or food) form a much higher share of low-income households' consumption baskets, policies that raise the prices of these goods can have distributional effects. If, for example, a carbon tax increases the cost of heating, the disposable income of low-income households might substantially shrink, while the effect on the disposable income of high-income households might be negligible.

In addition to differences in preferences, borrowing ability and consumption baskets, households with different incomes may also have different abilities to make expenditures that reduce their exposure to carbon prices or allow them to benefit from support schemes. For example, high-income households may be able to take advantage of a rooftop solar subsidy because they own a house.

3.3.3 Government Side

Governments collect a variety of taxes, including those on income from capital, labour and land and those on consumption. These revenues are used to fund the provision of public goods and services, such as streets and public transportation, as well as transfers to individuals, such as social security benefits. Climate policies that generate public revenue can enable governments to reduce other taxes, increase the provision of transfers and public services or use the revenue in other ways. In theory, governments can offset the distributional effects of regressive climate policies through targeted lump-sum transfers or by reducing other regressive taxes. The way in which governments

---

[6] A household might also invest in production factors or decide to consume more leisure instead of consuming more goods and services – so this is another complex optimisation.

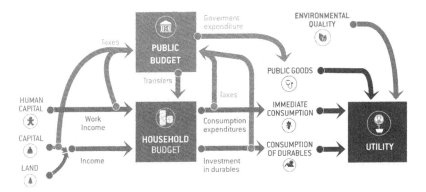

FIGURE 3.2 Stylised model of households in the economy
Source: Zachmann et al. (2018).

choose to use climate policy-related revenues can be progressive, that is, reduce existing inequality, or regressive, that is, exacerbate the disproportional effects of polices.

Figure 3.2 provides a high-level overview of the economic activities of households and individuals. Climate policies can affect the welfare of these groups by altering their income, the value of their investments and the utility they derive from their expenditures and consumption of public services. However, the impact of such policies may vary for low- and high-income households due to structural differences in their economic activities.

Therefore, it is important to analyse the distributional effects of a given climate policy on each economic activity in order to obtain fair policy guidance. Focusing on only one aspect of a policy's impact could bias the outlook. For example, a policy that has a disproportionate cost for low-income households on the expenditure side might decrease the returns to production factors held by high-income households on the income side, resulting in a roughly proportionate distributional effect. The type of policy, the targeted sector, the policy's design and the characteristics of the economy all play a role in determining the direction and extent of a policy's distributional impact.

3.4 DISTRIBUTIONAL EFFECTS OF CLIMATE POLICIES

3.4.1 *Carbon Pricing*

Many economists view the implementation of a carbon price, through the use of price-based instruments (e.g. taxes) or quantity-based instruments (e.g. emissions allowances), as the most economically efficient method of reducing emissions (e.g. Cramton et al., 2017). This approach can take the form of a single carbon price applied across all sectors, as seen in the European Union's Emissions Trading System (ETS), or a set of varying prices determined by sector, such as those implemented for aviation emissions.

The implementation of a carbon price can have two main distributional effects. Firstly, it increases the cost of emissions-intensive products for consumers, which is typically regressive as lower-income households spend a larger share of their income on these goods and may have fewer options for switching to less emissions-intensive substitutes. Secondly, a carbon price can alter the return to factors of production, such as capital and labour, with a slight tendency towards progressivity as emissions-intensive capital assets are more likely to be held by high-income households. However, these households also tend to own capital assets that may benefit from the implementation of a carbon price, such as shares in wind turbine manufacturers.

The distributional effects of carbon pricing differ across sectors based on factors such as the availability of low-carbon alternatives, the ability of producers to reduce prices and the consumption basket of households. First, the incidence of carbon pricing (i.e. how the cost is distributed between consumers and producers) will depend on the targeted product and its market conditions. In sectors where consumers can easily switch to low-carbon alternatives, producers of high-carbon products must either pay the carbon tax or lose market share. However, in sectors where no low-carbon alternatives exist, producers can pass the cost of the carbon tax on to consumers. Second, the extent to which producers can reduce prices will affect the distribution of the carbon price between them and consumers. For products that cannot be offered at lower prices, consumers will bear the cost of the carbon tax, while for products that can be offered at lower prices, producers will absorb a greater share of the carbon price. Finally, low-income households spend a disproportionally larger share of their expenditure on some products and services, such as electricity. A tax on these products and services may therefore be regressive. In contrast, services like aviation make up a larger expenditure share for high-income households and a tax on such services may be progressive (Table 3.1). This means that although the absolute expenditure of richer households for food or electricity is likely higher than that of poorer households, the effect of a tax may be felt most by the poor, given their higher relative expenditure share.

3.4.1.1 Road Fuel Emissions

Road fuels are a significant contributor to global emissions, and therefore decarbonisation policies in the road transport sector are a key area for policymakers. Initial effects of a carbon tax on households may include reduced consumption of fossil fuels as a result of increased prices and an increased incentive to invest in electric vehicles. The overall utility of households may be reduced, but this effect can be offset depending on how the government uses the additional revenue from the carbon taxes. As poor people often do not own a car and rich people spend a relatively low share of their budget on fuels and they are able to afford electric vehicles, the burden tends to fall on the middle class. Overall, literature on the distributional effects of road fuel taxes is mixed, with some studies finding it to be regressive (Brannlund & Nordström, 2004; Dumagan & Mount, 1992; Tovar Reaños & Wölfing, 2018; West & Williams, 2017) and others finding it to be progressive (Flues & Thomas, 2015; Tiezzi, 2005).

3.4.1.2 Electricity Consumption

In high-income countries, electricity taxes tend to be regressive. Flues and Thomas (2015) conducted a study of twenty-one Organisation

Table 3.1 *Summary table of greenhouse gas emissions and the share of overall household consumption expenditure for sectors affected by carbon pricing*

Category name in our report	Share of total emissions (EU-28) (%)	Share of expenditure on sector/product in overall household expenditure (Italy)			Engel curve slope estimate
		Bottom income quintile (%)	Average household (%)	Top income quintile (%)	
Air transport	4	0.2	0.3	0.4	0.07*
Road fuel	9	5.6	5.2	4.1	−0.89***
Agriculture	11	22.7	18.2	16.5	−1.25***
Electricity	21	3.9	2.4	2.4	−0.33
Heating		3.8	2.8	1.7	–

Note: An Engel curve slope estimate indicates how the expenditure on a particular good or service varies with income. Goods with a statistically significant positive slope estimate are consumed relatively more by high-income households, whereas low-income households spend a larger share of their income on goods with a statistically significant negative slope estimate. *** significant at 1 per cent level; ** significant at 5 per cent level; * significant at 10 per cent level. All data besides the Engel curve slope estimates are for 2019.

Source: Based on Eurostat (2022b), Italian National Institute of Statistics (2022) and Engel curve slope estimates from Faijgelbaum and Khandelwal (2016).

for Economic Co-operation and Development (OECD) countries and found that, on average, electricity taxes are regressive on both an expenditure basis and an income basis. A study by Tovar Reaños and Wölfing (2018) came to similar conclusions for the case of Germany. The regressive nature of electricity taxes has several drivers. The demand for electricity in high-income countries is inelastic. This means that households are unable to reduce their consumption significantly in response to price increases, because all modern households require a minimum amount of electricity for essential appliances. Additionally, credit constraints can prevent low-income households from switching to more efficient appliances, even if they would like to do so, further exacerbating the regressive nature of electricity taxes.

In low-income countries, however, similar policy measures can be progressive (Ohlendorf et al., 2021). Dorban et al. (2019) assess the expected incidence of moderate carbon price increases in eighty-seven low- and middle-income countries and find that poor households in low-income countries are less affected. They explain their findings with the inverse-U relation between energy expenditure and income. Poor households in low-income countries spend less on electricity since their level of income does not allow for many electrical appliances.

3.4.1.3 Residential Heating

The distributional effects of taxes on residential heating is another issue analysed by the two abovementioned studies. Both studies found that heat taxes are regressive. However, while Tovar Reaños and Wölfing (2018) estimate that heat taxes result in a welfare loss two to three times greater than that resulting from electricity taxes, Flues and Thomas (2015) find that electricity taxes tend to be more regressive than taxes on heating fuel. The impact of heating taxes on low-income households may be mitigated by the fact that these households are more likely to live in smaller dwellings or apartment blocks that require less heating and are more sensitive to increasing costs, leading them to use less heat. Overall, while heating taxes are likely regressive, the extent to which they disproportionately hurt low-income households compared to other taxes remains unclear.

3.4.1.4   Aviation Services

Existing evidence suggests that air transport taxes are unlikely to be regressive. This is because high-income households are more likely to fly and spend larger portions of their income on air travel. Furthermore, data from the United Kingdom suggests that people who travel by plane are generally wealthier than the general population, implying that an air travel fuel tax would likely primarily affect high-income households (Zachmann et al., 2018).

3.4.1.5   Maritime Transport

Maritime shipping is another significant contributor to greenhouse gas emissions, accounting for 2.2 per cent of global emissions in 2012.[7] However, according to Cames et al. (2015), this figure could rise to 17 per cent by 2050 if left unregulated. In 2018, over 100 nations agreed to halve their greenhouse gas emissions from shipping by 2050.[8] The implementation of a carbon price for maritime emissions could incentivise firms to reduce emissions but would also increase the cost of shipping goods. This could lead to an increase in the price of imported goods, potentially reducing demand for imports and the volume of trade. The impact of a maritime carbon price on final goods prices and on the disposable income of various socio-economic groups, however, is complex and difficult to predict (Kollamthodi et al., 2013; Zachmann et al., 2018).

3.4.1.6   Labour Markets

Decarbonisation policies are likely going to have consequences on labour income distribution, because of existing rigidities in the

---

[7] Ferries and passenger ships account for only 0.3 per cent of the dead-weight tonnage of all ships (UNCTAD, 2017, p. 25).

[8] See International Maritime Organisation (2018), 'UN Body Adopts Climate Change Strategy for Shipping', www.imo.org/en/MediaCentre/PressBriefings/Pages/06GHGinitialstrategy.aspx

labour markets and their different impacts on sectors and job categories. A detailed analysis of these effects is presented in Chapter 7.

3.4.2 Subsidies

Many governments provide incentives for low-carbon technologies in their pursuit of climate objectives. These incentives can be direct subsidies for research and development, tax breaks for the purchase of electric vehicles or para-fiscal instruments such as feed-in tariffs for rooftop solar panels. Because they benefit higher-income households and companies that have the capital to invest in new low-carbon assets, such subsidies are likely regressive.

Early findings by West (2004) show that subsidies for new vehicles are more regressive than taxes on gasoline. Grösche and Schröder (2014) similarly find that the German feed-in tariff system, which uses a levy on electricity consumption to subsidise solar panels for households, was mildly regressive. Tovar Reaños and Sommerfeld (2018) demonstrate that the regressive effects of subsidies can also be seen in Germany's 2016 implementation of a €4,000 subsidy for electric vehicle purchases, which was financed through increased fuel prices. This subsidy primarily benefited higher-income households because lower-income households were unable to afford the expense of a new electric vehicle even with the subsidy.

Overall, many low-carbon subsidies are regressive because they reduce the price of goods that are primarily purchased by higher-income households. Subsidising clean vehicles, for instance, primarily benefits those who can afford them, while the less affluent gain little.

3.4.3 Public Investment

Another example for widespread climate policies is government investment in low-carbon technologies or complementary infrastructure, such as public transport or charging infrastructure for electric vehicles. The literature on the distributional effects of such investment in developed countries is scarce. For developing countries, however, several studies have indicated that public investment can reduce inequality.

For example, Dercon (2014) finds that moving investment away from long-distance transport and allocating it to local development can reduce inequality, though the distributional impact depends on the details of the particular investment project and the economic context. Furceri and Li (2017) report that increased public investment reduces income inequality, though the effect depends on whether the infrastructure generates productivity gains only in the sector involved or also in other sectors. Evidence from China and Latin America also suggests that public investment in infrastructure such as roads, dams and telecommunications has contributed towards the alleviation of inequality and poverty (Calderón & Servén, 2004; De Ferranti et al., 2004; Fan & Zhang, 2004). By contrast, Chatterjee and Turnovsky (2012) find that government spending on public capital leads to a persistent increase in wealth inequality in terms of income dispersion, while spurring growth and average welfare. Similar findings by Khandker and Koolwal (2007) suggest that access to paved roads has had limited distributional benefits in rural Bangladesh.

The distributional consequences of public investment may depend on various factors such as the specifics of the investment, the economic context and the financing mechanism. It is important to carefully consider these factors in order to maximise the potential benefits and mitigate any adverse distributional consequences.

3.4.4 Trade Policy

According to Peters et al. (2012), approximately 22 per cent of global CO_2 emissions are a result of the consumption of goods produced in another country. In a globally integrated economy, the goods that are consumed usually contain parts that have been produced elsewhere. This is the result of long value chains, which increase economic efficiency and make our products cheaper and better. For climate policy to be effective, it is important that climate policies reduce emissions at all stages of the production process. If all countries implemented the same climate policies, emissions would be cut according to the same rules across the world. In practice, however, climate policies differ. As these policies differ, producers might find it profitable to shift carbon-intensive production to countries with less stringent climate policies. This type of carbon leakage can frustrate domestic climate policies. Empirically, we can observe that consumption-based and production-based emission footprints of countries differ.

Trade policy is therefore considered a potential instrument for decarbonisation, and the question for this chapter is how trade policy measures to fight carbon leakage would affect inequality. One potential approach is for countries to impose trade restrictions on imports from countries with less stringent climate policies in order to protect domestic producers from competitive disadvantages resulting from stricter environmental regulations and to incentivise trading partners to reduce emissions. Another approach is to reduce trade restrictions on environmentally friendly goods.[9]

On the expenditure side, the distributional impact of a tariff on carbon-intensive foreign products will be similar to that of a carbon tax, in that consumers who spend a disproportionate share of their income on these imported goods will be disproportionately affected. This effect may be compounded by the fact that many carbon-intensive products are intermediate goods used in the production of final consumer goods. Distributive effects will thus be shaped by the specific design of the policy, including the size of tariffs on individual imported goods. An analysis of trade data from forty countries by Fajgelbaum and Khandelwal (2016) found that low-income households gain the most from trade on the expenditure side. Therefore, limiting or restricting trade will disproportionately harm low-income households. This is because low-income households tend

---

[9] Since July 2014, several members of the World Trade Organization have been negotiating an Environmental Goods Agreement to remove barriers to trade in goods that are crucial for environmental protection and climate change mitigation.

to spend a larger fraction of their income on traded goods, while high-income households spend more on domestically produced services.

On the income side, producers of substitute goods for carbon-intensive imports will likely see an increase in income, as will the labour employed in these sectors. Also, there is some evidence suggesting that trade barriers can reduce the wage premium for high-skilled labour (Borusyak & Jaravel, 2018). Additionally, capital owners in sectors where foreign competitors are locked out may see significant gains as their newly acquired market power allows them to raise prices, transferring wealth from consumers to these firms and their owners.

3.4.4.1 The Carbon Border Adjustment Mechanism

The European Union has adopted a proposal to establish a system called the carbon border adjustment mechanism (CBAM).[10] The purpose of the CBAM is to prevent companies in the European Union from moving their production to countries with less strict carbon emission regulations, a process known as 'carbon leakage'. Such carbon leakage would present a risk to EU economies and undermine its efforts to limit global emissions. The CBAM requires companies in the European Union importing certain products that have high carbon emissions, such as cement, iron and steel, aluminium, fertilisers and electricity, to pay for allowances based on the carbon content of those products. This is meant to replace the current system of allocating free allowances in the EU ETS, which is also used to prevent carbon leakage. The CBAM applies to industries that are already part of the EU ETS, and the cost of the allowances is similar to the price of allowances in the ETS. The CBAM is expected to increase the price of the covered goods.

The European Commission conducted a study to understand the potential distributional effects of the CBAM, using a computational model for different scenarios. The overall conclusion was that

---

[10] The EU trilogues reached a provisional political agreement on the reform of the ETS and the establishment of the CBAM in December 2022.

the CBAM would be regressive, meaning it would disproportionately impact poorer households more than wealthier ones. However, the impact is expected to be small due to limited effects on household incomes and consumption prices. The study also looked at the effects on household spending and income separately. The CBAM was found to be regressive on the expenditure side, as the consumption of poorer households would become more expensive in most countries. On the income side, the CBAM was again generally regressive, as it increased capital returns and wages, which would disproportionately benefit wealthier households who receive a higher proportion of their income from capital and labour. It should be noted that part of the regressive income-side effect may have been due to the choice on how to recycle carbon revenues, which reduces labour income taxes and disproportionately benefits wealthier households.

3.4.5 Standards

Efficiency standards mandate or regulate products with certain characteristics, such as low energy consumption or emissions. Economists have long debated the relative efficiency of taxes versus standards in reducing vehicle emissions (e.g. Jacobsen, 2013; Levinson, 2016). Distributional consequences of standards are less controversial. The US Corporate Average Fuel Economy (CAFE), for example, can be seen as regressive when considering the impact on used vehicles (Davis & Knittel, 2016; Jacobsen, 2013). Fleet standards incentivise producers to increase the prices of less efficient cars, which trickles down to the second-hand market and imposes an implicit tax on cars commonly purchased by less-wealthy households. Efficient cars, primarily bought by wealthier households, on the other hand, are effectively subsidised as producers lower prices to increase sales to meet fleet-average emissions targets (Levinson, 2016).

In general, Levinson (2016) argues that standards in all sectors may be more regressive than carbon prices, due to the fact that they disproportionately affect less frequent users, who tend to have higher incomes, and do not allow for progressive revenue recycling schemes. However, it is worth noting that many studies on the regressive effects of standards do not take into account the long-term effects of these policies, such as their potential to drive innovation. Furthermore, in developing countries, some governments may find it difficult to collect taxes, making standards a more feasible option for enforcing regulations.

3.4.6 *Agriculture*

Food production, which includes land use, crop and livestock production, and supply chains, accounts for around one-quarter of global greenhouse gas emissions (Poore & Nemecek, 2018). Decarbonisation policies in the agricultural sector are therefore likely to be a focus in the future. In addition to the direct cost impact of reducing emissions in agriculture, decarbonisation policies in other sectors may also significantly affect food prices. The production of biofuels, for example, can lead to higher crop prices and subsequently higher food prices. If negative-emission technologies and bioenergy with carbon capture and storage become key components of global decarbonisation, food prices may increase. Since low-income households spend a higher share of their income on food, such an increase could be regressive.

Differences in food preferences and the effect of climate policies on individual products can further alter the cost faced by different income groups. Carbon-intensive food products are likely to become disproportionately more expensive when agricultural emissions are regulated. The greenhouse gas emissions from producing one kilogram of beef, for example, can be up to 70 kilograms of CO_2 equivalent (Zachmann et al., 2018).

In the United Kingdom, high-income households spend an additional 40 per cent or more on rice, salmon, chicken and beef, while the low-income households spend more on milk.[11] Zachmann et al. (2018) examine the share of carbon value in total food expenditure of different households in the United Kingdom and find that the shares are

---

[11] Zachmann et al. (2018) based on the Family Food 2016/17 survey of the United Kingdom (see Government of the United Kingdom, 2018).

similar for all household types, suggesting that while the general climate policy induced increase in food prices is regressive, the differentiated effects of climate policy on the cost of different food items may not be. In general, research on the distributional impact of regulating emissions from agriculture is scarce and further analyses are needed.

3.4.7 Summary of Within-Country Effects

Climate policies, such as electricity taxes, aim to address the issue of carbon emissions. A review of the empirical literature shows that different policies have varying distributional impacts, with some being more regressive than others. Thereby, the direction and size of the distributional effect depend not only on the chosen policy tool (e.g. standard vs tax) but also on its sectoral coverage (e.g. of carbon taxes), implementation (e.g. fleet standards vs absolute minimum standards) and the economic environment in which they are implemented (e.g. countries with different sector structures). In addition, policies may affect horizontal equity by affecting households differently based on factors other than income. This indicates that finding a combination of policy tools that mitigate adverse distributional effects while ensuring effective decarbonisation requires situation-specific analysis.

3.5 BETWEEN-COUNTRY INEQUALITY

For global climate change it is essentially irrelevant in which country a molecule of a greenhouse gas is emitted. But for the individual country's economies, it matters a lot if they have to decarbonise faster than others. Implicitly distributing a limited 'carbon budget' across time and between countries is the central aspect of international climate negotiations. All financial and technology transfers (e.g. loss and damage, climate finance, technology transfer, emission trading) primarily serve to enable a global compromise on what some might see as a zero-sum game. The UNFCCC process is based on the principle of 'common but differentiated responsibilities' but continues to struggle to translate it into generally accepted definitions. The challenge is that a 'fair' share of emissions can be distributed along

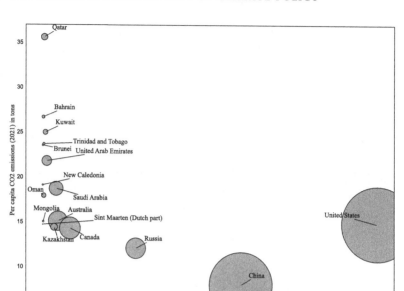

FIGURE 3.3 Cumulative and per capita emissions
Note: Circle size is proportionate to 2021 country GDP in current US$.
Source: Authors' calculations based on World Bank (2022a) data and
Global Carbon Project (2022).

many criteria like wealth of the countries, historic emissions, current
emissions and population. Figure 3.3 reveals that countries with currently high CO_2 per capita emissions may rank low on the list of historical emitters. In the 1997 Kyoto protocol, the world was split into
two types of countries – binding commitments (20 per cent reduction
from 1990 to 2020) for industrialised countries, no commitments for
other countries (including China). In the 2015 Paris Agreement all
countries have self-determined decarbonisation obligations, and tools
exist to encourage a ratcheting up of these ambitions. But the general
challenge of splitting the decarbonisation burden across countries in
a way each and every of them perceives as fair remains.

But the transition to a low-carbon economy in itself also holds
distributional implications across countries. The measures required
to achieve a green transition and their economic consequences will

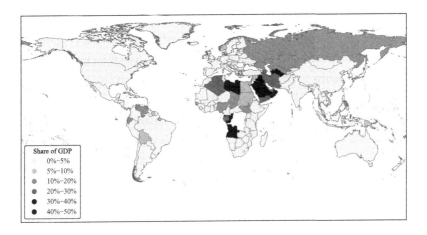

FIGURE 3.4 Average natural gas and oil rents as per cent of GDP, 2000–20
Source: Authors' calculations based on World Bank (2022b, 2022c) data.

differ between countries, depending on factors such as their level of economic development, industrial specialisations and political circumstances. Countries that have historically been reliant on the export of fossil fuels for their economic growth, for example, may find it difficult to pivot to an alternative economic model. However, the transformation of industry towards more low-carbon modes of production also holds opportunities for economic growth. Whether all countries can attract and benefit from the large-scale investments necessary to achieve this transformation, however, depends on their economic and political context. If climate policy investments disproportionately benefit developed countries, they may further the gap between richer and poorer countries. While the complexities and uncertainties connected to different transition scenarios make it difficult to give concrete prediction about distributional ramifications, it is possible to identify several influencing factors.

3.5.1 Dependence on Fossil Fuels

Some countries receive a significant share of their value added from the extraction of fossil fuels. Figure 3.4 shows the share of oil and natural gas rents in GDP of various countries since 2010. If in response to the green transitions the demand for fossil fuel falls, the economic models of countries most reliant on fossil fuels, like the Organisation of the Petroleum Exporting Countries (OPEC) members and Russia, will face substantial challenges (IRENA, 2019). The degree of exposure to this risk varies widely between countries. Countries importing fossil fuel, like the European Union, China, India and Japan, may even benefit from the reduced fuel expenditure (Mercure et al., 2018). The United States, despite having emerged as a gas exporter following its shale revolution, has a more diversified economic model. However, as noted by the International Energy Agency (IEA) in a 2018 report, most countries relying heavily on hydrocarbon revenues have less diversified economies and are more vulnerable. Past drops in the net income available from oil and gas and investment shortages already presented challenges to countries like Iraq, Nigeria and Venezuela. Projections based on the Paris Agreement suggest that future income losses faced by oil and gas producers are around $7 trillion. For example, Nigeria could experience a loss in future incomes of approximately $500 billion, Saudi Arabia nearly $2 trillion and the United Arab Emirates approximately $900 billion (IEA, 2018). Mercure et al. (2018), come to similar conclusions, with OPEC member states facing significant stranded fossil fuel assets and declining investment. A study by Makarov et al. (2017) on Russia stresses that sustained growth in low-carbon scenarios will depend on its ability to diversify and invest.

The ability of oil, gas and coal exporters to diversify away from fossil fuel revenues varies between countries. Low-cost fossil fuel producers like Saudi Arabia and the United Arab Emirates may still profit in declining markets, allowing them to adapt by investing in profits in downstream industries like petrochemicals (Goldthau & Westphal, 2019; IEA, 2018; Tagliapietra, 2019). Other, less competitive, fossil producer countries, however, would bear greater losses in revenue (Mercure et al., 2021). Goldthau et al. (2020) argue that many resource-rich countries in the Global South may also face declining terms of trade, as their exports decrease relative to imports, exacerbating the economic perils. However, predicting the dynamics that will unfold in response to a green transition is difficult, and the consequences may go well beyond fossil fuel industry. Cahen-Fourot et al. (2021), for example, find that the 'capital stranding' could be triggered in a much wider range of sectors and expose developed nations to greater risk.

3.5.2 Investments and Opportunities

Next to the obvious risks for economies currently relying on fossil fuel production, the transition to a low-carbon economy also holds opportunities for economic growth. The large-scale investments in policy changes that are required for the transition can provide stimulus to economies and reduce their dependence on fossil imports in favour of domestic and renewable energy sources. Based on models collected by the Intergovernmental Panel on Climate Change, scenarios leading to net zero by 2050 are expected to lead to a sizeable increase in real GDP. The average economic growth in these sixty-six scenarios is 2.8 per cent per year between 2020 and 2050 (see Chapter 5). While investments and policy changes are required across the board, some countries stand to benefit more than others. This is because the availability of renewable resources and investments depends on geographical, political and economic factors. As a result, countries in the Global South especially may struggle to reap the benefits of a global transition towards net zero. Figure 3.5 shows that the financing costs of many developing countries are higher than those of countries like the United States or Germany. Since 2022, inflation, high interest rates in developing countries and overall economic uncertainty have further exacerbated financing conditions in much of the developing world (IMF, 2022).

Increased reliance on renewable energy sources could bring a competitive advantage to southern countries with high solar energy potential or costal states with large offshore wind energy potential. Harvesting this renewable energy potential, however, requires

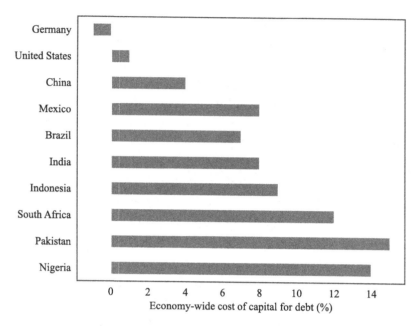

FIGURE 3.5 The cost of capital for the energy transitions, 2020
Note: Economy-wide cost of capital is calculated as the sum of ten-year local currency bond yield and the debt and equity market risk premiums required by investors to invest in the debt and equity securities of a given market.
Source: IEA (2022).

investment and technological know-how, both of which are often difficult to access for countries in the Global South. IRENA (2019) reports that, judging by the number of patents in the low-carbon technology domain, low-carbon technology remains concentrated in terms of ownership. So far only few developing economies, like Brazil, have joined the OECD and China among countries with renewable technology capacity. If countries in the Global South do not succeed in building up indigenous capacities, dependence on these countries will grow, risking trade and political tensions and monopolies (Goldthau et al., 2020).

Although increased demand in key minerals and metals needed for the development and deployment of renewable technologies may benefit countries in Latin America and Africa, as well as

China (World Bank, 2017), technology development, the most lucrative part of the supply chain, remains centred in the United States, the European Union, China and Japan (Curran, 2015; Nahm, 2017). In China, local industrial policies helped firms upgrade in the clean energy value chain (Gosens & Lu, 2013; Schmitz & Lema, 2015; Zhang & Gallagher, 2016). Similar policies, however, may not succeed in countries with smaller markets, poor regulation and lower innovative potential (Johnson, 2016). In addition, private developers may be hesitant to invest in politically unstable or poor countries due to the risk involved (Kirchherr & Urban, 2018). These risks raise the costs of transition away from high-carbon technology. Large existing investments in fossil fuel infrastructure in the Global South by countries like China (e.g. Zhou et al., 2018) and the growing energy demand in developing regions could further impede the ability of countries to transition to renewable energy and reap its long-term benefits (Mercure et al., 2018; Unruh, 2000; Unruh & Carrillo-Hermosilla, 2006). While efforts are being made by international institutions and public–private partnerships to facilitate technology transfers, they have so far fallen short of turning the tide, indicating a risk of continued divergence between the Global North and South (Goldthau et al., 2020).

Macroeconomic ramifications. The investments required to achieve the green transition could lead to large macroeconomic shifts. Luciani (2020) argues that the massive shift from consumption to investment necessary for the transition will not be achieved by simply redirecting existing savings but requires an increased rate of savings over GDP. Under normal circumstances, such increases in investment are expected to spur growth by expanding the economy's productive capacity. However, existing capital stocks may become obsolete, and investments abroad do not directly contribute to domestic growth, limiting the growth for those countries who bear the brunt of the investment burden. Economies that rely on export for their economic growth, like China and Germany, may especially struggle to uphold consumption and export growth when faced with large investment needs. The institutional shifts necessary to enable and accommodate investments could thus change the global economic landscape and lead to a redistribution of economic power.

3.5.3 Policy Examples

While distributional consequences for less competitive fossil fuel exporters and countries in the Global South that fail to mobilise sufficient investment are likely, their direction and magnitude remain largely uncertain. Analyses of individual policy responses have attempted to draw a more concrete picture of the consequences. Leonard et al. (2021), for instance, assess the distributional consequences of the EU Green New Deal. They find that while higher carbon prices will induce an abatement of fossil industries, the costs related to this shift differ widely across EU countries. Options for reducing emissions vary within and across sectors. For instance, some countries may be able to decommission polluting facilities that are no longer economically viable, while others may require significant investments to achieve emissions reductions within a sector. Additionally, the EU ETS, which covers emissions from the power and industrial sectors, shows that wealthier countries tend to have a greater share of industrial emissions, which can be costlier to abate, while poorer countries tend to have a larger share of emissions from the power sector, which may be more affordable to reduce.

To ensure a fairer sharing of the burdens of decarbonisation, despite substantial between-country inequalities, the UNFCCC process has early on established three classes of instruments: climate finance, technology transfer and international carbon trading. The massive distributional effects between sovereign countries that these three classes of policies can have, however, resulted in relatively slow progress in the corresponding international negotiations that essentially require unanimity. But those policies might eventually gain momentum (the $100 billion pledge for climate finance goes in that direction) as pieces of a 'grand bargain' to ensure sufficient mitigation action in emerging and developing countries too.

3.6 KEY TAKEAWAYS

3.6.1 What Is Inequality and Why Does It Matter for the Green Transition?

- Inequality matters because it has direct implications for the total welfare of a population as well as for a country's economic growth.
- In addition, political support for the green transition hinges on the (perceived) distributional consequences of policies both within countries and internationally.
- Measures of income inequality capture only parts of the unequal effects of policies. The natural environment, community life or personal circumstances are among many factors that are affected by climate change as well as by climate policy and are not typically captured by measures of income inequality.

3.6.2 Analytical Framework for Within-Country Inequality

- Households are affected by the transition to a zero-carbon economy both on the expenditure and income sides.
- On the expenditure side, households may, for example, face higher energy prices because of carbon pricing or other climate policies.
- On the income side, households may benefit or lose from changes in employment and wages in different sectors as a result of the transition.

3.6.3 Distributional Effects of Climate Policies

- Depending on the initial conditions, the chosen policy instrument, its sectoral coverage and its implementation, the economic impacts of decarbonisation policy can differ strongly between different population groups.
- Policies such as revenue recycling and instrument design can help to mitigate these negative effects and promote a more equitable transition.

3.6.4 Between-Country Inequality

- Climate change has unequal effects on different countries in the world. Many poor countries are directly affected by climate change, for example through droughts, floods, extreme weather events and changes in the natural environment. Reducing emissions in the industrialised world would therefore tend to reduce inequality.

- Climate policy also changes rents that can be extracted from selling fossil fuels. Some countries such as Russia, the countries of the Gulf and several African countries export oil and gas, which form the basis of large parts of their overall export and sometimes government revenues.
- In addition, not all countries may be able to invest in and economically benefit from low-carbon technologies in the same way. The investment and technological capacities in developing countries, especially, may need to be strengthened to ensure a more equitable outcome of the transition.
- The high degree of political and economic uncertainty makes the quantification of the magnitude of distributional consequences difficult. Considering the need for global political consensus and effective financing, however, the importance of economic and institutional shifts resulting from the transition cannot be overstated.

REFERENCES

Alvaredo, F., L. Chancel, T. Piketty, E. Saez, and G. Yucman (2017) 'Global Inequality Dynamics: New Findings from WID.world', *American Economic Review*, 107:5, 404–09.

Auclert, A., M. Rognlie, and L. Straub (2020) 'Micro Jumps, Macro Humps: Monetary Policy and Business Cycles in an Estimated HANK Model', Working Paper No. 26647, National Bureau of Economic Research, www .nber.org/system/files/working_papers/w26647/w26647.pdf

Australian Bureau of Statistics (December 2022) Australian National Accounts: Distribution of Household Income, Consumption and Wealth, www .abs.gov.au/statistics/economy/national-accounts/australian-national-accounts-distribution-household-income-consumption-and-wealth/latest-release

Balestra, C., and R. Tonkin (2018) 'Inequalities in Household Wealth across OECD Countries: Evidence from the OECD Wealth Distribution Database', OECD Statistics Working Papers, No. 2018/01, OECD Publishing, Paris.

Bilbiie, F., G. E. Primiceri, and A. Tambalotti (2022) 'Inequality and Business Cycles', PSE Working Paper, http://pseweb.eu/ydepot/seance/515181_Inequality&BC1-10.pdf

Borusyak, K., and X. Jaravel (2021) 'The Distributional Effects of Trade: Theory and Evidence from the United States', Working Paper No. 28957, National Bureau of Economic Research.

Brannlund, R., and J. Nordström (2004) 'Carbon Tax Simulations Using a Household Demand Model', *European Economic Review*, 48:1, 211–33.

Brannlund, R., and L. Persson (2012) 'To Tax, or Not to Tax: Preferences for Climate Policy Attributes', *Climate Policy*, 12:6, 704–21.

Cahen-Fourot, L., E. Campiglio, A. Godin, E. Kemp-Benedict, and S. Trsek (2021) 'Capital Stranding Cascades: The Impact of Decarbonisation on Productive Asset Utilisation', *Energy Economics*, 103, 105581.

Calderón, C., and L. Servén (2004) 'The Effects of Infrastructure Development on Growth and Income Distribution', Policy Research Working Paper No. 3400, World Bank.

Cames, M., J. Graichen, A. Siemons, and V. Cook (2015) 'Emission Reduction Targets for International Aviation and Shipping', European Parliament IPOL, Study PE 569.964, www.europarl.europa.eu/thinktank/en/document/IPOL_STU(2015)569964

Chatterjee, S., and S. J. Turnovsky (2012) 'Infrastructure and Inequality', *European Economic Review*, 56:8, 1730–45.

Church, C., and A. Crawford (2018) 'Green Conflict Minerals: The Fuels of Conflict in the Transition to a Low-Carbon Economy', International Institute for Sustainable Development Report.

Cingano, F. (2014) 'Trends in Income Inequality and Its Impact on Economic Growth', OECD Social, Employment and Migration Working Papers, No. 163, OECD Publishing, Paris.

Coibion, O., Y. Gorodnichenko, M. Kudlyak, and J. Mondragon (2014) 'Does Greater Inequality Lead to More Household Borrowing? New Evidence from Household Data', Working Paper No. 19850, National Bureau of Economic Research.

Cramton, P., D. J. C. MacKay, A. Ockenfels, and S. Stoft (2017) *Global Carbon Pricing: The Path to Climate Cooperation* (Cambridge, MA: The MIT Press).

Cronin, J. A., D. Fullerton, and S. Sexton (2019) 'Vertical and Horizontal Redistributions from a Carbon Tax and Rebate', *Journal of the Association of Environmental and Resource Economists*, 6:S1, S169–208.

Curran, L. (2015) 'The Impact of Trade Policy on Global Production Networks: The Solar Panel Case', *Review of International Political Economy*, 22:5, 1025–54.

Darvas, Z. (2019) 'Global Interpersonal Income Inequality Decline: The Role of China and India', *World Development*, 121:C, 16–32.

Davis, L. W., and C. R. Knittel (2019) 'Are Fuel Economy Standards Regressive?', *Journal of the Association of Environmental and Resource Economists*, 6:S1, S37–63.

De Ferranti, D., G. E. Perry, F. H. Ferreira, and M. Walton (2004) *Inequality in Latin America: Breaking with History?* World Bank Latin American and Caribbean Studies (Washington, DC: World Bank).

Dechezlepretre, A., A. Fabre, T. Kruse, B. Planterose, A. S. Chico, and S. Stantcheva (2022) 'Fighting Climate Change: International Attitudes toward Climate Policies', Working Paper No. 30265, National Bureau of Economic Research.

Dercon, S. (2014) 'Is Green Growth Good for the Poor?', *The World Bank Research Observer*, 29:2, 163–85.

Dietz, S., and G. Atkinson (2010) 'The Equity-Efficiency Trade-off in Environmental Policy: Evidence from Stated Preferences', *Land Economics*, 86:3, 423–43.

Dogan, E., M. Madaleno, R. Inglesi-Lotz, and D. Taskin (2022) 'Race and Energy Poverty: Evidence from African-American Households', *Energy Economics*, 108, 105908.

Dumagan, J. C., and T. D. Mount (1992) 'Measuring the Consumer Welfare Effects of Carbon Penalties: Theory and Applications to Household Energy Demand', *Energy Economics*, 14:2, 82–93.

Eurostat (2022a) Distribution of Income by Quantiles, https://ec.europa.eu/eurostat/databrowser/view/ilc_di01/default/table?lang=en

(2022b) Air Emissions by NACE Rev. 2 Activity, https://ec.europa.eu/eurostat/databrowser/view/ENV_AC_AINAH_R2__custom_7245994/default/table?lang=en

Fajgelbaum, P. D., and A. K. Khandelwal (2016) 'Measuring the Unequal Gains from Trade', *The Quarterly Journal of Economics*, 131:3, 1113–80.

Fan, S., and X. Zhang (2004) 'Infrastructure and Regional Economic Development in Rural China', *China Economic Review*, 15:2, 203–14.

Flues, F., and A. Thomas (2015) 'The Distributional Effects of Energy Taxes', OECD Taxation Working Papers, No. 23, OECD Publishing, Paris.

Furceri, D., and G. B. Li (2017) 'The Macroeconomic (and Distributional) Effects of Public Investment in Developing Economies', IMF Working Papers, No. 2017/217, A001.

Gagnebin, M., P. Graichen, and T. Lenck (2019) 'Die Gelbwesten-Proteste: Eine (Fehler-) Analyse der französischen CO2-Preispolitik', Agora Energiewende, https://static.agora-energiewende.de/fileadmin/Projekte/2018/CO2-Steuer_FR-DE_Paper/Agora-Energiewende_Paper_CO2_Steuer_FR-DE.pdf

Global Carbon Project (2022) Global Carbon Atlas, https://globalcarbonatlas.org/

Goldthau, A., L. Eicke, and S. Weko (2020) 'The Global Energy Transition and the Global South', in M. Hafner and S. Tagliapietra (Eds.),*The Geopolitics of the Global Energy Transition*, pp. 319–39 (Cham: Springer Nature).

Goldthau, A., and K. Westphal (2019) 'Why the Global Energy Transition Does Not Mean the End of the Petrostate', *Global Policy*, 10:2, 279–83.

Gornemann, N., K. Kuester, and M. Nakajima (2016) 'Doves for the Rich, Hawks for the Poor? Distributional Consequences of Monetary Policy', CEPR Discussion Paper No. DP11233, April.

Gosens, J., and Y. Lu (2013) 'From Lagging to Leading? Technological Innovation Systems in Emerging Economies and the Case of Chinese Wind Power', *Energy Policy*, 60, 234–50.

Government of the United Kingdom (2018) Family Food 2016/17, www.gov.uk/government/statistical-data-sets/family-food-datasets

Grösche, P., and C. Schröder (2014) 'On the Redistributive Effects of Germany's Feed-in Tariff', *Empirical Economics*, 46:4, 1339–83.

Hafner, M., and S. Tagliapietra (2020) 'The Global Energy Transition: A Review of the Existing Literature', in M. Hafner and S. Tagliapietra (Eds.), *The Geopolitics of the Global Energy Transition*, pp. 1–24 (Cham: Springer Nature).

Hafner, M., and A. Wochner (2020) 'How Tectonic Shifts in Global Energy Are Affecting Global Governance', in M. Hafner and S. Tagliapietra (Eds.), *Global Governance in Transformation*, pp. 147–62 (Cham: Springer Nature).

Hänsel, M. C., M. Franks, M. Kalkuhl, and O. Edenhofer (2022) 'Optimal Carbon Taxation and Horizontal Equity: A Welfare-Theoretic Approach with Application to German Household Data', *Journal of Environmental Economics and Management*, 116, 102730.

IEA (2018) *Outlook for Producer Economies 2018* (Paris: International Energy Agency).

(2021) Report: The Cost Of Capital In Clean Energy Transitions, www.iea.org/articles/the-cost-of-capital-in-clean-energy-transitions

IMF (2022) *Global Financial Stability Report* (Washington, DC: International Monetary Fund).

IRENA (2019) *A New World. The Geopolitics of the Energy Transformation* (Abu Dhabi: International Renewable Energy Agency).

Italian National Institute of Statistics (2022) Household Budget Survey, www.istat.it/en/archivio/180353

Jacobsen, M. R. (2013) 'Evaluating US Fuel Economy Standards in a Model with Producer and Household Heterogeneity', *American Economic Journal: Economic Policy*, 5:2, 148–87.

Jaumotte, F., and C. Osorio (2015) *Inequality and Labor Market Institutions* (Washington, DC: International Monetary Fund).

Jetten, J., F. Mols, and H. P. Selvanathan (2020) 'How Economic Inequality Fuels the Rise and Persistence of the Yellow Vest Movement', *International Review of Social Psychology*, 33:1, 2.

Johnson, O. (2016) 'Promoting Green Industrial Development through Local Content Requirements: India's National Solar Mission', *Climate Policy*, 16:2, 178–95.

Kaplan, G., B. Moll, and G. L. Violante (2018) 'Monetary Policy According to HANK', *American Economic Review*, 108:3, 697–743.

Khandker, S., and G. Koolwal (2007) 'Are Pro-growth Policies Pro-poor? Evidence from Bangladesh', mimeo, The World Bank.

Kirchherr, J., and F. Urban (2018) 'Technology Transfer and Cooperation for Low Carbon Energy Technology: Analysing 30 Years of Scholarship and Proposing a Research Agenda', *Energy Policy*, 119, 600–09.

Kollamthodi, S., A. Pueyo, G. Gibson, R. Narkeviciute, A. Hawkes, S. Cesbron, et al. (2013) 'Support for the Impact Assessment of a Proposal to Address Maritime Transport Greenhouse Gas Emissions', Report for European Commission – DG Climate Action, Ricardo-AEA/R/ED56985.

Leonard, M., J. Pisani-Ferry, J. Shapiro, T. Tagliapietra, and G. Wolff (2021) 'The Geopolitics of the European Green Deal', Policy Contribution No. 04/2021, Bruegel.

Levinson, A. (2019) 'Energy Efficiency Standards Are More Regressive than Energy Taxes: Theory and Evidence', *Journal of the Association of Environmental and Resource Economists*, 6:S1, S7–36.

Luciani, G. (2020) 'The Impacts of the Energy Transition on Growth and Income Distribution', in M. Hafner and S. Tagliapietra (Eds.), *The Geopolitics of the Global Energy Transition*. Lecture Notes in Energy, vol 73. (Cham: Springer).

Makarov, I., Y. H. H. Chen, and S. Paltsev (2017) 'Finding Itself in the Post-Paris World: Russia in the New Global Energy Landscape', MIT Joint Program Report Series, Report 324.

Mercure, J. F., H. Pollitt, N. R. Edwards, P. B. Holden, U. Chewpreecha, P. Salas, et al. (2018) 'Environmental Impact Assessment for Climate Change Policy with the Simulation-Based Integrated Assessment Model E3ME-FTT-GENIE', *Energy Strategy Reviews*, 20, 195–208.

Mercure, J. F., P. Salas, P. Vercoulen, G. Semieniuk, A. Lam, H. Pollitt, et al. (2021) 'Reframing Incentives for Climate Policy Action', *Nature Energy*, 6:12, 1133–43.

Nahm, J. (2017) 'Renewable Futures and Industrial Legacies: Wind and Solar Sectors in China, Germany, and the United States', *Business and Politics*, 19:1, 68–106.

Ohlendorf, N., M. Jakob, J. C. Minx, C. Schröder, and J. C. Steckel (2021) 'Distributional Impacts of Carbon Pricing: A Meta-Analysis', *Environmental and Resource Economics*, 78:1, 1–42.

Ostry, J. D., A. Berg, and C. G. Tsangarides (2014) *Redistribution, Inequality, and Growth* (Washington, DC: International Monetary Fund).

Peters, G. P., S. J. Davis, and R. M. Andrew (2012) 'A Synthesis of Carbon in International Trade', *Biogeosciences Discussions*, 9:3, 3949–4023.

Pizer, W. A., and S. Sexton (2020) 'The Distributional Impacts of Energy Taxes', *Review of Environmental Economics and Policy*, 13:1, 104–23.

Poore, J., and T. Nemecek (2018) 'Reducing Food's Environmental Impacts through Producers and Consumers', *Science*, 360:6392, 987–92.

Poterba, J. M. (2017) 'Is the Gasoline Tax Regressive?', in *Distributional Effects of Environmental and Energy Policy*, pp. 31–50 (Abingdon: Routledge).

Rausch, S., G. E. Metcalf, and J. M. Reilly (2011) 'Distributional Impacts of Carbon Pricing: A General Equilibrium Approach with Micro-data for Households', *Energy Economics*, 33, S20–33.

Schmitz, H., and R. Lema (2015) 'The Global Green Economy', in J. Fagerberg, S. Laestadius and B. R. Martin (Eds.), *The Triple Challenge for Europe*, 1st ed., pp. 119–42 (Oxford, UK: Oxford University Press).

Sommer, S., L. Mattauch, and M. Pahle (2022) 'Supporting Carbon Taxes: The Role of Fairness', *Ecological Economics*, 195, 107359.

Steckel, J. C., I. I. Dorband, L. Montrone, H. Ward, L. Missbach, F. Hafner, and S. Renner (2021) 'Distributional Impacts of Carbon Pricing in Developing Asia', *Nature Sustainability*, 4:11, 1005–1014.

Tagliapietra, S. (2019) 'The Impact of the Global Energy Transition on MENA Oil and Gas Producers', *Energy Strategy Reviews*, 26, 100397.

Tiezzi, S. (2005) 'The Welfare Effects and the Distributive Impact of Carbon Taxation on Italian Households', *Energy Policy*, 33:12, 1597–612.

Tovar Reaños, M. A., and K. Sommerfeld (2018) 'Fuel for Inequality: Distributional Effects of Environmental Reforms on Private Transport', *Resource and Energy Economics*, 51, 28–43.

Tovar Reaños, M. A., and N. M. Wölfing (2018) 'Household Energy Prices and Inequality: Evidence from German Microdata Based on the EASI Demand System', *Energy Economics*, 70, 84–97.

UNCTAD (2022) *Review of Maritime Transport 2022* (Geneva: United Nations Conference on Trade and Development).

United States Census Bureau (September 2022) Income in the United States: 2021, www.census.gov/library/publications/2022/demo/p60-276.html#:~:text=Highlights,and%20Table%20A%2D1

Unruh, G. C. (2000) 'Understanding Carbon Lock-in', *Energy Policy*, 28:12, 817–30.

Unruh, G. C., and J. Carrillo-Hermosilla (2006) 'Globalizing Carbon Lock-in', *Energy Policy*, 34:10, 1185–97.

Vona, F. (2019) 'Job Losses and Political Acceptability of Climate Policies: Why the "Job-Killing" Argument Is So Persistent and How to Overturn It', *Climate Policy*, 19:4, 524–32.

West, S. E. (2004) 'Distributional Effects of Alternative Vehicle Pollution Control Policies', *Journal of Public Economics*, 88:3–4, 735–57.

West, S. E., and R. C. Williams (2017) 'Estimates from a Consumer Demand System: Implications for the Incidence of Environmental Taxes', in D. Fullerton (Ed.), *Distributional Effects of Environmental and Energy Policy*, pp. 117–40 (Abingdon: Routledge).

World Bank (2017) *The Growing Role of Minerals and Metals for a Low Carbon Future* (Washington, DC: World Bank).

(2022a) World Bank national accounts data: GDP (current US$), https://data .worldbank.org/indicator/NY.GDP.MKTP.CD

(2022b) World Bank staff estimates: Natural gas rents (% of GDP), https://data .worldbank.org/indicator/NY.GDP.NGAS.RT.ZS

(2022c) World Bank staff estimates: Oil rents (% of GDP), https://data.world bank.org/indicator/NY.GDP.PETR.RT.ZS

Zachmann, G., G. Fredriksson, and G. Claeys (2018) 'The Distributional Effects of Climate Policies', Blueprint Series 28, Bruegel.

Zhang, F., and K. S. Gallagher (2016) 'Innovation and Technology Transfer through Global Value Chains: Evidence from China's PV Industry', *Energy Policy*, 94, 191–203.

Zhou, L., S. Gilbert, Y. Wang, M. M. Cabré, and K. P. Gallagher (2018) 'Moving the Green Belt and Road Initiative: From Words to Actions', World Resource Institute Working Paper, 08-18, www.wri.org/research/moving-green-belt-and-road-initiative-words-actions

4   Public Finances and Decarbonisation

4.1   INTRODUCTION

The window of opportunity to contain global warming is closing
rapidly. Governments will need to play a crucial role if they want
to fulfil their promise to substantially reduce global greenhouse gas
emissions to limit the global temperature increase in this century to
2°C while pursuing efforts to limit the increase even further to 1.5°C
as agreed during the UN Conference of the Parties (COP) Climate
Change Conference in Paris (COP21) in 2015 and confirmed in its
later climate change conferences.

Public authorities will need to use the whole range of their policy
toolkit to achieve this goal. The following chapters explore the role
of different public policies in the decarbonisation of our economies.
This chapter focuses on fiscal policy, while the other policies that
will also play a crucial role in decarbonisation – industrial, financial,
labour and monetary policies in particular – will be discussed in the
following chapters of the book.

What do we mean by fiscal policy here? In macroeconomics, the term 'fiscal policy' is often used in a narrow sense, focusing on the macroeconomic stabilisation role of the public budget to
dampen the cycle, ensure full employment and avoid the build-up
of inflationary or deflationary pressures (Samuelson, 1948). But in
this chapter we discuss fiscal matters in a broader sense and explore
all public finance aspects related to decarbonisation, as all three
main functions of public finances described originally by Musgrave
(1959) – allocation, stabilisation and distribution – should play a
role in the decarbonisation process. We thus discuss all the relevant
instruments directly affecting the government budget that are under
the control of fiscal authorities.

Two main questions are discussed in this chapter. First, what role can fiscal policy play in the transition to a carbon-neutral economy? In other words, how to design fiscal policy (both on the revenue and on the expenditure sides) to reach net zero emissions by mid-century in a credible, growth- and distribution-friendly way to ensure a smooth transition (or at least to avoid as much as possible a disruptive one)? And second, how will the transition impact public finances? Should we expect a radical change in tax revenues/expenditures? Should we fear any debt sustainability risk because of the transition?

There are, however, three main caveats that readers should keep in mind when reading this chapter. First, as in the remainder of the book, this chapter focuses on fiscal policy during the transition, taking as given the objective to decarbonise fully and to achieve net zero emissions by 2050 – even if it is becoming increasingly clear that Nationally Determined Contributions and even more so actual current policies are insufficient to meet this objective (UNFCCC, 2022). This chapter therefore does not discuss directly the potentially large fiscal costs of adaptation measures related to potential catastrophic effects of a global temperature increase by more than 1.5°–2°C. The idea is that stringent mitigation measures put in place between today and 2050 should reduce the long-term fiscal risks due to extreme weather and other climate-related disasters.

Second, the optimal mix of fiscal measures and their implications both for the main macroeconomic variables (output, inflation and employment) and for CO_2 emissions are still matters of much debate. One reason is that uncertainty characterises this field of research, and on some particular issues there is no clear consensus yet in the literature. The literature is still very much in its infancy, also because serious decarbonisation efforts are only starting. Moreover, 'first-best' solutions may not be attainable because of political economy considerations and the difficulties in coordinating various instruments and actors at different levels (local, national, global). These differences between optimal and actual solutions will have large effects on public finance and on citizens, whose support needs to be ensured to successfully implement climate policies. In particular, the parts of the population that will be most affected by climate policies will demand fiscal compensation, both within and between countries (these questions are discussed in Chapter 3). This chapter will therefore often discuss a menu of second-best options available to fiscal policymakers.

Third, the role of and the impact on public finances will vary a lot depending on the initial situation of each country: its economic development, its economic structure, its fiscal space, its ability to tax, the efficiency of spending, the location of brown activities that will be closed and of the green activities that will rise, and so on. For instance, given their specialisation and reliance on the export of carbon-intensive products, the public finances of oil-exporting countries will be much more affected than the ones of large and diversified economies such as the European Union, the United States, Japan or even China. We will mainly focus on the latter group of countries in this chapter, as their actions will prove critical in achieving decarbonisation at the global level.

4.2   TAX REVENUES AND DECARBONISATION

The level and composition of tax revenues will both be impacted significantly by the transition towards net zero.

4.2.1   Carbon Pricing Objectives and State of Affairs

The most important element that should affect public finances during the transition is the introduction of a meaningful carbon pricing. The reason why carbon pricing should be introduced is to solve an important market failure: greenhouse gas (GHG) emissions, including CO_2 emissions, represent what economists call a negative externality, as they impose a cost on society – global warming – not fully taken into account in their decisions by the companies or individuals responsible for the emissions. This difference between private and social cost means that emissions are higher than socially optimal

(Solow, 1971). The textbook tool to solve this market failure is a tax (Pigou, 1920), so that prices fully reflect the negative environmental cost of emissions.

The main objective of carbon pricing is to change relative prices in order to reduce emissions by incentivising a change in behaviours, by unleashing innovation in green technologies and by reallocating labour and capital from brown to green activities (including for the state itself in countries where brown assets are state-controlled). A high carbon price should indeed curb demand for fossil fuels and thus encourage to leave them in the crust of earth (as burning all known fossil fuel stocks is incompatible with the agreed temperature objective). It should induce substitution first from carbon-intensive to less carbon-intensive fossil fuel (e.g. from coal to gas, which produces half emissions) and then away from fossil fuel altogether to renewables. It should boost carbon capture and storage and limit deforestation. It should boost private research and development (R&D) into clean energy and into energy-saving technologies by making them profitable in the future and thus by facilitating their financing today. Finally, it should encourage households, firms and government to spend more on mitigation (e.g. in energy infrastructures compatible with renewables and in energy efficiency).

In practice, there exist two main mechanisms to implement carbon pricing: cap-and-trade schemes (such as the Emission Trading System (ETS) in place in the European Union since 2005, which covers industrial sectors representing around 40 per cent of EU emissions) and a carbon tax. In a cap-and-trade system, governments set an emission cap and issue emission allowances, also called permits, consistent with that cap. Emitters must hold allowances for every ton of emission. They may buy and sell allowances, and this market establishes an emission price. A carbon tax is simply a tax levied on each ton of emission.

How to choose between these two types of schemes? The main differences and pros and cons are discussed in Box 1.1, but the main trade-off can be summarised as follows. In principle the two should be equivalent, but in a world riddled with frictions and uncertainties the main advantage of cap-and-trade schemes is that they ensure certainty regarding emissions, as these are fixed by policymakers, but they leave economic agents to bear the risk in terms of price volatility (which can happen, for instance, because of varying economic growth rates that increase or reduce the demand for permits or because of a faster rollout of renewable technology).[1] On the contrary, a carbon tax path provides economic agents with certainty regarding the price they will face for emissions (and is simpler to administer as it can be built on existing taxes) but leaves society to face some uncertainty in terms of the quantity of emissions (in particular if the tax is not well calibrated).

Whether policymakers decide to go with a tax or a market-based scheme (or a combination of both) to price carbon emissions in their jurisdictions, two basic design principles should be respected to reduce emissions significantly: First, emission coverage should be comprehensive, both geographically and in terms of sectors. This is not the case for the moment in most countries. Second, ensuring some certainty about carbon price is crucial. Climate policies that are implemented need to be credible and predictable to really change behaviours and incentivise investment and innovation. Legal tools such as climate legislation or the creation of new institutions (such as independent bodies in charge of climate policies) might help solve this problem of credibility. Otherwise, the perceived risk of potential policy reversal could lead to a risk premium for decarbonisation projects, which could make them unprofitable and reduce the prospect that they are instigated.

Emissions covered by a tax or cap scheme have expanded significantly in the last three decades, from only four countries in 1990 to forty-seven today. A noteworthy number of countries (or states,

---

[1] An additional advantage of an ETS is that it appears to be better accepted by populations than a carbon tax because it takes place at the producer level, despite the fact that in the end producers pass through most of the additional cost related to the purchase of permits to consumers (Blanchard et al., 2022).

in the United States, such as California and Oregon) have now introduced a carbon price via either a cap-and-trade or a carbon tax or sometimes combining both. As of 2022, there are seventy carbon pricing instruments in operation: thirty-six carbon taxes and thirty-four ETS, and more are scheduled or considered to be put in place in the near future, as shown in Figure 4.1.

However, carbon prices are still very low: carbon pricing revenues have reached $84 billion in 2021 for around fifty billion tons of GHG emissions, that is less than 2$ per ton (World Bank, 2022a). In addition, this number hides a large heterogeneity between countries and reflects that most emissions are simply currently not priced at all in most jurisdictions. As Figure 4.2 shows, only around twelve billion tons (representing around 20 per cent of global emissions) are priced, and less than 4 per cent of global emissions are covered by a carbon price above $40 per ton of CO_2.

Carbon pricing is very effective in reducing emissions. For instance, the introduction of a carbon price floor in the energy sector in 2013 in the United Kingdom led to the almost complete phasing out of coal for electricity generation in only five years (Leroutier, 2022).[2] But the price in place in most countries (and/or in most sectors) in 2022 might not be sufficient to incentivise radical changes in behaviours and unleash the much-needed wave of investments and innovation in green technologies from the private sector (for more details on what the carbon price level should be and how it should evolve to ensure decarbonisation by 2050 see section 4.2.2).

However, there are many obstacles to the deployment of carbon pricing schemes (as detailed, for instance, in van der Ploeg, 2021). One of the main explanations why carbon prices still have a low coverage and too low prices despite the evidence that carbon pricing is successful in reducing emission is its unpopularity. This lack of support from the general public (documented in depth by Dechezlepretre

---

[2] Carbon pricing should also boost innovation and incentivise energy efficiency as the example of air conditioning, which got much more energy efficient after the oil shocks of the 1970s, suggests (Acemoglu et al., 2012).

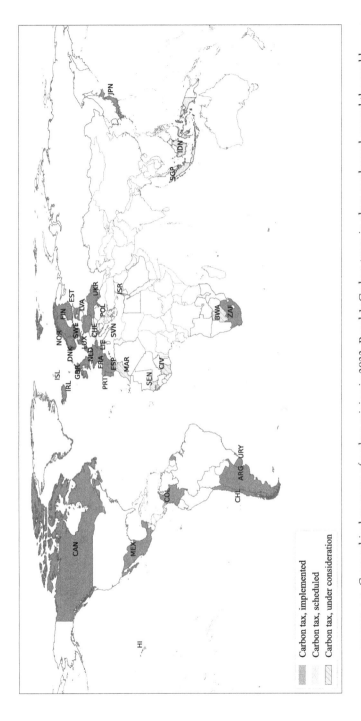

FIGURE 4.1 Geographical coverage of carbon pricing in 2022. Panel 1: Carbon taxes in place or planned around the world. Panel 2: ETS in place or planned around the world

Source: Authors, based on carbon pricing dataset of World Bank (2022b).

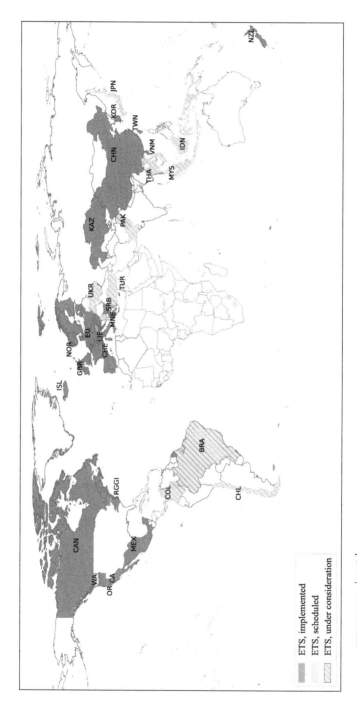

FIGURE 4.1 (cont.)

ETS, implemented

ETS, scheduled

ETS, under consideration

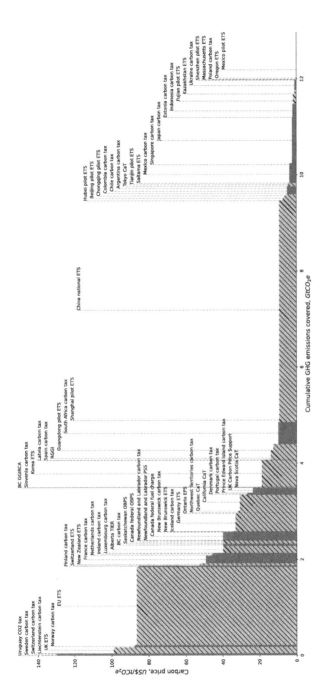

FIGURE 4.2 Cumulative coverage of emissions and prices applied in 2022 (in US$ and million tons of emissions)
Source: Authors, based on carbon pricing dataset of World Bank (2022b).

et al., 2022) is mainly driven by the citizens' fear of the regressive effects of carbon prices and by the absence of widespread alternative to carbon-intensive arrangements, for instance in transport or in heating systems (two important issues that will come back in Section 4.3), while firms fear mainly for their competitiveness at the international level.

Another important reason why carbon prices are low is related to potentially substantial free-riding problems at the international level. Indeed, given that each jurisdiction represents a relatively small share of emissions (except possibly China, the United States and the European Union) no one has an incentive to put in place a meaningful and comprehensive carbon pricing in its jurisdiction first (or to be more ambitious than the others). On the contrary, countries might have an incentive not to do anything in order to gain a competitive advantage over other countries. If coordination at the international level is impossible, countries will need instruments to solve potential 'carbon leakage' issues – that is, the fact that companies located in a jurisdiction imposing a high carbon price could move their carbon-intensive production to another country to take advantage of looser standards or that domestic goods could be replaced by cheaper but more carbon-intensive imports. Such a carbon leakage could shift emissions around the world and therefore undermine global climate efforts. That is why some jurisdictions, such as the European Union, intend to introduce the carbon border adjustment mechanism (CBAM) to equalise the carbon price between domestic products and imports and ensure that production is not relocated to countries with less ambitious policies (see Box 4.1).

Finally, the negative consequences associated with possible stranded assets that could create some financial risks (see Chapter 6) or have negative impact on employment in some sectors or regions (see Chapter 7) could make politicians susceptible to capture from firm or trade-union lobbying and thus make carbon pricing politically more difficult to implement.

BOX 4.1 **What is CBAM?**[1]

A central element in achieving the transition to a carbon-neutral economy is to put a significant price on all GHG emissions. Such a tax will incentivise producers and consumers to switch to less GHG-intensive alternatives. But if domestic producers were taxed heavily on their emissions, they would be put at a disadvantage compared to foreign producers that are not taxed heavily. A group of more than 3,000 distinguished American economists has therefore proposed to introduce CBAM (Climate Leadership Council, 2019).

Taxing domestic producers on their GHG emissions without taxing foreign producers would disadvantage domestic production because consumers would continue buying the same products but shift to suppliers from abroad instead of switching to more efficient domestic producers.

Imagine a plastic toy. Suppose there are two toy producers in the European Union. One (A) uses an efficient production process and therefore emits only 1 kg of CO_2 while the other (B) needs 2 kg to produce the same toy. There is also a third producer (C) in a country outside of the European Union that provides the same toy with 3 kg of CO_2. Finally, there is an efficient foreign producer (D) that also needs only 1 kg. Suppose the price of the four toys is equivalent to €10. Consumers will be indifferent to the four toys based on the price and will choose the toy that they like most for its colour or other characteristics.

Now suppose the European Union introduces a tax of €1 per kilogram of CO_2 but only on the domestic producers (this would be a very high price but let's use it for the sake of simplicity. The described logic fully applies also at lower prices, for example at €100 per ton, i.e. one tenth of the price used here). The result would be the prices documented in Table B4.1.1, which shows that the foreign producers C and D would gain a significant advantage relative to the two domestic producers. Domestic producer A would gain a price advantage relative to domestic producer B and consumers

---

[1] This box partly reproduces Wolff (2019).

would be incentivised to shift to A. However, only consumers that have a strong preference for domestic production would continue sticking to A while all others would shift to C and D. Depending on the respective elasticities, the domestic CO_2 tax might achieve very little in terms of consumption of CO_2 but it would destroy the domestic industry.

The obvious solution to this problem is to introduce a tax that would also apply to the foreign producer. The result is given in the last row and illustrates the power of CBAM. Dirty producers, domestic or foreign, would be penalised. Producers B and C would have to quickly render their production more efficient or risk losing their EU market share. Meanwhile, producers A and D would both gain market share.

Table B4.1.1 nicely illustrates why on first principle grounds the introduction of a CO_2 tax is a powerful instrument to change production patterns. It also shows why first principles require some form of CBAM if the tax is supposed to be effective in changing the consumption of CO_2 and not just in shifting production abroad. Obviously, moving production abroad would not only be bad for

Table B4.1.1 *Illustrating CBAM with the example of a plastic toy*

	Domestic producer A	Domestic producer B	Foreign producer C	Foreign producer D
Amount of CO_2 emitted per toy	1 kg	2 kg	3 kg	1 kg
Current price without taxing CO_2	€10	€10	€10	€10
Domestic price after a €1/kg CO_2 tax on domestic producers	€11	€12	€10	€10
Domestic price after a €1 /kg tax on all producers	€11	€12	€13	€11

Source: Authors

domestic industries but also be bad for the climate in that the relevant global GHG emissions would barely change with the introduction of the EU tax. In contrast, a tax combined with some form of CBAM would not only reduce domestic CO_2 consumption in the European Union but also prevent carbon leakage. It would also provide a strong incentive – due to the big size of the EU market to foreign producers – to innovate and update their production processes. Over time, these efficiencies would also reduce CO_2 consumption in third countries, in which there is no tax on CO_2. Finally, the CBAM would also relieve the domestic producers of the tax when they export abroad. It would provide a tax rebate for those exported goods so that in the foreign market the domestic producers would not be put at a disadvantage.

The strength of the described effects, that is the amount of carbon leakage, obviously depends on the price of carbon, the amount of carbon content in the respective products and the elasticities of demand to price changes. All three are a matter of empirical research. For some products, the respective numbers may be such that CBAM is irrelevant. But those products would likely also be the products for which the carbon content is rather low, thereby making them less of a problem for climate policy. Or put differently, to the extent that the carbon price will matter in decarbonising, it will also matter in putting a wedge between domestic and foreign producers in the absence of the CBAM.

There are three fundamental critiques of CBAM:

The first criticism is that emerging economies would be put at a disadvantage. This argument is undoubtedly wrong in theory but may be right in practice. Table B4.1.1 illustrates that the argument is wrong in theory. Foreign producer D is not put at a disadvantage to domestic producer A. The relative price of their products does not change as a result of the introduction of the CBAM. On the contrary, only introducing a domestic tax would have been putting the emerging market producer at an unfair advantage relative to the domestic producer. In practice, however, the argument may still be right, in that emerging market industrial processes might be less efficient than domestic ones. On a practical level, this will lead to opposition from emerging markets to introducing such a measure.

The second criticism is that the CBAM would not be compatible with the World Trade Organization (WTO) and be a form of green protectionism. There are two main replies to this critique. The first is that WTO compatibility depends on the precise design of the CBAM. A well-designed CBAM can be made WTO compatible. The second and more fundamental reply is that even if the CBAM was not WTO compatible, it may still be the right political choice to introduce the CBAM. The European Union is a strong advocate of the global multi-lateral and rules-based trading system. However, it is a political choice whether it is more important to support the WTO or to achieve ambitious reductions in GHG emissions. If there were to be a trade-off between the two and the global multi-lateral rules-based system were incompatible with achieving the necessary reductions in GHG emissions, couldn't and shouldn't even the European Union's choice be to pursue the latter?

The third, and perhaps the most pertinent criticism of the CBAM, is that it is practically unfeasible. The core of that practical argument is that it is relatively easy to measure the emissions domestically while it is difficult or even impossible to measure them in third countries. Domestically, the factory would be fully taxed based on the amount of all CO_2 emitted, which is relatively easy to measure as one can measure the input into the production of cement, chemicals, electricity and so on. Should one ask foreign producers to report on their emissions? Who would verify those reports? How deep into the value chain is one looking? Where did a car producer buy its steel? From which power plant did the electricity for a ton of steel come from? Could one find an international treaty framework establishing standards of measurement? Should there be a form of carbon rating measuring and confirming the CO_2 content of all products in the world? So how could one tax the foreign producer according to its true emissions?

The European Union is introducing a CBAM limited to a few products as the book is written. It will be interesting to study how the CBAM will work in practice.

This means that carbon pricing should not be implemented in isolation. Other fiscal tools (such as public investment and R&D subsidies) will act as necessary complements to change behaviours, while some form of redistribution will be decisive in gaining the general public's support, as will be discussed in Section 4.3.

4.2.2 What Should Be the Price of Carbon and How Should It Evolve over Time?

There is a clear consensus in the academic literature and across simulations about the fact that carbon prices are currently too low and that they need to increase significantly in the next thirty years. However, no consensus can be found on the exact path they should take. A strict Pigouvian tax sets the carbon price to the social cost of carbon, that is, the expected present discounted value of all present and future damages to the world economy resulting from emitting one ton of carbon today. However, this approach leads to a wide range of carbon price paths because of disagreements and of the fundamental uncertainty about the size of marginal damages from climate change, about the discount rate to use (and whether they should be market-based or ethically based) and about the sensitivity of temperatures to CO_2 emissions (van der Ploeg, 2021).

This is why policymakers and negotiators in COP conferences have not been using this approach to price carbon but adopted a simpler approach based on a temperature target, which can be equivalently translated on a cap on cumulative emissions, a so-called carbon budget (i.e. the maximum cumulative amount of emissions to limit temperature change to the agreed maximum global temperature rise). At the global level, our carbon budget, as of 2020, was estimated to be between 400 billion and 500 billion tons of CO_2 to stay below 1.5°C with a sufficiently high probability (IPCC, 2021).[3] This represents

---

[3] More precisely, research gathered by the Intergovernmental Panel on Climate Change (IPCC, 2021) shows that the world can emit only about 500 $GtCO_2$ starting in 2020 for a 50 per cent chance of limiting warming to 1.5°C. For a 67 per cent chance of avoiding 1.5°C, the budget will come down to 400 $GtCO_2$.

less than ten years of global carbon emissions at current levels (i.e. between 40 and 50 billion tonnes of carbon dioxide [$GtCO_2$] per year). This problem is thus equivalent to the problem of optimal extraction of an exhaustible resource studied by Hotelling (1931). His objective was to understand at which rate to extract the resource and at which price to sell it, and he showed that the optimal path for the price of that resource is to rise at a rate equal to the interest rate. How to use our remaining carbon budget can be seen as an exhaustible resource problem, meaning that carbon price should rise at the risk-free interest rate level, while the climate target and the anticipation of future technologies allowing to reduce emissions should determine the initial price but not the price growth rate itself (Gollier, 2021).

However, this is not what is often proposed either. For instance, in the United States, the Climate Leadership Council (2019) endorsed a plan to put in place a carbon tax at $40 per ton of emission (in 2017 prices) growing at 5 per cent per year above inflation. In France, a 2019 report recommended a carbon price growing from €69 in 2020 to €775 in 2050 (both in 2019 prices), that is a real growth rate of 8 per cent per year (Quinet, 2019). In the models collected by the Intergovernmental Panel on Climate Change (IPCC, 2021) the global carbon price is expected to grow on average by 9 per cent per year between 2022 and 2050 in scenarios leading to net zero by 2050 (as can be seen on the left-hand-side panel of Figure 4.3). These growth rates are much higher than the observed interest rates, which means that the carbon budget is not fully optimised, at least according to Hotelling's rule.[4]

The most probable reason behind this is the political unacceptability of a high carbon price in the short term (as discussed in Section 4.2.1), which incites policymakers to postpone climate efforts in the future as much as possible (Gollier, 2021). This means that they prefer to start with very low prices and promise to increase them quickly in the future, taking the risk that this promise will remain unfulfilled.

---

[4] Quinet (2019) explains in detail the two main approaches to carbon pricing and how they complement each other.

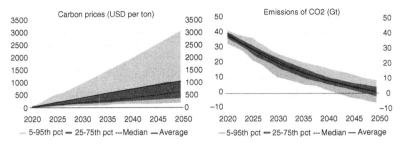

FIGURE 4.3 IPCC-reviewed models' estimates of carbon prices (in 2010 US$) and CO_2 emissions (in $GtCO_2$) in net zero scenarios
Note: Estimations of emissions and carbon price paths from all models collected by the IPCC assuming net zero scenarios, excluding outliers (top and bottom 5 per cent of the distribution).
Source: Authors, based on IPCC AR6 dataset (2021).

In practice, the large uncertainty around the desirable carbon price path and the exact impact that it will have on emissions means that the evolution of the carbon price and its effects will have to be monitored closely to ensure that it is consistent with net zero transition. This should guarantee that policies can be revised either because the chosen path fails to achieve the target (as it creates unforeseen and undesirable side-effects) or because of unexpected technological change (as new technologies will be the most crucial ingredient in determining the feasibility of a particular scenario). Indeed, if a new low-carbon technology turns out to be quickly available at a low cost, this could mean that the price of carbon could increase less than originally planned. However, even if some flexibility is needed given the considerable uncertainty, significant revision of carbon price paths over time could also lead to time-consistency issues.

4.2.3 *Government Revenues from Carbon Pricing*

Carbon pricing is above all a climate tool intended to change behaviours. It should thus not be perceived or presented as a way for governments to raise more resources permanently. One important reason is that these revenues should decrease over time with the reduction of emissions if the policy is successful in decarbonising the economy (*in fine* the tax base should disappear). But, in the meantime, the implementation of a meaningful carbon tax and/or the sale of comprehensive emission allowances should nonetheless lead to a significant increase in government revenues during the transition. Indeed, carbon pricing has already generated $84 billion in revenues at the global level in 2021, with the EU ETS representing the lion's share of these revenues at $34 billion (World Bank, 2022a).[5]

But how will these revenues evolve during the transition? This is a difficult question. The discussion in Section 4.2.2 emphasised the large uncertainty surrounding the emission path and even more around the carbon price path needed to reach net zero by 2050. The left-hand-side panel of Figure 4.3 – displaying the distribution of carbon price paths in the models collected by the IPCC in 2021 – highlights the significant heterogeneity of possible carbon price path across models (despite omitting the most extreme estimations), with carbon prices reaching between $250 and $3,000 per ton, and an average at around $1,000, by 2050 (in 2010 US$). Combining these with possible emissions paths (displayed in the right-hand side of Figure 4.3) allows us to obtain a range of possible revenues from carbon pricing at the global level for the whole period (as revenues = emissions x prices). As a result, and despite the very large uncertainty surrounding these numbers, Figure 4.4 suggests that carbon pricing could represent a significant source of revenues for governments for a couple of decades – that is between around 2 per cent and 5 per cent of GDP (focusing on the twenty-fifth/seventy-fifth percentile), with a median estimate at around 4 per cent, in 2030.[6]

---

[5] The World Bank (2022b) carbon price dashboard is a useful tool to find up-to-date and comprehensive information about carbon pricing, but another tool allows to compare details of ETS (and in particular the design aspects) in force or being considered in various jurisdictions across the globe: https://icapcarbonaction.com/en/compare/108/43

[6] Estimates for the first few years should be treated with even more caution because estimates from the models collected by the IPCC do not match historical numbers. One reason is that some models use carbon pricing as the only climate tool and thus the carbon price variable also incorporates the implicit price effect of non-price policies, including standards and other regulations. These estimates are therefore probably overestimating the actual revenues governments will make if they decide to use non-price measures.

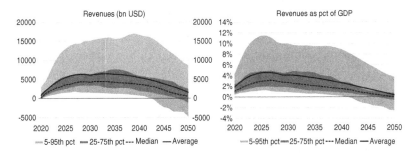

FIGURE 4.4 Revenues from carbon pricing (IPCC-reviewed models' estimates) in net zero scenarios. Panel A: Revenues in 2010 $. Panel B: As a share of global GDP
Notes: Estimates from models collected by the IPCC assuming net zero scenarios, excluding outliers (top and bottom 5 per cent of the distribution). Total revenues calculated as price times emissions (Panel A) and divided by real GDP estimates (Panel B).
Source: Authors, based on IPCC AR6 (2021).

In the European Union, public revenues from the ETS are already substantial. The total revenues generated in the EU-27 from the auctions selling the ETS allowances between 2013 and 2020 exceed €56 billion. The EU ETS Directive (Article 10) stipulates that member states should use at least 50 per cent of auctioning revenues (or the equivalent in financial value) for climate- and energy-related activities. As prices increase, so do the corresponding revenues. Germany, for example, raised €13 billion in 2022 by selling ETS allowances and domestic allowances. These revenues were used to fund climate and transition funds and were thus recycled primarily for domestic green investments. Compared to the simulation in Figure 4.4, the numbers are currently thus still low, as German revenues from selling emission permits still represent less than 0.4 per cent of GDP.[7]

Another significant change (and positive impact) on public finances should come from the elimination of subsidies and tax exemptions to fossil fuels and carbon-intensive activities, which effectively act as negative carbon prices. At the global level explicit fossil fuel subsidies represent $455 billion in 2020, that is 0.5 per

[7] Source: https://climate-energy.eea.europa.eu/topics/climate-change-mitigation/use-of-ets-auctioning-revenues/intro

cent of global GDP, around four times as much as the subsidies for renewables during that year (IMF, 2021a).[8]

Some jurisdictions, like the European Union, currently envisage to put in place CBAMs to prevent the risk of carbon leakage. Estimates of potential revenues from such mechanisms are scarce, but at the EU level, the European Commission estimated that CBAM revenues would initially represent €0.7 billion per year during the period 2022–30 (European Commission, 2021). This highlights the limited scope of the envisaged CBAM (and the difficulties about its implementation). A back-of-the-envelope calculation would suggest that a comprehensive mechanism covering all imports could yield up to €70 billion per year in revenues in the coming years (assuming that the EU imports 1 $GtCO_2$ per year, that a ton of CO_2 is priced at €70 as is the case at the time of writing in November 2022 and that the carbon embedded in imports is not priced at all in its country of origin).

Finally, decarbonisation could also have a negative impact on other sources of governments' revenues. Tax revenues coming from brown activities will be drastically curtailed as decarbonisation takes place. Revenues from carbon-intensive assets in public ownership will also be affected. This source of funding is generally negligible in the European Union but this is not the case everywhere in the world (Zenios, 2021). Even if the effect on public finances could be more or less neutral at the global level, there will be large differences between countries. The fall in demand for fossil fuels will reduce the economic activity and thus fiscal revenues of major fossil fuel exporters if they do not reorient their activity quickly. Despite the relatively high degree of diversification of its economy compared to other oil-exporting countries, Norway represents a prime example of a country for which the exploitation of natural resources (oil and gas in particular) is an important source of revenues for the state (since

---

[8] Implicit subsidies, reflecting undercharging for environmental costs and foregone consumption taxes, are estimated at $5.9 trillion or 6.8 per cent of GDP in 2020 (IMF, 2021a).

2000 it has represented between 10 per cent and 35 per cent of the state revenues but will reach almost 50 per cent in 2022–23 because of the rise of energy prices[9]). That's why the country decided in 1996 to transfer these revenues into a sovereign wealth fund, whereby the government can use only the real return from the investments of the fund to finance its yearly budgets.

However, more generally, in countries in which revenues coming from fossil fuel exploitation is negligeable and that fund themselves mainly through corporate, income and retail sales taxes, the overall change in revenues will depend mainly on the change in the level of output. If GDP remains largely unaffected by climate policies in the long run (as most models seem to suggest, see the discussion but also the limits of these models in Chapters 1 and 2) overall fiscal revenues could be unaffected too, assuming each unit of GDP can be taxed similarly.

4.3 PUBLIC EXPENDITURES AND DECARBONISATION

Decarbonisation will also lead to a significant change in both the level and the composition of public spending.

4.3.1 Recycling Carbon Pricing Revenues to Reduce Distorting Taxes or Public Debt

Initial ideas on green public spending focused mainly on how to use the revenues from carbon pricing to lower other distorting taxes in order to make the economy more efficient by taxing 'bad' inputs – CO_2 emissions – instead of taxing 'good' inputs – that is labour and capital (Goulder, 1995).

Indeed, in theory, this recycling mechanism could affect economic activity positively by reducing distorting taxes in the economy, such as capital taxes and consumption taxes to improve the efficiency of the tax system. For instance, reducing labour taxes could have beneficial macroeconomic effects, as it could increase the

---

[9] Source: www.norskpetroleum.no/en/economy/governments-revenues/

employment of low-income workers,[10] boosts income and improve overall economic activity.[11]

This positive gain is often referred to as 'double dividend', whereby decarbonisation not only successfully mitigates damages from climate change but in addition leads to net positive gains in output and employment from lowering distortions from pre-existing revenue-motivated taxes (Jaeger, 2013). However, this revenue recycling option could also lead to a lower drop in emissions compared to other options, highlighting the general trade-off between emissions and economic activity.

Another avenue for recycling carbon pricing revenues would be to reduce public deficits and debt levels. Apart from carbon pricing itself, this avenue would have no direct environmental benefits but it could have indirect beneficial effects by reducing debt-servicing cost and liabilities of the government that should eventually be covered with taxes in the future. This could also lead to a reduction in interest rates and allow more investment by the private sector in the transition. However, this should not have a first-order effect either on output or on emissions (Carbone et al., 2012).

In both cases, as discussed previously, given that revenues from carbon pricing are not supposed to be permanent, it could be complex and possibly counterproductive to replace temporarily other taxes with carbon pricing to finance the government or to rely on carbon pricing as a long-term strategy to improve the state of public finances.

Moreover, more recently, the debate on green public spending has shifted away from simply recycling carbon revenues and towards a more important discussion on the large-scale fiscal needs

---

[10] This is particularly important as significant mitigation measures (construction work in buildings to increase energy efficiency, installation and maintenance of renewable energy power plants, low-carbon agricultural practices) are generally considered more labour intensive than economic activities based on fossil fuels (see discussion in Chapter 7).

[11] For instance, Estrada-García and Santabárbara-García (2021) find that such a recycling scheme of carbon revenues in Spain could lead to a net gain of GDP by 0.2 per cent and a net gain of employment by 0.6 per cent compared to baseline after ten years.

to accelerate the transition, in particular on the spending needs for investment and for speeding up green R&D and on spending to solve distributional issues possibly induced by climate policies (see Chapter 3). This is what we will discuss in the next sub-sections.

4.3.2 Large-Scale Public and Private Investments in Green Technology and Infrastructure

Two kinds of investment will play a decisive role in the transition. First, decarbonisation will demand a lot of investment in intangible capital in the form of green R&D. Indeed, technological progress is the only way to put the world on a decarbonising path compatible with long-term growth.[12] Influencing the direction of research and putting innovation on a green path as quickly as possible is crucial to achieve decarbonisation in the limited time that we have left. Otherwise, the market size effect and initial productivity advantage of brown technologies would provide them with too large a head start, which would prevent green technologies to emerge and to be adopted massively, and ultimately lead to an environmental disaster (Acemoglu et al., 2012). For private R&D, public incentives matter considerably; for example Pisani-Ferry and Mahfouz (2022) note that there is a correlation between the increase in green patents and climate pledges by countries, suggesting that political commitment (about carbon pricing) and support (through subsidies) are important factors behind the behaviour of firms to invest in green R&D.[13] However, green research is still very low, as public and private R&D on green technologies represents only 4 per cent of total global R&D (Blanchard et al., 2022).

---

[12] Technological change is indeed a crucial determinant in the feasibility of the scenarios combining both growth and decarbonisation in the models collected by the IPCC (2021). The large difference in the pace of technological progress assumed in the various models is also one of the main drivers of the large differences between the estimates in terms of required carbon price paths and growth paths.

[13] In fact, firms that have been submitted to the EU ETS have increased their number of patents registration, in particular for green technologies (Calel & Dechezlepretre, 2016).

Second, decarbonisation will also create significant needs for physical investment in low-carbon infrastructure, mainly in energy, transport and buildings but also in adaptation infrastructures (e.g. flood defences, water management, wildfire management, which will be needed in some regions even if we manage to stay below 1.5°C as recent events suggest).

All sectors will need to invest massively to decarbonise. But the most important effort will have to take place in electricity generation from renewables and in electricity distribution. This could represent more than 60 per cent of the investment needs of the 2021–30 decade (IMF, 2021b). Even if energy efficiency is promoted in every sector and households adopt a more sober way of life, much more electricity will be needed for instance to electrify transport and heat buildings. And for sectors that will not run directly on electricity, the production of alternative fuels such as green hydrogen will also lead to considerably more electricity consumption. For instance, for aviation to be at the same level as today in 2050 while being decarbonised, solar energy to produce green synthetic fuels (such as hydrogen) for air travel would require a surface of between 140,000 km^2 – the size of Nepal – and 200,000 km^2 – the size of Uganda (Gössling et al., 2021). But other sectors will also have to invest massively, in particular manufacturing but also the agriculture sector.

Overall, the estimations on total investment needs at the global level to decarbonise fully by 2050 vary widely, as visible in Table 4.1. It is difficult to find precise and reliable estimates encompassing all investment needs at the global level (or even at the EU one). The reason is that some estimations are focusing only on particular sectors (energy, transport, etc.), some estimates are net, while others are in gross terms and thus not easily comparable. But, overall, what is clear is that capital expenditure should go up significantly over the next three decades (by around between 0.5 per cent and 3 per cent of global GDP per year on average until 2050, Table 4.1).

There are three main drivers of these large-scale needs. First, a decarbonised economy appears to be more capital intensive than

Table 4.1 *Annual investment needs estimates for decarbonisation for the world and the European Union*

	IEA (2021)	IRENA (2021)	McCollum et al. (2018)	OECD (2017)	IPCC (2021)	EC (2020)
Investment per year (bn $/€, different base years)	2030: 5,000 bn ($ 2019) i.e. 4.5% GDP 2040: 4,800 bn ($ 2019) 2050: 4,500 bn ($ 2019) i.e. 2.5% GDP	2021–30: 5,686 bn ($ 2020) 2031–50: 3,696 bn ($ 2020)	3,381 bn (USD 2015) [2,366–4,677 bn range]	6,900 bn ($ 2015)	2,400 bn–4,600 bn ($ 2015)	2021–30: 1,055 bn (€ 2015) 2031–50: 1,196 bn (€ 2015)
Description	Total investment	Total investment	Total investment	Total investment	Total investment	Total investment
Period	2021–50	2021–50	2016–50	2016–30	2020–30	2021–50
Scenario	NZE (net zero emissions) by 2050	1.5°C	1.5°C	2°C (with 66% probability)	1.5°–2°C	55% GHG reduction by 2030, NZE by 2050
Region	World	World	World	World	World	EU-27

Table 4.1 (cont.)

	IEA (2021)	IRENA (2021)	McCollum et al. (2018)	OECD (2017)	IPCC (2021)	EC (2020)
Sectors	Energy: buildings, transport, industry, electricity generation, fuel production	Energy	Energy as the sum of energy efficiency (demand) and low-carbon energy supply	All: energy from IEA; airports and ports, water and telecoms based on OECD data	Energy supply (electricity), energy efficiency, transport, land agriculture and forestry	Energy, all transport (aviation, rail, road, maritime) and building
Investment gap per year (NZE – BAU)	–	1,087 bn ($ 2020)	900 bn [481–1,663 bn] ($ 2015)	600 bn ($ 2015)	–	179.5 bn (€ 2015)
Investment gap per year (NZE – historical)	2,150 bn (USD 2019)	2,253 bn ($ 2020)	–	–	1,600–3,800 bn ($ 2015)	465.6 bn (€ 2015)

Investment gap per year (all in $ 2010)	1,835 bn ($ 2010)	BAU: 916 bn ($ 2010) Historical: 1,898 bn ($ 2010)	828 bn [443 bn–1,530 bn] ($ 2010)	552 bn ($ 2010)	1,500–3,500 bn ($ 2010)	NA
Average investment gap per year as percentage of GDP	vs historical: 1%	vs BAU: 0.5% vs historical: 1.04%	vs BAU: 0.48% [0.26%–0.89%]	vs BAU: 0.44% vs historical: 1.1%–2.6%	vs BAU: 1.1% vs historical: 2.8%	

Note: The estimates in the first line of the table are directly quoted from their respective publications and indicate the total investment in decarbonisation per year. In lines 4 and 5, the investment gap is computed as the difference between the total decarbonisation investment and the investment level under the business-as-usual (BAU) scenario or the historical level of investment. In order to make the estimates comparable, in line 6, they are converted in USD 2010 prices. Finally, in line 7, the investment level is reported as a share of GDP in purchasing power parity terms. For all studies except the one for the European Union, GDP forecasts is obtained from the IPCC AR6 database by averaging GDP levels across eighty models under the 2050 decarbonisation scenarios. For the EU estimates, we use the European Commission's model GDP estimates (PRIMES).

Sources: Authors, based on IEA (2021), IRENA (2021), McCollum et al. (2018), OECD (2017), IPCC (2021) and European Commission (2020).

a carbon-intensive economy, which requires less initial investment but has an ongoing need for fossil fuels to provide energy. In contrast, solar farms, wind farms, nuclear plants and hydroelectricity plants necessitate a large amount of initial capital but have low operating costs (Hirth & Steckel, 2016), as, in the case of solar and wind at least, the energy is available even at close to zero marginal cost. The same holds for building renovation and energy efficiency measures in general, which require some large immediate investment but will reduce costs and energy consumption once they are realised. This distinctive cost structure also means that low-carbon projects are highly reliant on the availability of financing (private or public) to fund these high upfront investments.

Second, the cost of low-carbon equipment might be higher than comparable 'brown' infrastructure. It may be more expensive to build a wind farm than a coal-fired power plant. However, the cases of solar panels or electric vehicles (EVs) suggest that technological progress and production at scale can bring down costs substantially. Indeed, for these two products, prices were initially much higher than their carbon-intensive alternatives but economies of scale and innovation have reduced their cost quickly.

Finally, brown assets that still operate well will need to be replaced in some sectors earlier than initially foreseen, resulting in substantial write-offs of these stranded assets. The faster and more disruptive green infrastructure replaces brown one, the bigger the costs. This would increase the amount of capital that will need to be installed in coming years. Moreover, this would not even increase the stock of capital but just compensate for a quicker than foreseen depreciation of the ageing (brown) capital stock. The necessary replacement of brown capital, combined with the high initial costs of low-carbon energy, explains why many estimates of investment needs are humped-shaped as more capital is needed in the next one or two decades (see, e.g. the estimates from the International Energy Agency (IEA) and International Renewable Energy Agency (IRENA) in columns 1 and 2 of Table 4.1).

4.3.3 What Spending Should Be Public and What Should Be Private?

The investment needs estimated and described earlier concern all investments. Yet, for fiscal policies, public investments are most relevant for public budgets. An important question is, therefore, which green investments need to be directly funded by the government. It is further important to understand which private investments would need to be incentivised by the public sector via guarantees. There is no simple answer to these questions as a lot depends on the way economies and the public sector are organised. Countries also have very different public policy traditions and different political economy constraints leading them to different choices.

It is certain that capital expenditure by the private sector is going to play a crucial role. Firms across the world are starting to play that role as do private households. They do so in response to public pressure but also simply in response to the incentives resulting from emissions taxes and higher fossil fuel energy prices. For instance, a UK survey run at the end of 2021 showed that a large share of UK firms (44 per cent) intended to increase climate-related investments over the next three years in response in response to climate change (Bank of England, 2022).

However, there are good reasons why the state will have to play a catalytic role to ensure that the very large investment needs discussed previously are met so that decarbonisation effectively happens. As we have seen in Section 4.1, carbon price is a crucial ingredient to alter behaviours towards a decarbonised economy. However, it will not be effective enough to generate sufficient investment or innovation to achieve net zero by 2050 if it is not credible and predictable, or simply if it is lower than what is required for political reasons, which unfortunately will probably be the case as the situation of the United States suggests (see Box 4.2 on what US climate policy will look like in the coming years).

Additionally, public investments are needed to deal with numerous market failures that go beyond the negative externality of

CO_2 emissions. The transition to a decarbonised economy is indeed riddled with issues related to technology lock-in (e.g. due to the long lifetime of gas-fired powerplants), time inconsistencies (e.g. the problem noted earlier about the carbon price path), limited foresight of households (also due to the large uncertainty characterising the transition), short-termism of firms, natural monopolies (e.g. because of large and upfront fixed costs of energy networks and renewables), positive externalities (such as knowledge spillovers arising from green R&D), coordination issues, network effects and chicken and egg problems (e.g. charging points are profitable if there is a large number of EVs in operation but EVs are a viable transport option only if there are enough charging points), economies of scale, path dependencies (e.g. of research), financial frictions (e.g. liquidity-constrained households that cannot purchase durable goods that are green and long-lasting). All these failures could lead to delays or outright under-provision of green capital and green R&D by the private sector.

This again stresses why public spending and carbon pricing are complements and not substitutes. Even if carbon pricing were to rise at a pace that should theoretically induce the desired change in behaviour, to be able to effectively shift from carbon-intensive behaviours economic agents will need affordable low-carbon alternatives to be available – for instance public transportation, trains, charging networks for EVs to move away from combustion engine cars, trucks, and airplanes. But if these alternatives are under-provided by the private sector (because of market failures), carbon pricing will not have the intended effect and will primarily affect the purchasing power of households instead of their behaviours.

How much of the green investments should be public? The share of public investment in total investment is around 15 per cent on average in Organisation for Economic Co-operation and Development (OECD) countries. But given the radical transformation that our economy will have to go through, this share might have to be higher in the next decades. The International Monetary Fund (IMF), for instance, uses historical average shares uniformly to calculate the amount of green investments that should be covered with public money (IMF, 2021b), but in practice it is difficult to say how much exactly governments will have to spend as this will depend on each country's specific situation. Looking at what is currently planned for the transition, there is a large variability across countries in terms of distribution between public and private, as far as green investments are concerned. For instance, in the European Union, national energy and climate plans for the period 2021–30 show that the share of public investment could vary considerably across the continent,[14] representing less than 3 per cent of total planned green investments in the Netherlands but almost 70 per cent in Lithuania, with an unweighted average at 45 per cent (EIB, 2021) and a weighted average at 28 per cent (Darvas & Wolff, 2022). These large disparities reflect different sectoral needs, distinctive involvement of the state in the economy in general or in particular sectors (especially in the energy sector), diverse historical traditions, statistical reporting differences and specific national political economy considerations.

So, in practice how to decide what investment should be public and what should be private? In addition to solving the various market failures discussed previously that should dictate how the state should intervene, other features should be considered. At the macroeconomic level, the fiscal capacity of countries – that is their ability to raise affordable funds to invest in green projects and later to collect taxes to repay their debt – should play a crucial role in this decision. At the microeconomic level, the capacity of a specific project to generate fees, or more generally cash flows, to reimburse the initial investment should obviously determine if it can be done by the private sector (Krogstrup & Oman, 2019). And, finally, from an institutional perspective, the existence of effective public institutions is crucial and should be taken into account to be sure that public money is well allocated and that large-scale public investment is effectively planned, well implemented and well managed.

---

[14] These plans have been released by EU countries in 2018 in order to coordinate their energy and climate strategies during the next decade.

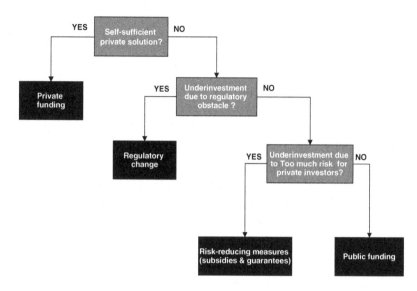

FIGURE 4.5 Multi-lateral institutions' approach on how to decide
which investments could be public or private
Source: Authors, inspired by Gabor (2021).

One possible approach to take into account projects' and countries' specificities to decide what can be financed by the private sector and what needs to be done by governments is the one promoted
by multi-lateral institutions like the World Bank, the IMF, and the
United Nations (e.g. in Krogstrup & Oman, 2019). This approach can
be formalised with the decision tree presented in Figure 4.5, as in
Gabor (2021).[15] For each project, the first step is to see if it can be
funded privately without public support. If that is the case the government does not need to intervene. If that is not possible, the second
step is to identify if there are some regulatory impediments to the
realisation of these investments. If so, the government should work
on those impediments. If not, the third step is to see whether the risk

---

[15] In her paper, Gabor (2021) uses this representation in a critical way to describe what
she calls the 'Wall Street consensus' as a system to reduce the role of governments in
green investments to the benefit of private actors. This approach could nevertheless
be interesting in practice given the major role played by these institutions in the green
investment landscape.

of the project is considered too high by private investors. If it is possible to reduce that risk enough to crowd in private investors using guarantees or other tools, the government should do it (see Chapter 6). Finally, if that is not possible the government should fund the project as long as it contributes to the decarbonisation of our economies. This approach could be particularly useful in countries that have limited fiscal or institutional capacity.

4.3.4 Fiscal Tools Used to Boost Investment for the Transition

As we have seen, governments will need to play a major role to unleash investment and innovation. But what form will public action take? The state will have to use the whole panoply of fiscal tools to accelerate decarbonisation in the next two decades.

Outright public investment will be indispensable in various sectors. First, in energy infrastructure, in particular in electricity production and distribution. Indeed, electricity networks will have to be more interconnected and more reliable, for instance not only because production of solar and wind energy will not necessarily take place near manufacturing sites but also because they will have to be more resilient to climate disasters. Second, in transport infrastructure, in particular in public transportation. A dense network of high-speed trains could be useful to replace long-distance car trips or short air travel, but the state will also have to invest in local railways and in clean transport (such as bike lanes) that allow to substitute daily-life car trips. Third, in the renovation of public buildings to improve their energy efficiency and make them carbon neutral. Fourth, in urban development to design more compact cities that will reduce commuting. Finally, and most importantly, investment will also need to be made in intangible assets as public R&D plays a decisive role in the innovation process as a necessary complement to private R&D, in particular in the form of fundamental research that is underprovided by the private sector. In some cases, some of these public investments will take the form of public–private partnerships (PPPs) to reduce the direct cost for public finances. PPPs generate fewer future cash flow and asset accumulation for the state but they can still be appropriate especially if initial costs are very large, as is often the case for low-carbon equipment.

Another important fiscal tool will be subsidies and tax breaks. They could help crowd in private investment from firms to accelerate the deployment of renewable energy power plants or to build dense network of charging stations for EVs. The goal is to make low-carbon energy sources more abundant and cheaper and improve the carbon efficiency of energy and production. Renewable energy has demonstrated significant learning-by-doing in the past decade, suggesting that subsidising the installation of these technologies could contribute to a decrease in their cost. Subsidies could also be used to reduce the costs for households that will have to invest in clean transport such as EVs and to renovate their homes. Subsidies and tax breaks could also be designed to support innovation in more novel green technologies that will improve emissions intensity further in the future, as risky R&D that is profitable only with a long lag might not be done without public support (despite the incentive of carbon pricing). They could be used for instance to kick start innovation to improve batteries (which will be much needed for EVs to become mainstream but also to deal with the intermittency of renewables), to make green hydrogen a reality (which will be needed for air travel but could also become a way to store the intermittent excess supply of energy from renewables) and in carbon capture and storage technologies. These technologies are already available but innovation is needed to make them more efficient and cheaper. Public intervention could also take the form of feebates, which combine a subsidy on clean activities with a levy on polluting activities. A typical example is a subsidy for EVs financed by a tax on high energy consuming sport utility vehicles.

Next, public guarantees on some investments could be used to reduce the risk taken by project developers in order to crowd in private investment. This could be particularly useful if carbon prices do not increase in line with what is required to ensure that low-carbon investments are profitable or if carbon pricing policies are not perceived as credible enough by investors.[16] The government could also guarantee specific prices. For instance, for the production of clean electricity, feed-in tariffs can be used to lock in prices for renewable electricity producers to reduce uncertainty around these investments and thus increase their share in electricity generation. These guarantees could then act as a commitment device for governments (which could reduce time inconsistency issues discussed previously), as it could become very costly for governments to honour these guarantees if they do not put in place carbon pricing.

Public procurement could also play a role in the decarbonisation process as green criteria in government purchases could lead to an increase in market size thanks to a reliable demand for low-carbon industrial products from the state. This in turn could lead to considerable economies of scale, in particular in sectors in which government demand is significant. Green public procurement can incentivise firms to innovate and introduce more environmentally friendly products. This is particularly true for small and medium-sized firms (Krieger & Zipperer, 2022). However, caution is needed as green criteria could also make decisions in public tenders more opaque, which would be costly for taxpayers. Moreover, the ability to tilt procurement could expose officials to lobbying and electioneering (Blanchard et al., 2022)

Finally, public development banks and public funds will also play a role in boosting the transition through targeted lending programmes (towards firms but also towards liquidity-constrained households), public equity and co-investment with private investors. This will be discussed in Chapters 5 and 6 of the book.[17]

---

[16] In the end, the level of carbon price needed to decarbonise by 2050 also depends on other policies in place: if a sufficient battery of complementary measures (subsidies for R&D, public investment, non-price measures, etc.) are put in place in parallel then carbon price could be lower. This is also why carbon price paths can differ so much in IPCC models.

[17] Public development banks do not directly affect the balance sheet of the government, except when they are created to build their capital or exceptionally if they need to be recapitalised.

4.3.5 *How to Deal with the Distributional Effects of Climate Policies?*

Low-income households spend a higher share of their income on energy than their richer counterparts, meaning that they are likely to be more affected by climate policies. Given the overall regressive nature of climate pricing (even if there also exist some progressive aspects to the transition, see Chapter 3), distributional issues will need to be tackled to ensure electoral support in democracies. To make carbon pricing credible and predictable, and thus effective in changing behaviours, it needs to be acceptable to citizens, which makes compensatory spending a part of the discussion. Fortunately, one major difference between an increase in carbon prices and an external energy price shock – such as the oil shocks from the 1970s or the 2022 energy crisis – is that the increase in carbon prices is not a term-of-trade shock making households poorer, so carbon pricing revenues can be redistributed domestically.

One avenue to do this is through transfers to alleviate the burden of a high carbon price and restrictive standards for low-income households. These households tend to spend a larger share of their budget on energy expenditures and to have fewer resources (and are often credit constrained) to invest in low-carbon durable goods, such as EVs, heat pumps or home insulation. Loosening the budget constraint of households not only could dampen the drop in demand created by carbon pricing and make carbon pricing more acceptable but more importantly it would effectively allow them to change their behaviours.

In terms of design, directly offsetting the increases in energy bills would be a bad idea as it would reduce the incentive to curtail energy consumption and allow for more emissions. This is why most economists favour direct transfers in a lump-sum manner, with varying degrees of universality. For instance, the Climate Leadership Council (2019) proposed for the United States a universal transfer to return all net proceeds from carbon pricing to all citizens on a quarterly basis. However, more targeted instruments could also be

BOX 4.2   **Green expenditures in practice, the examples of the US Inflation Reduction Act bill and the EU Recovery and Resilience Facility packages**

The Inflation Reduction Act (IRA) is a US federal law signed in August 2022. The Act provides additional spending in three main areas, which are a reform of the Internal Revenue Service, the temporary extension of the Affordable Care Act and, most prominently, spending and tax incentives for the adoption of green technologies. The spending envelope of the Act over the period 2022–31 amounts to $579 billion, or 2.5 per cent of US GDP in 2021 (Committee for a Responsible Federal Budget, 2022). Of these, two thirds, or $391 billion (1.7 per cent of US GDP), will be allocated to the green transition. Given the length of the plan, this means around 0.2 per cent per year in new green expenditures over the next decade.

Among green investments, $234 billion will be employed in tax credits to corporations and, to a lesser extent, consumers. The aim is to promote private investments in clean energy generation, electrification and energy efficiency of buildings and to promote the use of EVs and green fuels. Figure B4.2.1 (left panel) shows a breakdown of these investments.

The sector benefitting the most from the IRA, as depicted in Figure B4.2.1 (right panel), is the energy sector to which are allocated almost $250 billion, or almost two thirds of the green investments included in the bill, followed by manufacturing ($47 billion) and environment ($46 billion).

In Europe, the Recovery and Resilience Facility (RRF) is an instrument providing EU countries funds to support reforms and investments as part of the common EU-wide response to the COVID-19 pandemic. It consists of €312.5 billion in grants and €360 billion of loans for a total envelope of €672.5 billion, in 2018 prices (around 5 per cent of EU GDP).

In order to foster the green transition, at least 37 per cent of the spending of each country financed through the RRF must be allocated to climate measures. The European Commission estimates

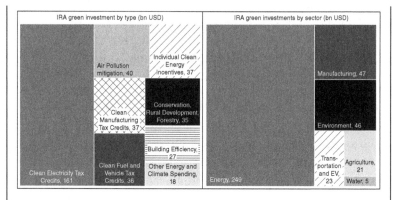

FIGURE B4.2.1   US IRA green spending by type and by sector
(in US$ bn)
Source: Authors, based on Committee for a Responsible Federal
Budget (2022) and McKinsey (2022).

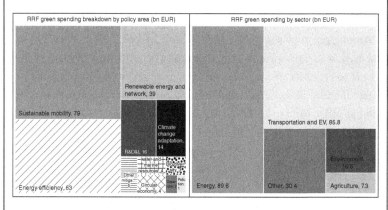

FIGURE B4.2.2   EU RRF green spending by policy area and sectors
(in € bn 2018 prices)
Notes: Darvas et al. (2021) estimate the total green spending under
the RRF to be €230 billion under different categories, here grouped by
sector by the authors to be comparable with the IRA breakdown by
sector in Figure B4.2.1. Additionally, European Commission (2022)
provides a breakdown of green spending under the RRF by policy area
as share of total green spending. Volumes of green spending per policy
area have been calculated by multiplying the shares provided by the
European Commission by the total green spending measured by
Darvas et al.
Source: Authors, based on European Commission (2022) for the LHS
and Darvas et al. (2021) for the RHS.

that this target has been exceeded and provides a breakdown of the expenditures towards climate objectives as illustrated in Figure B4.2.2 (left panel). Sustainable mobility, or transportation, is the most prominent recipient of funding (34 per cent of the green spending in the RRF) followed by energy efficiency (27 per cent) and renewable energy (17 per cent). Overall, this means around 0.3 per cent per year in new green expenditures over six years.

Because granular information concerning the spending plans is not broadly available yet, Darvas et al. (2021) developed a dataset that aims at collecting and harmonising each country's reforms and investment plans. Figure B4.2.2 (right panel) reports a breakdown of the green spending by sector.[1] Similar to the IRA, the sector benefitting the most is the energy sector (€89.6 billion), followed by transportation and environment.

[1] It estimates that countries will spend €230 billion in green investments, which is smaller than the original European Commission number because not all loans available under the RRF have been requested by EU countries.

used to help low-income populations – for example either through targeted transfers or through an expansion of the social safety net. In particular, there should also be significant expenditures devoted to job reskilling in order to help displaced workers from brown industries acquire the needed skills to transition to green jobs (see details of labour market issues and possible policies in Chapter 7).

Distributional effects are also going to be geographical given the concentration of brown activities in particular regions or the difference in lifestyle between metropolitan areas and suburban/rural areas. This means that there could also be transfers between regions to help the most-affected regions adjust to a decarbonised economy or that localisation could be one of the parameters of the determination of individual transfers (see, e.g. Bureau et al., 2019).

How much would it cost to compensate climate policies? Given the uncertainty surrounding carbon prices themselves, it is very difficult to know how much compensation would cost. However, the

IMF (2020) estimated that, for example, with a carbon price of $50 per ton in the United States and in China, recycling between 17 per cent and 25 per cent of carbon revenues would be needed to fully compensate the poorest 20 per cent of households, and between 40 per cent and 55 per cent to compensate the bottom 40 per cent.

Finally, as discussed at length in Chapter 3 there is also an international dimension to this distributional issue. For decarbonisation to happen, it is crucial that it happens at the global level. Since historical cumulative emissions have been generated in large part in the industrial North, developed countries will be called upon to help poorer countries to decarbonise, which will also impact their public finances. The loss and damage fund agreed at the COP27 of Sharm El Sheikh is a reflection of this history of emissions. Moreover, coordinated policy across the world could have a positive macro impact as it could lead to demand spillovers and knowledge spillovers, create larger market size for low-carbon technologies, and so on.

4.4 EFFECT ON DEBT AND DEBT SUSTAINABILITY OF DECARBONISATION

Previous sections suggest a larger role for the state than today during the transition to a decarbonised economy through fiscal measures. However, given the large uncertainty surrounding both the revenues from carbon pricing and the needs in terms of public expenditures to complement it, the overall impact on public finances remains unclear. On the one hand, there should be significant additional revenues from carbon pricing; on the other hand, the magnitude of the new spendings to boost green investment and innovation and to compensate those most negatively affected by climate policies should also be very high.

The rough estimates discussed in Section 4.3 suggest that magnitudes are in the ballpark of several points of GDP in both cases, but it is safer not to expect that they will perfectly match. Given that both types of policies are necessary in their own right, it is important that spending policies are not constrained by the level of revenues from carbon pricing. In particular, given the political risks surrounding the implementation of climate pricing in some important countries like the United States, most climate action may actually result from public spending and regulation, funded through general tax revenues and debt. It is also not clear if the revenues and expenditures would be well synchronised so that revenues can be 'recycled' into expenditures. Again, it is probably safer to expect that they will possibly be asynchronous, meaning that in a given year green revenues and green spending do not necessarily match.

These two elements point towards the possible need to increase deficits and probably debt-to-GDP ratio during the transition. The alternative would be to crowd out other types of public spending. However, this might not be easy because of the magnitude of the fiscal needs for climate spending and also because of the other challenges to be faced in the next couple of decades, for instance related to ageing and health issues.

Would increasing public debt for climate be justified from an intergenerational perspective? Current generations must make sacrifices to curb global warming for future, perhaps much richer, generations that will be better off inheriting a preserved climate. Seen like this, intergenerational redistribution through public debt appears to be a legitimate tool to achieve what would be an intergenerational win-win outcome (Kotlikoff et al., 2021).[18]

However, a significant increase in the debt-to-GDP ratio could potentially raise some doubts about the sustainability of public finances in some countries (Zenios, 2021). Public debt is considered sustainable if it is not on an explosive debt path with a high probability, with the dynamics of the debt ratio given by the following debt accumulation equation (see e.g. in Blanchard, 2023):

$$d_t - d_{t-1} = (r - g)\, d_{t-1} - b_t$$

---

[18] Another argument in favour of debt financing of mitigation is the irreversibility of climate change. It will be easier for future generations to pay back debt on a planet capable of sustaining complex modern economies than to reverse climate change once it becomes out of control.

where d_t is the debt-to-GDP ratio at time t, r is the interest rate paid on the stock of debt, g is the nominal growth of GDP and b_t is the primary budget balance as a share of GDP in t.

To make it simple, this means that debt sustainability depends mainly on the level of the difference between r and g and on the capacity of governments to generate primary surpluses b large enough to put the dynamic on a non-explosive path if this difference is positive. This is assumed to be the case in normal times, meaning that to stabilise debt governments would generally need to run primary surpluses. However, for a decade after the 2008 Global Financial Crisis, $(r - g)$ turned negative in large parts of the developed world. If $(r - g)$ were permanently negative, it would mean that governments could run primary deficits forever while keeping the debt on a non-explosive path, a very favourable condition for public finances. It is difficult to know if $(r - g)$ will remain negative during the next thirty years of decarbonisation efforts. In fact, it may well be possible that interest rates will rise as a result of increased investments in green infrastructure and that growth will slow in a period of difficult transition with many stranded assets. In any case, governments are well advised to be cautious about public finances: (i) a sign reversal of $(r - g)$ remains possible, and interest rates can rise rapidly as the large increase in interest rates in 2022 shows and (ii) even if $(r - g)$ stays negative, in practice, financial markets might find it difficult to distinguish a large but sustainable increase of the debt ratio from an actual debt explosion (Blanchard, 2023).[19]

What does this imply in our case? What will be the effect of the climate transition on these variables and therefore on debt sustainability? Could it lead to a favourable situation in which $(r - g)$ remains negative? This is a very difficult question that has not yet been answered by the literature, but a first qualitative analysis might give us a first idea of whether debt sustainability could be a significant challenge during the transition. As far as the primary balance b

---

[19] See chapter 4 in Blanchard (2023) for a detailed discussion on this point.

is concerned, the previous discussion on revenues and expenditures highlights that there is a lot of uncertainty but that it is possible that the transition will result in higher primary deficits during the next three decades as green investments increase while carbon pricing is either not used or used only to a limited extent in some countries.

Concerning the interest rate, r, numerous possible channels through which the transition to net zero will impact interest rates can be identified. Additional green investment should put an upward pressure on interest rates during the transition. But other forces could push the interest rate in the other direction. For example, productivity could be impacted by the radical change that the transition will bring forward, and could impact r. Monetary policy could be also affected in a world in which negative supply shocks become more frequent and persistent, thereby driving up rates (see Chapter 8). Unfortunately, the overall effect is ambiguous at this stage. The literature on this question is still in its infancy and more research work is needed to understand fully and quantify the effects of the different channels (see Chapters 1 and 2 for a more detailed discussion).

Finally, as far as g is concerned, Chapters 1 and 2 have highlighted the ambiguous overall effect of the transition on economic growth during the transition. Most models predict a negligible impact of the transition (either slightly positive or negative) in comparison to what would happen in case of unchanged policies. In all likelihood, the green transition will not be significantly growth enhancing. Once achieved, the lower energy costs might be positive for activity. Concerning the models collected by the IPCC, all scenarios leading to net zero by 2050 forecast a sizeable increase in global real GDP during the decarbonisation process, as visible in Figure 4.6. The average economic growth in these sixty-six scenarios is at 2.8 per cent per year between 2020 and 2050 (with a relatively low range between 2.4 per cent and 3 per cent if we exclude the top and bottom 5 per cent of the distribution). This would entail a nominal growth rate g of around 5.8 per cent (assuming inflation around 2 per cent but it could end up being a bit higher during the transition, see Chapters 2 and 8)

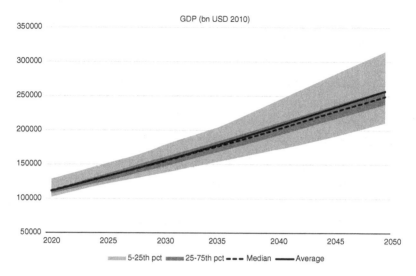

FIGURE 4.6 Global real GDP (IPCC-reviewed models' estimates) in net zero scenarios
Notes: Estimates from models collected by the IPCC assuming net zero scenarios, excluding outliers (top and bottom 5 per cent of the distribution).
Source: Authors, based on IPCC AR6 (2021).

and could thus probably be higher than r in many countries, even if interest rate were to rise meaningfully (as it has been the case in most EU countries since the end of the 1990s; Claeys & Guetta-Jeanrenaud, 2022).

These first back-of-the-envelope calculations and their implications in terms of debt sustainability assessment need to be taken with a grain of salt, as they rely on highly uncertain growth forecasts. Unfortunately, this means that debt sustainability risks are difficult to assess ex ante and will need to be monitored carefully in real time, as the transition unfolds, to discover which scenario will materialise.

4.5 KEY TAKEAWAYS

4.5.1 *Carbon Pricing Objectives and State of Affairs*

- The level and composition of the revenues of the governments around the world will be impacted by the transition towards net zero. The most important element that will affect tax revenues during the transition should be the introduction of meaningful carbon pricing.

- The objective of carbon pricing is to change relative prices in order to reduce emissions. The empirical literature suggests that carbon pricing is an effective tool in reducing emissions. Carbon prices in place in 2022 are not sufficiently broad and encompassing to achieve the global transition. In fact, large parts of global emissions are not even covered by carbon prices. Moreover, even jurisdictions with carbon pricing are often not setting the prices at levels sufficient to incentivise radical changes in behaviours and unleash the much-needed wave of private investments and innovation in green technologies. The main reason why the carbon price is too low is probably that it is politically difficult to put it in place.

4.5.2 Tax Revenues from Carbon Pricing

- Carbon pricing is a climate tool that should not be perceived or presented as a way for governments to raise more resources. One important reason is that these revenues should disappear over time with the reduction of emissions if the policy is successful. But, in the meantime, the implementation of a meaningful carbon tax and/or the sale of comprehensive emission allowances should lead to a significant increase in government revenues during the transition.
- The uncertainty surrounding estimates is very large but, if a meaningful carbon price is implemented, its revenues could represent several points of GDP (between 2 per cent and 5 per cent of GDP at the 2030 horizon)

4.5.3 Large Investment Needs in Green Technology and Infrastructure

- Decarbonisation will also lead to a significant change in both the level and the composition of public spending. Initial ideas focused mainly on using the revenues from carbon pricing to lower other distorting taxes in order to make the economy more efficient. However, the debate has shifted towards a discussion on the large-scale fiscal needs to accelerate the transition, in particular on the spending needs for investment and for speeding up green R&D and on spending to solve distributional issues possibly induced by climate policies.
- Overall, estimates for total investment needs at the global level to decarbonise fully by 2050 vary widely. But what is clear from the

literature is that capital expenditure should go up significantly over the next three decades, by around between 0.5 per cent and 3 per cent of global GDP per year on average until 2050.

- Three main reasons for increased investments can be identified. A decarbonised economy will be more capital intensive than a carbon-intensive economy, the cost of low-carbon equipment might be higher and brown stranded assets will need to be replaced in some sectors earlier than initially foreseen.

- Capital expenditure by the private sector is going to play a crucial role. However, the state will have to play a catalytic role to ensure large investment effectively happens. Public spending and carbon pricing are complements, not substitutes. Even if carbon pricing were to rise at a pace that should theoretically induce the desired change in behaviour, to be able to effectively move away from carbon-intensive behaviours, economic agents will need affordable low-carbon alternatives to be available. If these alternatives are under-provided by the private sector because of market failures, carbon pricing will not have the intended effect and will primarily affect the purchasing power of households instead of their behaviours.

4.5.4 Public Spending and Fiscal Tools

- In practice it is difficult to say how much exactly governments will have to spend as this will depend on each country's specific situation. This will reflect different sectoral needs, distinctive involvement of the state in the economy in general or in particular sectors, diverse historical traditions and specific national political economy considerations. At the macroeconomic level, the fiscal capacity of countries should play a crucial role in this decision. At the microeconomic level, the capacity of a specific project to generate cash flows to reimburse the initial investment should determine if it can be done by the private sector. And from an institutional perspective, the existence of effective public institutions should be taken into account to be sure that public investments are well allocated and well managed.

- The state will have to use its whole panoply of fiscal tools to accelerate decarbonisation in the next two decades: outright public investment, subsidies and tax breaks, public guarantees, green criteria in public procurement and public development banks could all play an important role in boosting green investment and kick-starting green innovation.

4.5.5 How to Deal with Distributional Issues?

- Low-income households spend a higher share of their income on energy than their richer counterparts, meaning that they are likely to be more affected by climate policies. Distributional issues will need to be tackled not only for ethical reasons but also for political economy reasons. To make carbon pricing credible and predictable, and thus effective in changing behaviours, it needs to be acceptable to citizens.
- One avenue to increase acceptability is through transfers to alleviate the burden of a high carbon price and restrictive standards for low-income households. Most economists favour direct transfers in a lump-sum manner, with varying degrees of universality. However, more targeted instruments could also be used to help low-income populations either through targeted transfers or through an expansion of the social safety net, for example via expenditures devoted to job reskilling. Distributional effects are also going to be geographical. This means that there could also be transfers between regions to help the most-affected ones adjust to a decarbonised economy.

4.5.6 Decarbonisation and Debt Sustainability

- All of this suggests a larger role for the state during the transition to a decarbonised economy through fiscal measures. However, given the large uncertainty surrounding both public revenues and expenditures, the overall impact on net public finances remains unclear. The debt-to-GDP ratio might well increase during the transition.
- Current generations must make sacrifices to curb global warming for future generations that would be better off inheriting a preserved climate. Intergenerational redistribution through public debt thus appears to be a legitimate tool.
- However, a significant increase in debt could raise doubts about the sustainability of public finances in some countries. Unfortunately, the large uncertainty about the main variables of the debt dynamic equation – with respect to r and g in particular – makes it very difficult to assess these risks ex ante. We consider risks to sustainability large enough that sustainability will need to be monitored carefully as the transition unfolds.

REFERENCES

Acemoglu, D., P. Aghion, L. Bursztyn, and D. Hemous (2012) 'The Environment and Directed Technical Change', *American Economic Review*, 102:1, 131–66.

Bank of England (2022) 'Climate Change: Possible Macroeconomic Implications', Quarterly Bulletin, Q4 2022, 21 October, www.bankofengland.co.uk/quar terly-bulletin/2022/2022-q4/climate-change-possible-macroeconomic-implications

Blanchard, O. (2023) *Fiscal Policy under Low Interest Rates* (Cambridge, MA: MIT Press).

Blanchard, O., C. Gollier, and J. Tirole (2022) 'The Portfolio of Economic Policies Needed to Fight Climate Change', Peterson Institute for International Economics Working Paper No. 22-18, www.piie.com/publications/work ing-papers/portfolio-economic-policies-needed-fight-climate-change

Bureau, D., F. Henriet, and K. Schubert (2019) 'A Proposal for the Climate: Taxing Carbon Not People', Note du Conseil d'Analyse Economique, No. 50, March, www.cae-eco.fr/staticfiles/pdf/cae-note050-env3.pdf

Calel, R., and A. Dechezlepretre (2016) 'Environmental Policy and Direct Technological Change: Evidence from the European Carbon Market', *Review of Economics and Statistics*, 98:1: 171–91.

Carbone, J., R. Morgenstern, and R. Williams III (2012) 'Carbon Taxes and Deficit Reduction', Resources for the Future working paper, www.rff.org/publica tions/reports/deficit-reduction-and-carbon-taxes-budgetary-economic-and-distributional-impacts/

Claeys, G., and L. Guetta-Jeanrenaud (2022) 'How Rate Increases Could Impact Debt Ratios in the Euro Area's Most-Indebted Countries', Bruegel blog, 5 July, www.bruegel.org/blog-post/how-rate-increases-could-impact-debt-ratios-euro-areas-most-indebted-countries

Climate Leadership Council (2019) 'The Four Pillars of Our Carbon Dividends Plan', https://clcouncil.org/our-plan/

Committee for a Responsible Federal Budget (2022) 'CBO Scores IRA with $238 Billion of Deficit Reduction', Committee for a Responsible Federal Budget blog, 7 September, www.crfb.org/blogs/cbo-scores-ira-238-billion-deficit-reduction

Darvas, Z., M. Domínguez-Jiménez, A. Devins, M. Grzegorczyk, L. Guetta-Jeanrenaud, S. Hendry, et al. (2021) 'European Union Countries' Recovery and Resilience Plans', Bruegel Dataset, www.bruegel.org/dataset/european-union-countries-recovery-and-resilience-plans

Darvas, Z. and G. Wolff (2022) 'A Green Fiscal Pact for the EU: Increasing Climate Investments While Consolidating. Budgets', Climate Policy, https://doi.org/10.1080/14693062.2022.2147893

Dechezlepretre, A., A. Fabre, T. Kruse, B. Planterose, A. Sanchez Chico, and S. Stantcheva (2022) 'Fighting Climate Change: International Attitudes toward Climate Policies', https://scholar.harvard.edu/files/stantcheva/files/international_attitudes_climate_change.pdf

Estrada García, A., and D. Santabárbara García (2021) Recycling Carbon Tax Revenues in Spain: Environmental and Economic Assessment of Selected Green Reforms (Banco de Espana, 14 May), https://repositorio.bde.es/handle/123456789/16552.

European Commission (2020) 'Commission Staff Working Document Impact Assessment Accompanying the Communication Stepping up Europe's 2030 Climate Ambition Investing in a Climate-Neutral Future for the Benefit of Our People', COM(2020) 562 final, 17 September, https://eur-lex.europa.eu/resource.html?uri=cellar:749e04bb-f8c5-11ea-991b-01aa75ed71a1.0001.02/DOC_2&format=PDF

(2021) 'Commission Communication: The Next Generation of Own Resources for the EU Budget', COM(2021) 566, 22 December, https://ec.europa.eu/info/sites/default/files/about_the_european_commission/eu_budget/com_2021_566_1_en_act_part1_v8.pdf

(2022) 'Recovery and Resilience Scoreboard', https://ec.europa.eu/economy_finance/recovery-and-resilience-scoreboard/green.html

European Investment Bank (2021) 'EIB Investment Report 2020/2021: Building a Smart and Green Europe in the COVID-19 Era', www.eib.org/en/publications/investment-report-2020

Gabor, D. (2021) 'The Wall Street Consensus', Development and Change, 52:3, 429–59.

Gollier, C. (2021) 'The Cost-Efficiency Carbon Pricing Puzzle', TSE Working Paper No. 952.

Gössling, S., A. Humpe, F. Fichert, and F. Creutzig (2021) 'COVID-19 and Pathways to Low-Carbon Air Transport until 2050', Environmental Research Letters, 16:3, 034063, https://doi.org/10.1088/1748-9326/abe90b

Goulder, L. H. (1995) 'Effects of Carbon Taxes in an Economy with Prior Tax Distortions: An Intertemporal General Equilibrium Analysis', Journal of Environmental Economics and Management, 29:3, 271–97.

High-Level Commission on Carbon Prices (2017) Report of the High-Level Commission on Carbon Prices (Washington, DC: World Bank).

Hirth, L., and J. C. Steckel (2016) 'The Role of Capital Costs in Decarbonizing the Electricity Sector', *Environmental Research Letters*, 11:11, 114010.

Hotelling, H. (1931) 'The Economics of Exhaustible Resources', *Journal of Political Economy*, 39:2, 137–75.

IEA (2021) *World Energy Outlook 2021* (Paris: International Energy Agency), https://iea.blob.core.windows.net/assets/4ed140c1-c3f3-4fd9-acae-789a4e14a23c/WorldEnergyOutlook2021.pdf

IMF (2020) 'Mitigating Climate Change – Growth- and Distribution-Friendly Strategies', WEO Chapter 3, October, www.imf.org/-/media/Files/Publications/WEO/2020/October/English/ch3.ashx

(2021a) 'Fossil Fuel Subsidy Database', www.imf.org/en/Topics/climate-change/energy-subsidies

(2021b) 'Reaching Net Zero Emissions', June, www.imf.org/external/np/g20/pdf/2021/062221.pdf.

IPCC (2021) 'Sixth Assessment Report', www.ipcc.ch/assessment-report/ar6/

IRENA (2021) 'World Energy Transitions Outlook: 1.5°C Pathway', International Renewable Energy Agency, Abu Dhabi, www.irena.org/publications/2021/Jun/World-Energy-Transitions-Outlook

Jaeger, W. K. (2013) 'Double-Dividend Definition', Encyclopedia of Energy, Natural Resource, and Environmental Economics, www.researchgate.net/publication/259486847_Encyclopedia_of_Encyclopedia_of_Energy_Natural_Resource_and_Environmental_Economics

Kotlikoff, L., F. Kubler, A. Polbin, and S. Scheidegger (2021) 'Can Today's and Tomorrow's World Uniformly Gain from Carbon Taxation?', Working Paper No. 29224, National Bureau of Economic Research, https://kotlikoff.net/wp-content/uploads/2021/09/Optimal_carbon_tax_in_multiregional_climate_OLG_model-17.pdf

Krieger, B., and V. Zipperer (2022) 'Does Green Public Procurement Trigger Environmental Innovations?', *Research Policy*, 51:6, 104516.

Krogstrup, S., and W. Oman (2019) 'Macroeconomic and Financial Policies for Climate Change Mitigation: A Review of the Literature', IMF Working Paper No. 19/185.

Leroutier, M. (2022) 'Carbon Pricing and Power Sector Decarbonization: Evidence from the UK', *Journal of Environmental Economics and Management*, 111, 102580.

McCollum, D. L., W. Zhou, C. Bertram, H.-S. de Boer, V. Bosetti, S. Busch, et al. (2018) 'Energy Investment Needs for Fulfilling the Paris Agreement and Achieving the Sustainable Development Goals', *Nature Energy*, 3, 589–99, https://doi.org/10.1038/s41560-018-0179-z

McKinsey (2022) 'The Inflation Reduction Act: Here's What's in It', www.mckin sey.com/industries/public-and-social-sector/our-insights/the-inflation-reduction-act-heres-whats-in-it

Musgrave, R. A. (1959) *A Theory of Public Finance* (New York: McGraw Hill).

OECD (2017) 'Technical Note on Estimates of Infrastructure Investment Needs, Background Note to the Report *Investing in Climate, Investing in Growth*', www.oecd.org/environment/cc/g20-climate/Technical-note-estimates-of-infrastructure-investment-needs.pdf

Pigou, A. C. (1920) *The Economics of Welfare* (London: Macmillan).

Pisani-Ferry, J., and S. Mahfouz (2022) *L'action climatique: un enjeu macroéconomique* (France Stratégie).

Quinet (2019) *La valeur de l'action pour le climat* (Paris: France Stratégie), www.strategie.gouv.fr/sites/strategie.gouv.fr/files/atoms/files/fs-the-value-for-climate-action-final-web.pdf (English)

Samuelson, P. (1948) *Economics: An Introductory Analysis* (New York: McGraw Hill).

Solow, R. (1971) 'The Economist's Approach to Pollution and Its Control', *Science*, 173:3996, 498–503.

UNFCCC (2022) 'Nationally Determined Contributions under the Paris Agreement. Synthesis Report by the Secretariat', https://unfccc.int/ndc-synthesis-report-2022?gclid=EAIaIQobChMIxoXquKmWgQMVP12RBR2u swi0EAAYASAAEgJNYPD_BwE

Van der Ploeg, F. (2021) 'Carbon Pricing under Uncertainty', *International Tax and Public Finance*, 28, 1122–42, https://doi.org/10.1007/s10797-021-09686-x

Wolff, G (2019) 'Demystifying Carbon Border Adjustment for Europe's Green Deal', Bruegel blog, www.bruegel.org/blog-post/demystifying-carbon-border-adjustment-europes-green-deal

World Bank (2022a) *State and Trends of Carbon Pricing* (Washington, DC: World Bank), https://openknowledge.worldbank.org/handle/10986/37455

    (2022b) 'Carbon Pricing Dashboard', https://carbonpricingdashboard.world bank.org/

Zenios, S. (2021) 'The Risks from Climate Change to Sovereign Debt in Europe', Bruegel Policy Contribution No. 16/2021, www.bruegel.org/policy-brief/risks-climate-change-sovereign-debt-europe

5.1   THE GREAT DECOUPLING CHALLENGE AND THE BET ON TECHNOLOGY

The fundamental challenge of the global decarbonisation process is to entirely decouple economic activity from the production of greenhouse gas (GHG) emissions. As shown by the Kaya identity discussed in the Introduction, this challenge is complex and multi-faceted. Unsurprisingly, the economic literature is profoundly divided regarding whether such decoupling is feasible at all (Lenaerts et al., 2021).

On one side of the debate, proponents of 'degrowth' argue that observed trends show that decoupling is happening much too slowly to avoid an environmental disaster and hence economic activity itself must be curtailed. On the other side, proponents of 'green growth' argue that these trends are not indicative of what is feasible and that a combination of technological innovation and smart policies can lead to an accelerated rate of decoupling, thereby allowing living standards to be maintained and even improved, while drastically shrinking emissions.

Degrowth scholars argue that perpetual economic growth is impossible on a planet with a finite quantity of resources. They highlight that this is a fundamental flaw of classical models of economic growth, which focus on replicating a pattern of exponential growth of gross domestic product (GDP). Economic policies based on these models will therefore inevitably lead to environmental and climate disaster. Green growth scholars, on the other hand, point to the fact that much of growth has become immaterial and based on services requiring little to no material resources. They also point to the fact that energy from the sun is practically infinite and recycling allows the re-use of final resources.

5.1.1 Zooming In on Degrowth

Beyond this basic premise, there is a broad range of interpretations in this literature around what exactly should degrow and how this can be achieved. While decreasing the use of resources, especially raw materials and energy, is clearly an objective of degrowth, reducing the size of the economy is often considered an inevitable consequence of this. However, realising the negative social consequences commonly associated with recessions, degrowth scholars set out to define a path to actively 'guide' GDP downward, rather than passively let the world slip into a depression and cause widespread suffering (Demaria et al., 2013).

To achieve a managed transition to a smaller economy, proponents advance a myriad of policies as part of a systemic change. The most common proposal is to limit the supply of production factors. Emphasis is often placed on reducing labour, especially working hours. Degrowth scholars argue that this can even increase social welfare by increasing leisure time and achieving higher levels of employment. The latter must also be supported by shifting employment towards labour-intensive sectors and steering innovation to increase resource productivity rather than labour productivity (Kallis, 2011; Kallis et al., 2018). The other lever for achieving degrowth is to limit capital accumulation. This can be done by reducing aggregate investment by firms to the point where it just replaces depreciation.

In this context, the reduction of consumption, working hours and capital accumulation is both a means to this end and an objective in and of itself. The aim is to arrive at a steady state in which the whole economy is consumed, which would end growth (Loehr, 2012). However, in the transition period, some sectoral growth is permitted, as the clean sectors are promoted at the expense of dirty sectors (Kallis et al., 2018).

Overall, the degrowth narrative raises several questions. First, it assumes a positive relationship between income and energy use. However, the relationship between income and GHG emissions is more complex. First, lower average incomes, especially in developed economies, push individuals to switch to cheaper, often dirtier, sources of energy, such as firewood or coal. Additionally, lower incomes also mean fewer resources for developing and installing clean technologies and for investing in energy efficiency. Second, from a technical perspective, it is difficult to estimate what should be the targeted level of income per capita to which rich and poor countries should converge. This depends on the evolution of the four factors of the Kaya identity and the interactions between them.[1] Finally, it is clear that at least ceteris paribus the global average income should be lower than it is today. This will not offer much solace to countries trying to lift large shares of their population out of poverty and is very unlikely to find support in wealthy liberal democracies. It is difficult to imagine that a critical mass of the global population will voluntarily agree to it.

5.1.2   Green Growth: The Decoupling Challenge

The crucial question is therefore how to concretely achieve the decoupling of economic activity from GHG emissions. In contrast to proponents of degrowth, 'green growth' scholars argue that this can indeed be achieved. A carefully crafted set of policies is needed to redirect economic activity towards low-emission and resource-efficient modes of production, thereby maintaining, or in the more optimistic scenarios even increasing, economic growth.

At the core of the 'green growth' narrative stands a positive view of technological development being able to deliver absolute decoupling.

---

[1] In particular, global population growth would theoretically offer a way to reconcile GDP per capita growth and emissions reductions. However, neither proponents of degrowth nor of green growth devote much attention to limiting population growth, because most authors view it as undesirable, especially when non-voluntary, and point out that the large and growing populations of the Global South put relatively little stress on the environment (Cosme et al., 2017).

That is, 'green growth' proponents are confident that climate objectives can be reconciled with economic prosperity thanks to technological developments allowing the global economy to keep growing while reducing its environmental footprint. This techno-optimism places the spotlight on the importance of fostering breakthrough innovation, as well as on creating and expanding markets for innovative green products. In short, it places the spotlight on rapid technological progress and green industrial policy as a way to achieve it.

To be clear, important challenges exist in this area. For instance, a key challenge is to ensure that the overall burden of the transition remains manageable. The required massive reallocation of resources needs to be done with minimal waste. Companies need to change the way they produce, occasionally retiring carbon-intensive assets before the end of their economic lifetime. Consumers need to reduce their carbon footprint by replacing carbon-intensive consumption with carbon-neutral products. Workers and capital need to be shifted from brown to green sectors.

Another challenge for the transition is to create an environment conducive to experimentation in order to unlock the development of new solutions. Indeed, there is a lot of uncertainty around what will eventually be the most economic technologies (e.g. hydrogen vs biofuel aviation), the most efficient systems (e.g. hydrogen vs electric), the best mix of reducing demand and adding carbon-neutral supplies (e.g. energy renovation vs more clean fuels) and the optimal share of domestic and imported clean fuels.

Given the high degree of uncertainty over the future trajectories of technological development, the magnitude of potential mistakes is not small. Individual projects will completely fail; specific technology solutions might cost twice as much as alternatives; and complete systems might be dozens of percentages more expensive than others.[2]

---

[2] The energy sector – with its quickly changing regulatory and market conditions – offers several examples of projects that completely failed, such as the German coal plants (Moorburg, Datteln) that were built but never entered into operation. Moreover, some large energy projects turn out to be unprofitable such as the big European

When constraints on production factors (e.g. land, capital and labour) are binding – which they will likely be – any misallocation will slow down the transition and withdraw these production factors from other more important uses. In other words, the transition to net zero emissions needs to be as efficient as possible, both in how factors of production are allocated statically and in how resources are allocated dynamically for the development of innovative solutions.

An increased number of governments and institutions have been arguing that turning the decarbonisation imperative into an opportunity for green growth requires stronger and smarter public policies to foster job creation and industrial development. This is the case, for instance, of the European Commission – which defines its European Green Deal as 'Europe's new growth strategy'. Likewise, the supporters of the Green New Deal in the United States have pitched it as a tool to create high-skilled, well-paid, sustainable jobs. After all, the United Nations' Sustainable Development Goals also represent a green growth agenda, as they combine targets of economic growth and decent jobs with deep decarbonisation and environmental protection.

For governments, one of the greatest challenges in the decarbonisation process thus is to organise this decoupling in an effective and efficient manner. A key aspect of the public policy debate is on how much government intervention and even entrepreneurship are necessary and to what extent the private sector will achieve decarbonisation and technological progress once the emission externality is appropriately priced in. Advocates of a more activist role for the state aim to put in place a workable green industrial policy, which is able to foster the creation of good jobs and sustainable economic growth while GHG emissions are being rapidly and decisively cut. This truly is a challenge of great importance, because a failure to do so – for instance, entailing that brown jobs do not get replaced by

Pressurized Water Reactor (EPR) projects in Finland and Flamanville, which had huge cost overruns.

green jobs – might ultimately jeopardise the transition and put the overall decarbonisation process at risk.

This chapter will unpack this complex set of issues by taking the following approach. First, it will define what green industrial policy is. Second, it will provide an overview about how green industrial policy works in practice. Third, it will dive into each of the three concentric circles of green industrial policy: (i) green innovation, (ii) green market creation and (iii) green market expansion. For each of them, the respective market failures justifying public intervention and relevant policy tools will be discussed. The chapter will then conclude discussing the risks entailed by green industrial policy and potential governance solutions to tackle them.

5.2 HOW TO DEFINE GREEN INDUSTRIAL POLICY?

Defining industrial policy is per se a challenge. Any government policy will have some impact on the economic structure of a country. Hence, the ontological limits of the definition can be the limits of the definition of 'policy' itself.

Looking at the established literature in the field (Ambroziak, 2017), it is possible to recognise that a common factor in all definitions of industrial policy is that of targeting a set of economic activities to achieve long-term benefits to society. New tendencies in the literature on industrial policy (Aiginger & Rodrik, 2020; Cherif & Hasanov, 2019; Lane, 2019; Rodrik, 2014), which we will label as 'new industrial policy', stress that the objectives of industrial policy should look beyond short-term competitiveness and economic growth to go for a broader multi-dimensional objective, which can be captured in the notion of long-term 'social welfare'. This is the case, for instance, of Rodrik (2014), who aims at rethinking and investigating a set of interventions by the public sector – or its delegated agencies – directly in the productive sphere and in direct collaboration with the most productive segments of the private sector. In Rodrik's view, this set of interventions should aim at building a 'good jobs economy' (2).

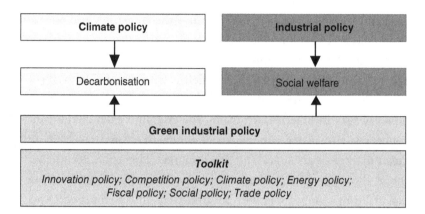

FIGURE 5.1 Green industrial policy
Source: Authors' elaboration.

The necessity of a green characterisation of industrial policy comes into play once decarbonisation is set as a societal goal, like in the case of Europe with the European Green Deal. While climate policy targets decarbonisation and industrial policy targets social welfare, green industrial policy has to reconcile the goal of decarbonising the economy (like climate policy) with the social welfare goal (like industrial policy) (Figure 5.1). It is thus possible to define green industrial policy as an industrial policy where climate change mitigation becomes a binding constraint in the social welfare policy objective.

As it combines decarbonisation and social welfare objectives, green industrial policy is different from climate policy, whose objective is solely decarbonisation. It is also different from industrial policy, whose objective is solely social welfare more broadly – or economic growth more narrowly. This combination of objectives identifies green industrial policy differently. It also immediately identifies the challenge of green industrial policy, namely to reconcile both objectives simultaneously, which becomes particularly challenging when they would conflict[3] – when trade-offs will have to be made

---

[3] An example of when decarbonisation and social welfare objectives diverge might be the case where energy efficiency standards for buildings increase construction costs (materials, skilled labour), slowing down the rate of new buildings, thereby worsening an eventual housing crisis situation.

and costs will have to be attached when one of the objectives is not being met.

Figure 5.1 also makes clear that green industrial policy will operate next to climate policy and industrial policy more generally and therefore raises the issue of coordination among the various policies, particularly when these different policies reside in different institutions or departments. Climate policy and industrial policy each have their own instruments. Would a coordination of already existing instruments from climate change and industrial policy be sufficient for a green industrial policy? Does green industrial policy need its own dedicated policy instruments? And if so, how to coordinate with existing instruments?

As for any form of economic policy more generally, green industrial policy represents a public intervention aimed at correcting market failures. Industrial policy addresses problems ranging *from* research externalities imposing access to knowledge constraints *to* financial capital market imperfections imposing access to finance constraints, or again *from* labour market imperfections imposing access to skills constraints *to* network externalities imposing access to partnerships imperfection. These constraints may lead to not only failures of existing markets to grow but also a failure of new markets to emerge and develop.

In addition to market failures at the core of classic industrial policy (Box 5.1), green industrial policy also has to address market failures associated with climate change, mainly. the GHG externality. GHG emissions are a side effect of economically valuable activities. Most of the impacts of emissions do not fall on those conducting the activities, so those responsible for the emissions do not pay the cost. The adverse effects of GHGs are therefore external to the market, which means there is usually only an ethical – rather than an economic – incentive for businesses and consumers to reduce their emissions. As a result, the market fails by over-producing GHGs. Economists have argued for a long time that the first-best policy to correct this market failure is to apply a cost to GHG emissions

---

BOX 5.1   **Classic examples of market failures**

- *Knowledge spillovers*: Companies tend to underinvest in developing new technologies, when these can be reproduced by competitors that did not spend money on research and development (R&D).
- *Dynamic scale efficiencies*: Learning-by-doing decreases the cost of wind and solar technologies, creating incentives to wait for other companies to start investing.
- *Imperfect information*: Banks do not know whether innovators will generate enough profits to pay back loans and hence ask for higher interest rates.
- *Coordination problems*: Landlords have less incentive to improve the energy efficiency of the apartments of their tenants than that of their own apartment.
- *Market power*: Companies that face too little competition might provide less of their product to increase market prices and hence earn higher revenues.
- *Network effects*: Building an electric charger network has positive spillovers to other actors that do not fully benefit the investor.
- *Behavioural biases*: Consumers buy durable goods that are too energy intensive as they care more about the upfront price than the total running costs over the long run.
- *Time inconsistency*: Companies and consumers might not believe that governments carry through with the announced stringent climate policies (e.g. rising carbon prices) – inefficiently delaying investments in emission-free production, infrastructure and appliances.

Source: Authors' elaboration.

---

in order to encourage emitters to reduce the amount of their emissions into the atmosphere. Absent a sensible carbon price, policymakers must recur to second-best policy interventions to correct the GHG externality, such as regulation. In addition, being general and technology-neutral, carbon pricing represents a superior policy tool also because it avoids the risk presented by more targeted policies to select wrongly.

As externalities have complex reinforcing interactions, the combination of classic market failure externalities and the GHG externality represents a significant challenge for green industrial policy. This implies that green industrial policy requires the deployment of specific instruments that go beyond the general industrial policy toolkit. These instruments do not need to be new, but they should at least be specifically tailored to fit in a green industrial policy. A green industrial policy mix should in any case be developed in coordination with the policy instruments used by climate policy and industrial policy, such as for instance, carbon pricing.

5.3 HOW DOES GREEN INDUSTRIAL POLICY WORK IN PRACTICE?

As previously illustrated, green industrial policy is a multi-faceted discipline, entailing a wide range of policy interventions. For the sake of simplicity, these can be grouped on three main areas of intervention, which can really be conceived as the three concentric circles of green industrial policy (Figure 5.2).

As usual in industrial development, everything starts with innovation. Developing green innovative products and solutions is the first, necessary, step to build the industries of the future. To speed up the process, green industrial policies need to overcome a number of market failures. For example, knowledge spillovers mean that, because firms can learn from other firms' R&D efforts, endeavours devoted to research are sub-optimal from a societal point of view. Moreover, while costs of innovation can be quite high in the beginning, the returns usually come later. When financial markets do not work perfectly, for example due to imperfect information regarding potential profitability, alternative sources of financing are needed to bridge the time gap. Governments can try to correct these market failures by providing public money for innovation and by creating a stronger incentive for innovation by firms through competition policy.

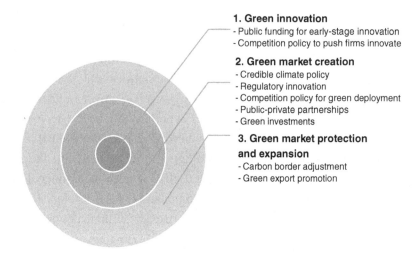

1. Green innovation
- Public funding for early-stage innovation
- Competition policy to push firms innovate

2. Green market creation
- Credible climate policy
- Regulatory innovation
- Competition policy for green deployment
- Public-private partnerships
- Green investments

3. Green market protection and expansion
- Carbon border adjustment
- Green export promotion

FIGURE 5.2   The three concentric circles of green industrial policy
Source: Authors' elaboration.

But innovation itself is not sufficient. Once developed, innovative green products and solutions need to find a receptive market to be deployed – and thus developed further. Here, a number of risks have to be carefully managed. Firstly, as market structures adjust to decarbonisation, market power could arise in a few sectors. Secondly, while strong efficiencies of scale and scope playing into the hands of single, big, networks can be useful in reducing the cost of the green transition, this needs to be reconciled with competition concerns. Thirdly, sometimes entire value chains have to make investments to adjust to new green technologies, which presents markets with coordination problems. Governments have a role in actively helping with market design or transformation through competition policy, innovative regulation, public–private partnerships and even direct state control in some circumstances.

Finally comes the international dimension of green industrial policy: green market expansion. On the one hand, this entails the prevention of carbon leakage risks with the adoption of carbon border adjustment measures. On the other hand, this also entails the promotion of the export of green innovative products and solutions, focusing especially on the developing world. Firms can face barriers to exporting caused by information failures, meaning that they have to incur high sunk costs to work out firstly whether exporting is profitable and secondly how to go about it. This can be beyond the means of especially smaller firms, so a global network of support is needed. Expanding business abroad, particularly to developing countries, can also be made difficult by institutional risk in destination countries, which can be mitigated through blended financial support. Another rational for export promotion is given by the fact that firms do not take into account the benefits their export decisions may have on society at large, causing them to make sub-optimal decisions. Supporting exports in this way does not only represent a way to foster the entry of green innovative industries into rapidly growing markets but it also is an important way of fostering global decarbonisation – in line with the climate finance, technology transfer and capacity building commitments undertaken by developed countries in the context of the Paris Agreement.

In the following sections we will dive into each of these three concentric circles, discussing the market failures justifying public intervention and providing an overview of the policy tools that might be utilised in the area.

5.4 GREEN INNOVATION

Most emissions reduction scenarios that predict continued economic growth rely to varying degrees on the use of technologies that are not yet available. This is frequently used by degrowth proponents as an argument to question the feasibility of green growth. The International Energy Agency (IEA, 2021a) net zero pathway, for instance, relies to a great extent on future innovation: 15 per cent of the emissions reductions by 2030 and 46 per cent of the reductions between 2030 and 2050 are to be achieved with technologies that are currently in a demonstration or prototype phase, such as carbon capture and storage, green hydrogen and advanced batteries.

Table 5.1 *Green innovation: main market failures and policy tools*

Market failures	Policy tools
Knowledge spillovers	Public funding for early stage risky
Dynamic scale efficiencies	innovation
Imperfect information	Improvement of European capital
	markets in fostering high-risk
	investments
	Competition policy to push firms to
	innovate

The breakthroughs achieved in the current decade will therefore be crucial. Unfortunately, none of the technologies needed beyond 2030 are currently on track to being deployed in time (IEA, 2021b), as the road from concept to commercialisation is typically long and winding. To accelerate the development of these innovative technologies, governments must overcome several market failures that keep private investments in R&D below optimal levels. This can be done by providing public funding instead or by using competition policy to spur innovation.

Here, it is important to underline that fostering green innovation entails the need of accepting failures (Table 5.1). Experimentation is central to green innovation in specific and to green industrial policy in general. Keeping in mind that governments do not start with the presumption that solutions are known, a green industrial policy built on experimentation ensures that the focus is not on 'picking winners' anymore but much more on 'letting losers go' on time (Hallegatte et al., 2013). Openness to failure should in fact be a characteristic of the design of industrial policy, which should incorporate uncertainty in its process. As Rodrik (2014) puts it, 'failure is part and parcel of a successful industrial policy effort'. This is particularly true for green innovation. In this sense, a successful green innovation action must be intended as a portfolio, and it is key to recognise and accept that some projects in the portfolio will fail. That is, a portfolio with no failures entails no risks.

5.4.1 Market Failure #1: Knowledge Spillovers

Perhaps the most often used argument for green industrial policy has to do with market failures arising from knowledge spillovers: markets do not provide sufficient incentives for private investment in research because of the non-appropriable, public good and intangible character of knowledge and its risky nature. New knowledge arising from R&D is non-rivalrous and only partially excludable: others may learn and use the knowledge, without necessarily paying for it. It is these spillovers that lead to social rates of return above private rates of return and private investment levels below socially desired levels. Hence, the quantity of knowledge created under laissez-faire is lower than what would be socially optimal.

In the case of green technologies, the sub-optimal level of innovation is further compounded by a misdirection of innovation effort away from green sectors. Underinvestment in green as opposed to brown innovation is not strictly speaking a market failure, because it is driven by the more limited market opportunities of green technologies. When the green sector of an economy is in its infancy, namely when it represents a small market and when the technologies are unproductive, green innovation will not offer interesting rewards and profit opportunities and therefore will not attract R&D spending. Acemoglu et al. (2019) report evidence that green innovation is at a disadvantage when fossil fuels are relatively cheap. Looking at the shale gas boom in the United States, they find that the fall in the price of natural gas caused firms to direct innovation away from green towards fossil fuel innovation.

Furthermore, Acemoglu et al. (2012, 2016) argue that path dependency makes the catch-up of green innovation very slow, even in the presence of carbon pricing. They argue that carbon pricing should be complemented by subsidies to the green sector in order to accelerate the rate of improvement in green technologies. This will ensure a much faster catch-up to brown technologies and a much shorter transition until green technologies become profitable in their own right.

It should also be mentioned that green technologies seem to be more complex than non-green technologies. Green technologies are a combination of a larger and more diverse set of other technologies, compared to non-green ones. Studies based on firm-level data (Ghisetti & Pontoni, 2015) and patent data (Barbieri et al., 2020) indeed find that green technologies are more complex than non-green ones. In addition, Barbieri et al. (2020) also find that these technologies tend to have larger spillovers and that these inventions affect a higher variety of other domains. The higher risks and uncertainty and the higher externalities from clean technologies make the case for a green industrial policy, calling for a more directed approach, directed at supporting investments in clean technologies. It also directs the selection of tools and projects for green industrial policy to those with the highest clean market failures, where private and public returns diverge the most.

5.4.2   Market Failure #2: Dynamic Scale Efficiencies

Beyond knowledge spillovers, the case for introducing policies that direct technical change towards the green sector is further strengthened by the presence of dynamic scale efficiencies. If production costs of new green technologies are initially higher compared to more established brown technologies, as may be the case in electricity generation, but decrease as firms learn by doing and achieve greater critical scale over time, there may be arguments to stimulate the initial deployment of the technologies.

Yet if future returns outweigh initial losses, and it is only a matter of bridging, capital markets could finance the necessary investment (Baldwin, 1969). For industrial policy to be justified, failings in the capital market are therefore also needed. Such capital market imperfections are likely to be present in the case of green technologies, as these are innovation areas subject to high uncertainty and important informational asymmetries.

5.4.3   Market Failure #3: Imperfect Information

Imperfect information tends to create inefficiencies in the allocation of credit. Innovators tend to have much better information about the chances of success of their projects than their financiers, such as banks. Banks that have difficulty determining in advance whether a project will generate enough profits to pay back loans will therefore ask for higher interest rates. This might price out of the market certain innovative projects that would have been profitable under the lower, 'perfect information', interest rate.

Lack of information around green technology also creates issues beyond financial markets. Parties along the supply chain may have different levels of access to information. Issues may also arise when there is incomplete information for everyone, such as for new projects in situations of high uncertainty. For new activities, the innovators themselves may simply not know if their project will be profitable. In the presence of informational externalities, a free-rider problem arises between different generations of innovators. Early innovators cannot recover their sunk costs when the outcome is unfavourable. But this information about profitability becomes public knowledge once the project is realised. If there is free entry ex post, no entrepreneur may be willing to make the initial investment and a socially beneficial market will not be established.

5.4.4 Policy Tool #1: Public Funding for Early Stage Risky Innovation

Developing green industrial policy requires leveraging public resources and policy toolkits to scale up national and regional public resources that go into climate innovation, but especially private investment in climate innovation. Furthermore, policymakers need to pay attention to the destination of innovation funds, either public or private, that are not explicitly 'green' and ensure that these are not going towards supporting investments that work against the climate goals.

It should be emphasised that fostering green innovation is not only about the availability of public finance resources. It is also about allocating public finance to the best areas and projects, meaning those with the largest socio-economic and climate returns that could not have been reached without public support. In this respect, particular emphasis should be placed on high-risk early stage technologies with potential for general-purpose breakthroughs. Green innovation requires a significant dose of risk-taking by public institutions and an acceptance that there will be failures. New support models that provide numerous and still sizeable grants and R&D subsidies in a relatively non-bureaucratic way are crucial to unleash frontier ideas. Green industrial policymaking should avoid deploying money only to safe bets with only average returns.

At the global level, a case that is frequently presented as a flagship initiative with regard to public funding for early stage risky innovation is the Defense Advanced Research Projects Agency (DARPA), an agency of the US Department of Defense responsible for the development of emerging technologies. Over the last decades, DARPA has significantly contributed towards many technologies embedded in our computers and smartphones, from microchips to the Global Positioning System, from voice recognition technologies to the Internet itself. The success of DARPA relates to the overall US economic ecosystem, which strongly favours innovation, and to its capability in translating disruptive innovations into marketable products – also through public procurement. That is, DARPA is an illustration of how public funding for innovation alone does not guarantee industrial development. DARPA's limited budget, around $3 billion per year, shows that creating the conditions for making innovative products marketable – also through public purchase of goods and services – is as important as public funding itself.

At the European level, there have been various initiatives aimed at replicating the DARPA success story. Back in 2005, the French government established a DARPA-like agency aimed at investing in disruptive technologies such as nanotechnology and biotech. Notwithstanding the initial endowment of €2 billion, the initiative proved not to be successful and quickly vanished. In 2018, the German government set up the Agentur zur Förderung von Sprunginnovationen, an agency aimed at promoting breakthrough innovations, again modelled on DARPA. More recently, the European

Union established the European Innovation Council to support disruptive innovators, also working on green technologies.

However, the main EU tool in this area is Horizon Europe, which can be seen as a key component of the European Union's green industrial policy toolbox not only for its focus on green technologies and projects but also due to its attempt to put into practice a new industrial policy vision of an institutionalised process of collaboration between institutions, the private sector and civil society. Horizon Europe is indeed built on missions, and each one has a mission board of fifteen high-level experts and an assembly that brings together a larger number of experts from academia, industry, civil society, finance and end-users to foster iterative collaboration.

5.4.5 Policy Tool #2: Competition Policy to Push Firms to Innovate

Beyond the role of the public sector in funding early stage risky innovation, companies have a crucial role to play in translating this research into new products.[4] Ensuring that companies have the right incentives to invest in R&D is a key parameter of the transition, and the degree of competitive pressure is an important determinant.

Innovation helps companies earn extraordinary profits by having better production processes, products and services than their competitors. It also supports their ability to maintain these profits through time by staying ahead of the competition. Competitive pressure allows for an efficient allocation of innovation effort because it encourages companies to target resources to the most commercially promising innovative ideas and, crucially, to cut resources when these activities cease to look promising. Finally, it also spurs innovation by punishing non-innovators with shrinking market shares and profits.

---

[4] Measuring private R&D devoted to green technology is difficult. According to IEA three quarters of clean energy R&D is done by business while one quarter is by governments: www.iea.org/reports/clean-energy-innovation/global-status-of-clean-energy-innovation-in-2020

However, the relationship between the degree of competition and innovation activity is not straightforward. The relationship between market power and innovation is a long-standing research topic with diverse theoretical and empirical results (e.g. Aghion et al., 2021; Arrow, 1962; Cohen, 2010; Gilbert, 2020; Gilbert & Newbery, 1982; Schumpeter, 1942). Overall, the literature indicates that market structure impacts innovation in a complex way.

While more competition increases the incentives to innovate, it reduces the means to do so. Neck-and-neck competition reduces the free cash flow of companies and their ability to fund innovation activities internally (Aghion et al., 2005). The ability of firms to attract external finances to fund innovation then becomes all the more important.

More generally, the market structure also affects which companies innovate. High fixed costs of entry tend to generate oligopolistic market structure as seen in many decarbonisation-related sectors (e.g. energy industry and energy-intensive manufacturing). This seems to affect the locus of innovation effort within complex supply chains. There tends to be more innovation in the non-oligopolistic segments, where more modular technologies ensure contestability. This can be seen, for example, in electricity production, where wind and solar photovoltaic compete against large complex power plants. In sectors that do not easily support multiple providers – such as electricity transmission and distribution, railroads and logistics services – we observe very little R&D by incumbents. In those parts of the supply chain where market incentives for innovation are weak, regulation or public ownership might have to step in to foster innovation.

This divergence in the innovation incentives between different actors also affects the type of innovation,[5] while larger incumbents

---

[5] Market power over a complementary asset may allow a firm to capture value from innovative effort. One might expect more innovation from incumbents in sectors where businesses can create market power through complementary assets. By the same token, however, an incumbent's dominance of a necessary complementary input may dissuade entry by others, potentially resulting in less innovation and dynamism in the sector. The sector-wide effect is ultimately unclear.

are suited to developing incremental innovations, small new firms are better at developing radical innovation (Christensen & Bower, 1996; D'Estea et al., 2011; Hamilton & Singh, 1992; Henderson, 1993). This is particularly relevant in the case of the transition to net zero, as it will involve the emergence of new business models and new technology solutions. Start-ups have an important role to play in contributing disruptive ideas that enable more efficient transition pathways. Policies should ensure that new market players with different backgrounds can bring new ideas and different capabilities to old sectors that are dominated by incumbents.

Finally, having more integrated markets across regions or countries not only increases the degree of competition that innovators are exposed to but it also guarantees higher benefits from investments in successful technologies. This is particularly important in sectors with high upfront costs in R&D and subsequently in infrastructure, such as energy provision and electricity generation. In fact, increasing the potential customer base of energy companies makes risk-taking more appealing because the returns of fruitful investments will be higher.

As innovation is so crucial for an efficient transition, policymakers, especially competition authorities, should put a high value on protecting and encouraging competition in green sectors in the many cases where it is good for innovation.

5.5 GREEN MARKET CREATION

Once a new green technology has been developed, it is necessary to bring it to the market. But scaling up new technologies is not straightforward. Prototypes need to be tested and demonstrated in real-world situations to become the first commercial-scale generation of the technology. If successful, this might mark the early adoption of the technology in niche markets. Thanks to further innovation, technological enhancements and efficiency gains, new generations of the technology can then be developed at lower costs and through economies of scale become mature and scalable. The market alone might not deliver on this, because of market failures such as abuse of market power, network effects and coordination failures. Policy intervention is required to tackle these issues.

The politically but also technically most challenging intervention in this regard possibly is designing efficient markets. Well-designed markets with robust regulatory oversight will often be the only realistic option for benefiting from the efficiencies of markets, without falling for the inefficiencies arising from market power especially in sectors dominated by network economies. This is not made easier by the fact that there is a constant risk of capture by the incumbents.

Many of the sectors relevant for the green transition have characteristics (network effects, scale and scope economies, platform effects, high capital specificity, etc.) that imply that either unregulated markets underinvest in socially desirable capital (e.g. back-up capacities) or that market concentration makes resource allocation inefficient. Coordination problems are likely to further exacerbate inefficiencies. To produce efficient results, market rules need to be put in place that provide market actors with incentives that are aligned with maximising citizens' welfare. Moreover, governments can pursue different degrees of engagement with the private sector, all the way to direct state control.

Finally, a huge expansion in green investment is needed. For instance, the IEA's (2021a) net zero pathway estimates that global energy capital investments must increase from a current yearly average of about $2 trillion to $5 trillion (2019 prices) by 2030, after which they must stay at almost the same level until 2050. As a fraction of global GDP, this would be an increase from 2.5 per cent today to 4.5 per cent in 2030, followed by a gradual decline back to 2.5 per cent. The private sector will need to cover most of the investments. By creating efficient markets for green capital goods with different forms of public funding, governments can pave the way for the private sector to take over the investment burden (Table 5.2).

Table 5.2 *Green market creation: main market failures and policy tools*

Market failure	Policy tools
Market power created by decarbonisation	Credible climate policy
	Regulatory innovation
Network effects	Competition policy for green tech deployment
Coordination failure	
	Public–private partnerships
	Direct state control
	Green investments

5.5.1 Market Failure #1: Market Power Created by Decarbonisation

The policies and transitions needed to achieve decarbonisation are likely to change the functioning of markets and lead to the emergence of market power in some areas. The need for energy and material efficiency might require a level of coordination that current market structures would be unable to provide. Hence, one scenario is the emergence of more market structures with a very limited number of potential competitors.

For instance, decarbonisation will require a reduction in economic activities related to fossil fuel. Shrinking markets might result in the exit of market players. It is conceivable that this process results in increasing market concentration in the whole market (e.g. when the number of players decreases faster than the volume) or the disintegration of relevant markets leading to highly concentrated market segments.

5.5.2 Market Failure #2: Network Effects

Leveraging economies of scale and scope, greatly aided by the use digital technologies, can help achieve the efficiency gains needed for the transition. The result is that in a number of areas a potential role is emerging for centralised platforms or networks to coordinate economic behaviour with the ability to extract significant rent.

An example illustrates this. One vision for the electricity system of the future foresees that passive users turn into prosumers that reduce the cost of the electricity system by supplying, consuming, producing or storing electricity based on real-time system information. Several overlapping networks (standardised appliances, power-lines, data network, information aggregation and payments/billing) would be required to efficiently run a system with a massive number of distributed energy resources. For several years, big players in some of these networks have been trying to position themselves in this market in the hope of benefiting from the value that can be created by managing these systems.

Hence, the better these complex multi-actor systems can be optimised, the less expensive infrastructure, energy and resources will be required for the transition. Single companies that can coordinate many actors, most notably through digital platforms, exhibit strong scale economies (i.e. the bigger they are, the more efficiently they can operate). As a result, the same efficiency gains that will help with the transition might potentially result in sectors characterised by reduced competition. Some of the current platform economy incumbents are potentially well positioned to extend their market power to these potentially very big new services.

Having said that, the promise of high excessive rents in a long-term future might create a welcome competitive race in the short term. This would be competition for ownership of the infrastructure ('for the market' competition) rather than competition between individual projects ('in the market' competition). However, as seen in the case of smart grids such a competition for a new market can also lead to an unproductive paralysis – when different actors each possessing essential infrastructure try to secure a central position in the new value chains – making it difficult to quickly find good compromises on standards.

Consequently, economic policy will have to strike a balance between, on the one hand, ensuring that the most productive systems are speedily selected and economic actors have incentives to invest in the necessary complementary infrastructure and, on the other hand, making sure that the regulatory framework allows the new systems to be efficiently used and developed.

5.5.3 Market Failure #3: Coordination Failure

The coordination failure argument for industrial policy is based on the idea that many projects require simultaneous investment in different parts of the value chain. Unless all agents along the value chain (e.g. both downstream and upstream firms) make these investments, individual investment projects might not be profitable. This happens particularly for complex early stage projects with large externalities and significant information asymmetries.

A critical question over the coordination failure argument for industrial policy is whether the government is able to solve this problem better than the market. Vertical integration or long-term contracts between intermediate and final goods producers can help resolve coordination problems, although there are clearly limits to the extent to which firms can adjust to solve coordination problems, exemplified by the classic hold-up problem.

5.5.4 Policy Tool #1: Credible Climate Policy to Provide a Clear Direction to Companies and Investors

Climate targets are an important tool of green industrial policy, as they give a clear direction to companies and investors in terms of the decarbonisation trajectory. Setting strong climate targets for tomorrow, if backed up by legislation to effectively turn them into practice, can have a major influence over the behaviour of the private sector already today. It should be noted that the difference in time horizons between policy planning and political cycles makes achieving coherent and sustained green industrial policy efforts extremely challenging. In this sense, clear climate targets – particularly if enshrined into law – also protect green industrial policy from significant uncertainty.

For example, the European Union's pledge to reach climate neutrality by 2050 and its target of reducing emissions by at least

55 per cent by 2030 compared to 1990 send a clear signal to market players about the irreversibility of its climate trajectory. But to be credible these targets need to be supported by detailed legislation. Changes are needed, for example, in the design of the Emissions Trading System (ETS), the Effort Sharing Regulation (ESR) for non-ETS emissions and the energy taxation directive. Major challenges include how to cut the number of ETS allowances given out for free (a concern for industry), how to put a price on emissions coming from the transport sector (e.g. inclusion in the ETS vs national taxation), how to use ETS revenues (allocated to the central EU budget or to national budgets, support for green investments or alleviation of the distributional effects of climate policy) and how to design a functional carbon border adjustment mechanism.

Always to remain in the European case, EU legislation on renewable energy and energy efficiency will also need a substantial upgrade. EU 2030 targets for renewable energy and energy efficiency at the time of writing (respectively, a 32 per cent share of final energy consumption and a 32.5 per cent improvement against a baseline) will only deliver GHG emissions reductions of 45 per cent by 2030. The European Union must find ways for its countries to deliver on higher targets in the absence of nationally binding commitments and for private investment to be really mobilised (one example is the simplification of permitting procedures for renewables). Other important areas of EU legislation, including transport and agriculture, will have to be revised to push the decarbonisation of these sectors.

5.5.5   Policy Tool #2: Fostering Regulatory Innovation

Innovation is needed not only for technological solutions but also in terms of policies and regulations to bring about the transition. Hence, competition between different regulatory systems also has the potential to let new solutions emerge.

Different regulatory and policy approaches between countries have improved the common understanding and selection of the most effective policies for the roll out of low-carbon technologies. For example, comparing different regulations in Germany and in Sweden, Midttun and Gautesen (2007) infer the appropriateness of the two policies according to the maturity phase of renewable technologies. Feed-in tariffs or specialised auctions, preferred in Germany, seem to be particularly good for technologies in early deployment, following the R&D phase. In contrast, certificates, preferred in Sweden, appear to be better in later stages of development. In fact, Midttun and Gautesen (2007; 1420) note that

> tariffs have the advantage of allowing differentiation and specific pricing of individual technologies, thereby permitting simultaneous development of a broad spectrum of technologies. In later phases, where some technologies develop performance characteristics closer to established incumbent technology, niche markets, such as the certificate markets will probably provide a more adequate stimulus to further commercialisation before full competitiveness in the mainstream market is achieved.

Such normative competition between systems has probably sped up convergence towards more efficient and politically workable tools while fostering the adoption of the fittest renewable energy sources. For instance, countries at the forefront of solar energy production, including Denmark, Germany, the Netherlands and Spain, have shown how solar photovoltaic can win technology-neutral tenders against any other renewable technology. Regulatory convergence is now emerging around the auctioning of feed-in premiums as the most common policy framework for incentivising the adoption of renewable energy sources. This is the standard price-setting mechanism in the Czech Republic, Denmark, Germany, Italy, the Netherlands, Estonia, Finland, Slovenia, Slovakia and Spain.

5.5.6 Policy Tool #3: Competition Policy to Facilitate an Efficient Green Tech Deployment

Relatively light-handed interventions to protect virtuous competition, such as adjusting the competition authority toolkits, can contribute to the decarbonisation objective. For example, reshaping market definitions (e.g. when investigating decline in brown sectors), clear rules on how to evaluate green efficiencies (e.g. to prevent greenwashing) or state-of-the-art market monitoring (e.g. in certificate markets) can go a long way to prevent abuses of market power that threaten efficient resource allocation.

Competition rules are primarily devised to address the strategic behaviour of companies with market power that result in inefficient allocation of resources. The main powers given to competition authorities in advanced economies are to prohibit anti-competitive agreements between companies (e.g. cartels), to punish or prevent abusive practices by powerful firms and to block mergers that threaten to significantly reduce competition.

But competition policy tools interact with other externalities. In the course of their work, competition authorities may find that some ostensibly anti-competitive practices have environmental benefits. An industry-wide agreement to phase out energy-intensive washing machines may restrict competition, for example, but promise to reduce carbon emissions. Conversely, competition authorities may find some industrial actions acceptable on pure competition grounds but alarming for environmental reasons. They could, for instance, be called to rule on an acquisition by a dirty incumbent that wants to delay greening its production process by eliminating a competitor – one that exerts little competitive pressure but commands green potential.

Consumers often care about purchasing sustainably, and they are willing to pay for it (Volpin, 2020). Consuming more sustainable products thus increases consumers' welfare. Nine in ten Europeans (94 per cent) say that protecting the environment is important to them personally and a third believe that changing consumptions patterns is the most effective way of tackling environmental problems (Eurobarometer, 2017). This is a strong motivation for companies to distinguish themselves from competitors by offering more sustainable products.

Competition for sustainability is hence a driver for innovation and a speedier transition – and policy should encourage it. Under current competition policy practices, environmental protection is not treated as a standalone non-economic goal to be defended in the same way that market integration is. Nor has environmental protection justified derogation from competition rules.

In Europe, where the competition authority has considered environmental concerns, it has done so as an element of consumer welfare, more specifically as a 'quality' of products. That is, competition policy is not blind to consumers wanting not only cheap but also sustainable products, as sustainability is clearly a dimension of the 'quality' of products and services that consumers care about. 'Quality' is a key dimension of competition under EU law. When firms compete on quality, any agreement or behaviour that artificially weakens it may be subject to a prohibition. In the context of mergers, for example, the European Commission states that 'competitive harm caused by a reduction of quality [is] on an equal footing with an increase of prices, or a reduction of output, choice of goods and services' (European Commission, 2013).

Degradations of sustainability as a result of mergers, acquisitions and the abuse of market dominance can already be considered by competition authorities, by referring to the negative impact on 'green quality'. But it becomes very difficult for competition authorities if such degradations need to be balanced against potential benefits for consumers (e.g. lower cost) from the same case. Marginal sustainability gains should not automatically allow companies to engage in anti-competitive behaviour to the detriment of all economy resource allocation. Hence, the assessment will remain an exercise in the weighting of the arguments – with more visibility of the sustainability effects.

5.5.7 *Policy Tool #4: Developing Public–Private Partnerships*

To develop a successful green industrial policy, policymaking has to be embedded in the private sector. Public–private partnerships are not only about activating co-funding but also ways to access skills, knowledge and information. This requires a high degree of interaction between the public and private sectors, and collaboration should be iterative since the solutions are not assumed as known but only as discoverable. The literature and case studies show that the design of public–private partnerships can take different forms. Deliberation councils, investment advisory councils, round tables, public–private venture funds and public development banks are all examples of ways in which governments can make operational the principles described earlier.

One example of a fruitful public–private partnership is the format of European Alliances, which has been employed since 2017 for batteries and since 2020 for clean hydrogen. The principles for a new green industrial policy should serve as guidelines when selecting and governing new alliances. Alliances should focus on addressing mega-problems covering the whole value chains of all relevant clean markets, rather than solving more discrete problems. In general, green industrial policy should also employ a balanced mix of alliances involving already-connected value chains that need to be scaled up and very early stage emerging value chains with still-to-be-connected stakeholders, even if the latter are higher risk choices that will result in higher failure rates.

Given the complexities of both green industrial policy and the policymaking machinery in advanced economies, strong governance is a prerequisite for effective green industrial policy. It is crucial for efficient coordination of different types of stakeholders and for the management of different policy governance areas, different instruments and different projects. First, the various partners must be incentivised with a set of balanced, clear, credible and time-consistent commitments. Second, clear and realistic intermediate goals must be set throughout the process to promote more risk-taking. Third, flexible policy design is required to cope with the uncertainties of new green technologies, with clear intermediate targets and milestones that can be monitored in order to strengthen policy measures over time. Fourth, accountability must be ensured, with incentives and penalties where needed.

Implementing all this requires strong governance, which should be based on three principles: competence, ownership and political independence. This could be provided through a governance body that is politically independent but still fully accountable. Ensuring the coordination and cooperation of multiple government players, each responsible for various aspects of policy needed for green industrial policy, and ensuring that they will work together require a central figurehead. This person should be selected externally, based on their skills, and given political independence and broad powers to coordinate and run dedicated green industrial policy. The various administrations in charge of the wide array of policy tools needed to activate green industrial policy should also be closely connected. These include the energy, transport, cohesion and reform, budget, trade, innovation and competition policy portfolios.

5.5.8 Policy Tool #5: Direct State Control

The economics in some sectors make it very difficult to engineer virtuous competition between companies, even with sophisticated market rules. Moreover, it is difficult to design markets such that they produce the most politically desired resource allocation and distributional results. Direct state control of essential pieces of infrastructure might end up being optimal, but the costs and benefits need to be evaluated on a case-by-case basis.

The level of state ownership in the economies has varied across countries and over time, reflecting different understandings of the relative importance of market imperfections, trust in indirect tools to address them and imperfections of direct public management. Striking examples of these differences are the energy sectors of France and Germany, where state ownership has remained constant in the former while it went through a phase of liberalisation in the 1990s and some re-communalisation in the 2010s in the latter.

Furthermore, as indicated by the discussion on new industrial policy, state control in specific sectors comes in degrees. It can range from (i) very light touch provision of company coordinating services that actually even shield companies against certain policies (ii) via medium level interventions such as strongly regulating the activities of private companies through specific agencies, public–private partnerships and minority shareholdings to (iii) very heavy handed direct control through majority shareholding in essential companies (e.g. platforms or network providers) or even complete value chains (electricity and rail sector in several EU countries).

One way of intervening here is to allow governments to take some temporary coordination role, as, for example, tried by the EU with 'EU industrial alliances', being careful that these initiatives do not end up protecting incumbents. Another example is regulation. Since a regulatory agency can never be completely independent of political influences, its intervention can shift *from* providing a solution to market failures *to* creating a barrier to entry protecting the market position of regulated firms. As in standard network utilities, regulation can become a form of barrier against technological change that may create inefficient path dependence and reduce dynamic competition.

5.5.9   Policy Tool #6: Stimulating Green Investments

Investment for the deployment of existing technologies will be important to realise the green transition. This includes mobilising funds from national budgets and from the private sector, for example with feed-in tariffs, which attract initial private investment in clean energy production by temporarily offering guaranteed above-market prices for the output, or with tax credits and purchasing subsidies for green capital goods. National budgets can also directly contribute to kick-starting green markets through the use of green public procurement (e.g. governments can electrify their car fleet, allowing producers of charging infrastructure to scale up and lower prices).

Clear public spending targets, such as the European Union's decision to devote 30 per cent of its budget for 2021–27 to climate action, are necessary steps. But these goals need to be well defined. In particular, it is important to ensure that the shares of public budgets that are not targeted towards green activities do not actively counteract green spending by going into activities that increase emissions. In addition, current international accounting rules need to clearly define which activities can truly be considered green investment. The risk of greenwashing is high, especially given that emissions reducing activities are very diverse, ranging from agricultural subsidies to research and innovation funding. For all these reasons, a solid methodology for monitoring and regularly reporting climate spending should be developed (Claeys & Tagliapietra, 2020).

Mazzucato and Penna (2016) propose a revived role for public development banks (PDBs) as channels for entrepreneurial states to direct finance towards ambitious societal goals, such as the green transition. Fernandez-Arias et al. (2020) study smart PDBs in more detail as facilitators of new activities within a new industrial policy perspective. Well-designed PDBs can help governments discover where problems and failures lie. They should engage in the search for nascent economic activities that face obstacles from market or government failures. This requires intelligence gathering and dissemination of lessons learned rather than simply providing credit. PDBs should transmit information on market and government failures to the relevant agencies. Fernandez-Arias et al. (2020), in a survey of PDBs, concluded that current practice is very far from what they propose. Nevertheless, they believe that PDBs can be reoriented to exploit the complementarities between their lending and intelligence gathering. In the European context, the European Investment Bank can take on this role, as the European Union's 'smart climate development bank'.

Finally, Important Projects of Common European Interest, a vehicle for channelling public funding into priority industries, is an example of European industrial policy.

5.6   GREEN MARKET PROTECTION AND EXPANSION

After having established a receptive domestic market for green technologies to grow, it is then important to ensure a level playing field vis-à-vis third countries with weaker climate policies and to expand this green market beyond national borders. This external dimension of green industrial policy might be conceived along two main directions.

On the one hand, there is a need to make sure that climate policies do not compromise a country's industrial competitiveness vis-à-vis third countries with less ambitious climate targets. In this regard, a potential solution that has been advanced in recent years is to impose an import tariff on carbon-intensive goods, which is discussed in this section.

On the other hand, even when domestically competitive green markets are already in place, firms that wish to export to other markets have to overcome several hurdles, which include a lack of knowledge about how to navigate foreign regulations and finding foreign partners. These firms also need to get public support in the form of blended finance instruments (e.g. guarantees, concessional loans, grants) to cover part of the country risk (i.e. the uncertainty inherent to investing within a given country, due to macroeconomic, regulatory or political issues). Furthermore, it is also important to consider that there might be a misalignment of incentives to make socially optimal export choices (Table 5.3).

5.6.1   Market Failure #1: Carbon Leakage

When it comes to the international dimension of green industrial policy, the first market failure to be discussed is that of carbon leakage.

Table 5.3 *Green trade: main market failures and policy tools*

Market failure	Policy tools
Carbon leakage	Carbon border adjustment
Information failure	measures
Positive externalities	Green export promotion

This concept refers to a situation where a producer shifts the production of carbon-intensive goods to another country with lower carbon taxes to save costs and then imports back the products from there – in short, a situation where a strong domestic climate policy ends up damaging the country's own industrial competitiveness. The risk of carbon leakage arises because climate action is still led by individual national and subnational jurisdictions that advance at very different speeds, despite the well-recognised benefits that could emerge from a globally harmonised approach. As a result of this, industries located in climate-ambitious countries might be put in a disadvantaged position vis-à-vis their peers located in countries with a weak climate policy. Critics say that the risk of carbon leakage is more theoretical than practical, as we do not have significant evidence for it so far. This might well be true, but for a good reason. Only around 20 per cent of global GHG emissions are currently covered by carbon pricing instruments, and the average price is $3 per ton (IMF, 2021) – that is, far below the $40–$80/ton of CO_2 equivalent range needed in 2020 to meet the Paris Agreement goals (World Bank, 2021). Given this low carbon price, the risk of carbon leakage has thus remained limited so far. However, as climate policies become more stringent, the risk of carbon leakage will likely rise. This will pave the way for the introduction of carbon border adjustment measures, aimed at preventing the risk of carbon leakage or – to use an expression dear to policymakers – at ensuring a level playing field.

5.6.2   Market Failure #2: Information Failure

Before firms that produce green technologies or goods can export to other countries, they must assess whether doing so is profitable and feasible. This requires incurring large fixed costs to collect information about the costs and benefits of entering a foreign market, about specific market characteristics and about how the process of exporting itself works. These costs cannot be recovered in case the firm decides against exporting. This represents a barrier for some enterprises, particularly smaller ones that do not have economies of scale, to engage in potentially profitable export opportunities. Moreover, the benefits of exporting are often underestimated.

5.6.3   Market Failure #3: Positive Externalities

While information collected for exporting purposes can be kept private and is thus excludable, there can still be positive spillover effects on other firms. For example, other firms can observe the success or failure of 'pioneer' exporters and draw conclusions from that. Moreover, successful export practices can pave the way for other firms to enter the market too, for example by lowering costs of setting up supply chains (e.g. when a regular shipping service is set up for the pioneer firm). Enterprises therefore do not factor in all social benefits when deciding whether to try exporting or not and might even wait for others to do it first.

Other export promotion services are simply not excludable, in the sense that all firms seeking to export benefit from it automatically, such as when the country of origin itself is promoted as an exporting country, for example with quality labels. Because of the public good nature of such services, these would be best provided by governments.

5.6.4   Policy Tool #1: Carbon Border Adjustment Measures

Carbon border adjustment measures are aimed at preventing the risk of carbon leakage. This policy tool entails placing a tariff on imported goods on the basis of their carbon content – that is, the GHG emitted during their manufacture. The amount of this tariff should mirror the level of the domestic carbon price. Consequently, goods with low or zero carbon content will pay low or zero carbon border adjustment accordingly. On the other hand, a fair carbon border adjustment measure would be discounted according to the carbon price paid in the country of origin, if there is one. High-carbon goods can thus pay a low or zero carbon border adjustment, provided that their production is located in a country where the carbon price is similar or even higher.

Carbon border adjustment will be necessary in any country that intends to seriously scale up its climate action. That is, carbon border adjustment is not about protectionism but about ensuring a level playing field in a situation in which some countries are doing more than others to implement their decarbonisation pledges. In fact, such measures are compatible with the provisions of the World Trade Organization (WTO). The General Agreement on Tariffs and Trade indeed allows a charge 'equivalent' to an internal tax on 'like domestic products' to be imposed on imported products (Article II:2 (a) and Article III:2). Furthermore, pursuant to Article XX, measures that are 'necessary to protect human, animal or plant life or health' may always be imposed if they are not applied in an arbitrary or discriminatory manner. To be WTO-compliant, carbon border adjustment measures need to be commensurate only with domestic climate efforts and must be designed in a clear and transparent manner to minimise the risk of protectionist abuse (Mehling et al., 2018).

5.6.5 Policy Tool #2: Green Export Promotion

Green export promotion concerns services to facilitate exports by domestic firms. This can entail providing information and advice to bridge cultural gaps, to understand administrative processes in foreign markets and to reduce trade costs, as well as matching buyers and sellers. It can also entail providing blended finance support to stimulate exports and green investments in developing countries.

In principle, such services could be provided cheaply to multiple firms by a private consultancy or by an industry organisation, thus overcoming the problem of information failure affecting individual firms. But governments are often seen as more reliable intermediaries and as having more privileged access to information and relations with governments of destination markets than private entities. Moreover, very few private organisations have the means to provide export support across the whole world like governments do through their embassies and consulates.

Blended finance support plays a very important role in fostering the export of green technologies and the undertake of green investments in developing countries characterised by high country risk. The rationale for blended finance is motivated by a series of market failures and market imperfections in receival countries – such as regulatory instability, lack of workable financing institutions and currency volatility. The provision of guarantees, concessional loans or grants might help overcome these issues – generally referred to as country risk – and allow firms to export their green technologies in rapidly growing markets. This is also how international development policies can assist in the creation of global green tech markets while at the same time meeting international climate commitments and sustainable development goals.

Promoting green exports can also be achieved through means such as environmental standards and green provisions in trade agreements. Big economies such as the European Union could, for example, use their status as an international standard setter to create the foundation for international green tech markets in which their own green technologies can easily be traded. They can also require compliance with strict environmental regulations as a condition to access their markets, which represents a strong incentive for trading partners to green their production processes. This in turn can stimulate foreign demand for domestically produced green tech (Leonard et al., 2021).

5.7 GREEN INDUSTRIAL POLICY NEEDS GOOD GOVERNANCE

As we have now amply illustrated, green industrial policy is a highly complex area, which encompasses a wide range of policy interventions spanning from innovation policy to competition policy, from fiscal policy to trade policy. This complexity, coupled with the overall sensitive issue of public intervention into the economy, does entail risks. Governments are indeed not omniscient, efficient and benevolent actors. Bureaucracies and policymakers have their own sources of 'failures' that sometime prevent them from achieving efficient results.

As the experience of industrial policy shows, especially in the traditional vertical style that prevailed during the 1960s and 1970s, public intervention raises three related challenges. The first is the capacity of bureaucrats and administrators to access information to allocate public resources correctly (by picking winners and subsidising them). The second is the inherent bias of public administrations to favour the status quo. The third challenge stems from the incentives for rent-seeking and 'capture' inherent in any policy that redistributes rents.

The market failure justification of industrial policy emphasises lack of information as a key obstacle for the functioning of the economy. This implies that to implement a first-best correction policymakers would have to master an extraordinary range and depth of knowledge and information, which the market participants themselves do not possess, at least individually. Policymakers would have to be knowledgeable about firms and industries that generate knowledge spillovers, the relative amount of learning by individual firms from others and from their own experience, the precise path of such learning over time, the magnitude of the cost disadvantage at each stage of the learning process and the extent to which early entrants generate benefits for future entrants. The breadth of knowledge and skills needed to implement an optimal policy would exceed that possessed by almost any institution.

More generally, government decisions, about resource allocation (e.g. R&D budgets) or regulations (e.g. on market rules), do not follow the logic of price-based resource allocation. Politicians compete for voters and campaign funding, bureaucracies for power, and decision-makers for careers. These incentives are often more aligned with the interests of incumbents than with those of the general public that might benefit from a fairer treatment of new entrants. Accordingly, administrations are, for example, worse at stopping projects that turn out inefficient, which is a prominent problem in a transition with a lot of uncertainty. They also set standards and regulations that tacitly form barriers against technological change.

For example, rules to protect specific rights in a status quo market might become so complex that only large players can safely navigate them. As government decisions shape the structures of competition in markets that will be crucial for an efficient resource allocation in the transition, preventing an undue bias towards the interest of incumbents goes far beyond the role of competition authorities and courts.

Finally, distortions could arise from lobbying efforts through which vested interests try to capture rents arising from public finances. Where accountability and transparency are lacking, pervasive lobbying efforts and corruption have resulted in inefficient and socially sub-optimal allocation of rents (Altenburg et al., 2015).

The presence of implementation challenges that place first-best policies out of reach does not entirely rule out policy intervention. The effectiveness of industrial policy ultimately has to be evaluated on the basis of its realised outcomes compared to no intervention. However, even on this criterion, the justification for industrial policy is equivocal. The history of industrial policy in Europe provides many examples of failures, such as the loss to the United States of the race to develop computers in 1960s and 1970s, the loss to Japan of the race to develop semiconductors in the 1980s and 1990s and the failure of Concorde, the British–French project, to develop the first supersonic passenger aircraft. Such examples of failed programmes have strengthened the case for a laissez-faire approach to industrial policy.

At a more systematic level, large-scale evaluation studies most often have looked at the impact of trade protection, R&D subsidies and tax credits, and general subsidies. Also in these studies one can find cases – such as subsidies for specific industries or public procurement programmes – which have distorted the market, resulted in the picking of the wrong firms and burdened the taxpayer with disappointing returns.[6] The big problem with evaluation studies is determining what would have been the outcome if no intervention

[6] For a review, see Noland and Pack (2003), Rodrik (2014) and Aiginger and Rodrik (2020).

had taken place. More recent studies, which try to deal better with causal identification and to correct for the non-random selection of projects, show that industrial policy can be effective in stimulating activities, but much depends, unsurprisingly, on the policies used and the institutional context.

A long-standing tension exists between the ability of markets to allocate resources efficiently and that of governments to intervene to improve rather than worsen market mechanisms. The main conclusion is that policymakers need to get away from simplistic state-or-market narratives. The focus should be on developing politically feasible frameworks for leveraging the benefits of competition that go beyond a focus on static efficiency to encourage useful investments in new systems and innovation. The role of institutions that determine resource allocation in the transition is an underappreciated but crucial area of policy action. A new wave of academic debate has sought to improve the design of industrial policy and proposed a new framework.

This new industrial policy perspective, which started with the work of Rodrik (2014), is an attempt to move beyond the ideological division between state-driven intervention and purely market-based solutions. It argues for a smart combination of both. Going back to the fundamental role of markets as institutions to mobilise resources, new industrial policy is best understood as a process. In the words of Rodrik (2014), new industrial policy should strive to be a 'process of institutionalised collaboration and dialogue rather than a top-down approach' in which the government picks sectors or firms and transfers money to them. The private sector has to be one of the three fundamental stakeholders in this collaboration, in which the other two elements are the government and civil society.

That is, green industrial policy should be designed in a way that makes it easier for the state to build policies based on the knowledge that resides in the private sector, while being legitimate from the point of view of civil society. The state's role should be to identify constraints and opportunities, in order to develop solutions that bring together private and public capacities and information, with aligned public and private motives, in a very pragmatic way. A modern framework should address the issues of rent-seeking and political capture, and all the inefficiencies and risks that lie at the intersection between the public and the private sectors, by effectively combining incentives and regulatory constraints and building in accountability and transparency.

Rodrik (2014) posits three pillars for this theoretical framework: (i) embeddedness; (ii) discipline and (iii) accountability.[7]

The concept of embeddedness (or embedded autonomy) dates back to the work of Evans (1995). It starts from the notion that individual stakeholders have different characteristics and that governments do not know in advance where market failures will occur. Therefore, government agencies have to be embedded in the private sector and have access to their information in order to leverage it to design policies. Embeddedness thus requires a high degree of collaboration between the public and private actors, which should work closely to discover solutions. In the Rodrik interpretation, new industrial policies by definition assume that trust and competences can be developed over time. Embeddedness relies on a continuous, fair and open dialogue between the different stakeholders, something that could be defined as policy learning.

To avoid the risk of moving too slow or staying inactive in the face of high uncertainties and high risks of failure, experimentation is crucial. Policies designed as learning experiments can help to reduce risks, provided that they are closely monitored and adjusted when new information arises. Monitoring will be required to deal with failures and mistakes. The instruments and tools used by industrial policy might initially not be the correct ones or might not work as planned. Testing and learning can offset these problems if built into the design of the policy.

---

[7] This framework is also used in Altenburg and Rodrik (2017), Ambroziak (2017), Altenburg and Assmann (2017), Andreoni and Chang (2019) and Fernández-Arias et al. (2020).

While embeddedness and collaboration represent a way to solve the information problem, they also entail the risk of capture and of provision of distorted information. While embedded, government agencies should not be 'in bed' with the private sector. The implementation of embeddedness must take into account informational asymmetries between different partners and how asymmetries change over time. To deal with the risk of political capture, industrial policy should include monitoring and transparency mechanisms, as well as mechanisms to align private and public incentives. To activate private agents and prevent 'cheating', proper incentives and accountability need to be in place.

Transparency on incentives and accountability mechanisms should be facilitated by roadmaps and clear government communication (Kemp & Never, 2017). A process of open policy dialogue should ensure a high degree of accountability. Accountability will be critical to the success or failure of industrial policy exercises. Civil society will play an important role in new industrial policy (Bowles & Carlin, 2020). In the bottom-up policymaking that the embedded model involves, civil society, including non-government organisations, trade unions, activist groups and citizen lobbying initiatives, must be as engaged as the private and public sectors in policy design.

So far, this discussion on the design of new industrial policy has focused on promoting and improving existing economic activities. Designing industrial policy for activities that do not yet exist is a very different challenge, and one that is particularly relevant in the domain of green innovation.

Mariana Mazzucato (2011) introduced the notion of the 'entrepreneurial state', whereby the role of the state should not be conceived merely as stepping into the economy to solve market failures but also to act as market creator when markets for the most innovative solutions do not yet exist. She furthermore proposes a broader 'mission-oriented' approach to industrial policy (Mazzucato, 2018). Society should set itself a restricted number of ambitious missions, taking into account the diverse range of stakeholders. The prominent mission used to illustrate this argument is the Apollo programme of the United States, which set the goal of landing humans on the Moon.

Policies should then be designed to direct economic and technical changes towards reaching these missions. Broad acceptance of the missions would be rooted in citizen engagement, via multi-stakeholder consultations. This system also implies setting concrete but ambitious milestones during the process. The United Nations' Sustainable Development Goals would be examples of missions, according to Mazzucato (2018). Meeting these goals requires a new toolkit that goes beyond fixing failures in existing markets. Strategic public investment in many different sectors should open up new industrial opportunities, to be developed further by the private sector.

This new stream of work on a new industrial policy provides fresh ideas on how to put in place a workable green industrial policy to help markets reconcile economic prosperity and climate objectives. The good news is that, notably in the European Union, these concepts are now well understood. It is now a matter of good policymaking and good governance to implement them. Should the world be able to embark into such a process, achieving the green growth – techno-optimistic – view about global absolute decoupling of economic growth and GHG emissions will be at hand.

5.8   KEY TAKEAWAYS

5.8.1   The Great Decoupling Challenge and the Bet on Technology

- Economists are divided about whether decoupling economic activity and emissions is feasible.
- Degrowth scholars argue that perpetual economic growth is impossible on a finite planet.
- They propose systemic economic changes to manage the transition to a much smaller economy.
- Green growth proponents say technology can reconcile prosperity and climate objectives.

- Implementing degrowth seems unfeasible; yet green growth also poses important challenges.
- Most importantly, green growth requires an environment conducive to experimentation.
- A workable green industrial policy is key, but the potential for mistakes is significant.

5.8.2 How to Define Green Industrial Policy?

- Industrial policy targets a set of economic activities to achieve long-term benefits to society.
- Green industrial policy must do this within the binding constraint of climate change mitigation.
- It is an intervention aimed at correcting market failures, including the GHG externality.
- Classic market failures are knowledge spillovers, dynamic scale efficiencies, network effects and so on.
- Green industrial policies should be coordinated with climate and industrial policy instruments.

5.8.3 How Does Green Industrial Policy Work in Practice?

- Green industrial policy entails a wide range of interventions, pertaining to three main areas.
- Green innovation must be accelerated as a first step by providing stronger incentives and funding.
- Green market creation is needed to deploy and further develop new technologies.
- Green market expansion refers to the international dimension of green industrial policy.

5.8.4 Green Innovation

- Breakthroughs achieved in the current decade will be crucial for timely decarbonisation.
- Fostering green innovation must be based on a portfolio approach and entails accepting failures.
- Knowledge spillovers from innovation are the most common argument for green industrial policy.

- Where capital markets fail to bridge financing gaps, dynamic scale efficiencies also warrant policy.
- Imperfect information can impede access to private finance.
- Public funds to foster innovation must focus on promoting high-risk, high-return green projects.
- Market structures affect innovation. Promoting competition in green sectors is often beneficial.

5.8.5   Green Market Creation

- Developing efficient markets with robust regulatory oversight is key but difficult.
- Many relevant sectors suffer from market power, network effects and coordination failure.
- Credible and clear climate targets protect green industrial policy from significant uncertainty.
- Competition between various regulatory systems can lead to better insights and decision-making.
- Competition policy must consider green arguments for both enforcement and derogations.
- Policymakers can access skill resources of the private sector through public–private partnerships.
- On a case-by-case basis, various degrees of direct state control can sometimes be optimal.
- Huge private investment in green capital goods must be mobilised through various instruments.

5.8.6   Protection and Expansion

- Carbon leakage arises when production in countries with stronger climate policies moves abroad.
- Carbon border adjustment measures are necessary to address this risk and are WTO compatible.
- Climate action requires expanding green markets beyond national borders.
- Yet information failures and positive externalities can result in sub-optimal export decisions.
- Governments are well placed to provide green export promotion services to firms to remedy this.

- Blended finance support can be used to overcome risks specific to destination countries.
- Finally, environmental standards are powerful tools to promote green exports by big markets.

5.8.7   *Green Industrial Policy Entails Risks: Good Governance Is Essential*

- Administrations have their own sources of failure: information constraints, bias and rent-seeking.
- Optimal policies require information beyond the capacity of almost any institution.
- Policymakers are biased towards the status quo and can unknowingly set barriers to innovation.
- Vested interests try to capture rents from public finances.
- Even when evaluated against a no-intervention scenario the case for industrial policy is equivocal.
- Policymakers must move away from a state/market narrative towards institutionalised dialogue.
- Government, the private sector and civil society are the three fundamental stakeholders.
- Embeddedness, discipline and accountability are the three pillars of this relation.
- Finally, industrial policy can be conceived as pursuing broad 'missions' agreed by society.

REFERENCES

Acemoglu, D., P. Aghion, L. Barrage, and D. Hemous (2019) 'Climate Change, Directed Innovation, and Energy Transition: The Long-Run Consequences of the Shale Gas Revolution', Working Paper, Harvard University, https://scholar.harvard.edu/files/aghion/files/climate_change_directed_innovation.pdf

Acemoglu, D., P. Aghion, L. Bursztyn, and D. Hemous (2012) 'The Environment and Directed Technical Change', *American Economic Review*, 102:1, 131–66, http://dx.doi=10.1257/aer.102.1.131

Acemoglu, D., U. Akcigit, D. Hanley, and W. Kerr (2016) 'Transition to Clean Technology', Working Paper, MIT, https://economics.mit.edu/files/11668

Aghion, P., R. Bénabou, R. Martin, and A. Roulet (2021) 'Is Market Competition Clean or Dirty?', *American Economic Review: Insights*, 5:1, 1–20, www .aeaweb.org/articles?id=10.1257/aeri.20210014

Aghion, P., N. Bloom, R. Blundell, R. Griffith, and P. Howitt (2005) 'Competition and Innovation: an Inverted-U Relationship', *The Quarterly Journal of Economics* 120:2, 701–28.

Aghion, P., A. Dechezlepretre, D. Hemous, R. Martin, and J. Van Reenen (2016) 'Carbon Taxes, Path Dependency and Directed Technical Change: Evidence from the Auto Industry', *Journal of Political Economy*, 124:1, 1–51, https:// doi.org/10.1086/684581

Aiginger, K., and D. Rodrik (2020) 'Rebirth of Industrial Policy and an Agenda for the Twenty-First Century', *Journal of Industry, Competition, and Trade*, 20, 189–207, https://link.springer.com/article/10.1007/s10842-019-00322-3#citeas

Altenburg, T., and C. Assmann (Eds.) (2017) 'Green Industrial Policy: Concept, Policies, Country Experiences', Working Paper, United Nations and Deutsches Institut für Entwicklungspolitk, https://stg-wedocs.unep.org/handle/20.500.11822/22277

Altenburg, T., O. Johnson, and H. Schmitz (2015) 'Rent Management – The Heart of Green Industrial Policy', *New Political Economy*, 20:6, 812–31.

Altenburg, T., and D. Rodrik (2017) *Green Industrial Policy: Accelerating Structural Change towards Wealthy Green Economies*, https://drodrik .scholar.harvard.edu/publications/green-industrial-policy-accelerating-structural-change-towards-wealthy

Ambroziak, A. (2017) *The New Industrial Policy of the European Union* (Cham: Springer).

Andreoni, A., and H. J. Chang (2019) 'The Political Economy of Industrial Policy: Structural Interdependencies, Policy Alignment and Conflict Management', *Structural Change and Economic Dynamics*, 48, 136–50.

Arrow, K. (1962) 'Economic Welfare and the Allocation of Resources for Invention', in National Bureau Committee for Economic Research (Ed.), *The Rate and Direction of Inventive Activity: Economic and Social Factors*, pp. 609–26 (Princeton: Princeton University Press).

Baldwin, R. (1969) 'The Case against Infant-Industry Tariff Protection', *Journal of Political Economy*, 77, 295–305.

Barbieri, N., A. Marzucchi, and U. Rizzo (2020) 'Knowledge Sources and Impacts on Subsequent Inventions: Do Green Technologies Differ from Non-green Ones', *Research Policy*, 49:2, www.sciencedirect.com/science/article/abs/pii/S0048733319302197#:~:text=We%20find%20that%20green%20 technologies,partially%20by%20novelty%20and%20complexity.

Bowles, S., and W. Carlin (2020) 'Shrinking Capitalism', *American Economic Review Papers and Proceedings*, 110, 372–77.

Cherif, R., and F. Hasanov (2019) 'The Return of the Policy That Shall Not Be Named: Principles of Industrial Policy', Working Paper No. 2019/074, International Monetary Fund.

Christensen, C., and J. Bower (1996) 'Customer Power, Strategic Investment, and the Failure of Leading Firms', *Strategic Management Journal*, 17, 197–218.

Claeys, G., and S. Tagliapietra (2020) 'Is the EU Council Agreement Aligned with the Green Deal Ambitions?', Policy Contributions 07/2020, Bruegel, www.bruegel.org/2020/07/is-the-eu-council-agreement-aligned-with-the-green-deal-ambitions/

Cohen, W. (2010) 'Fifty Years of Empirical Studies of Innovative Activity and Performance', in B. H. Hall and N. Rosenberg (Eds.), *Handbook of the Economics of Innovation*, pp. 129–213 (Amsterdam: Elsevier), https://doi.org/10.1016/S0169-7218(10)01004-X

Cosme, I., R. Santos, and D. O'Neill (2017) 'Assessing the Degrowth Discourse: A Review and Analysis of Academic Degrowth Policy Proposals', *Journal of Cleaner Production*, 149, 321–34, https://doi.org/10.1016/j.jclepro.2017.02.016

Demaria, F., F. Schneider, F. Sekulova, and J. Martinez-Alier (2013) 'What Is Degrowth? From an Activist Slogan to a Social Movement', *Environmental Values*, 22:2, 191–215, https://doi.org/10.3197/096327113X13581561725194

D'Estea, P., S. Iammarino, M. Savonac, and N. von Tunzelmann (2011) 'What Hampers Innovation? Revealed Barriers versus Deterring Barriers', Research Policy, https://iris.luiss.it/retrieve/handle/11385/197495/101980/Research%20Policy

Eurobarometer (2017) 'Eurobarometer Survey – Protecting the Environment', https://ec.europa.eu/commission/presscorner/detail/en/QANDA_20_330

European Commission (2013) 'The Role and Measurement of Quality in Competition Analysis – Submission by the European Union', submission to the OECD, www.oecd.org/competition/Quality-in-competition-analysis-2013.pdf

Evans, P. (1995) *Embedded Autonomy: States and Industrial Transformation* (Princeton: Princeton University Press).

Fernandez-Arias, E., R. Hausmann, and U. Panizza (2020) 'Smart Development Banks', *Journal of Industry, Competition, and Trade*, 20:1, 395–420, https://doi.org/10.1007/s10842-019-00328-x

Ghisetti, C,. and F. Pontoni, (2015) 'Investigating Policy and R &D Effects on Environmental Innovation: A Meta-Analysis', *Ecological Economics*,

118:C, 57–66, www.sciencedirect.com/science/article/abs/pii/S0921800915003006

Gilbert, R. J. (2020) *Innovation Matters – Competition Policy for the High-Technology Economy* (Cambridge, MA: MIT Press).

Gilbert, R. J., and D. Newbery (1984) 'Preemptive Patenting and the Persistence of Monopoly: Reply', *The American Economic Review*, 74:1, 251–53, www.jstor.org/stable/1803330

Hallegatte, S., M. Fay, and A. Vogt-Schlib (2013) 'Green Industrial Policy: When and How', Working Paper No. 6677, World Bank Policy Research.

Hamilton, W., and H. Singh (1992) 'The Evolution of Corporate Capabilities in Emerging Technologies', *Interfaces*, 22:4, 13–23.

Henderson, R. (1993) 'Under Investment and Incompetence as Responses to Radical Innovation: Evidence from the Photolithographic Alignment Equipment Industry', *Rand Journal of Economics*, 24, 248–70.

IEA (2021a) 'Net Zero by 2050. A Roadmap for the Global Energy Sector', International Energy Agency, www.iea.org/reports/net-zero-by-2050

(2021b) 'Tracking Clean Energy Progress', International Energy Agency, www.iea.org/topics/tracking-clean-energy-progress\

International Monetary Fund (2021) 'Five Things to Know about Carbon Pricing', www.imf.org/en/Publications/fandd/issues/2021/09/five-things-to-know-about-carbon-pricing-parry

Kallis, G. (2011) 'In Defence of Degrowth', *Ecological Economics*, 70:5, 873–80, https://doi.org/10.1016/j.ecolecon.2010.12.007

Kallis, G., V. Kostakis, S. Lange, B. Muraca, S. Paulson, and M. Schmelze (2018) 'Research on Degrowth', *Annual Review of Environment and Resources*, 43, 291–316, https://doi.org/10.1146/annurev-environ-102017-025941

Kemp, R., and B. Never (2017) 'Green Transition, Industrial Policy, and Economic Development', *Oxford Review of Economic Policy*, 33:1, 66–84.

Lane, N. (2019) 'Manufacturing Revolutions: Industrial Policy and Industrialization in South Korea', Working Paper, Institute for International Economic Studies.

Lenaerts, K., S. Tagliapietra, and G. Wolff (2021) 'Can Climate Change Be Tackled without Ditching Economic Growth?', Policy Contributions 09/2021, Bruegel, www.bruegel.org/comment/can-climate-change-be-tackled-without-ditching-economic-growth

Leonard, M., J. Pisani-Ferry, J. Shapiro, S. Tagliapietra, and G. Wolff (2021) 'The Geopolitics of the European Green Deal', Policy Contribution 04/2021, Bruegel, www.bruegel.org/2021/02/the-geopolitics-of-the-european-green-deal/

Loehr, D. (2012) 'The Euthanasia of the Rentier – A Way toward a Steady-State Economy?', *Ecological Economics*, 84, 232–39, https://doi.org/10.1016/j.ecolecon.2011.11.006

Mazzucato, M. (2011) 'The Entrepreneurial State', *Soundings*, 49:131–142.

(2018) 'Mission-Oriented Research & Innovation in the European Union', Publications Office of the European Union, Luxembourg, https://op.europa.eu/en/publication-detail/-/publication/5b2811d1-16be-11e8-9253-01aa75ed71a1/language-en

Mazzucato, M., and C. C. Penna (2016) 'Beyond Market Failures: The Market Creating and Shaping Roles of State Investment Banks', *Journal of Economic Policy Reform*, 19:4, 305–26.

Mehling, M., H. van Asselt, K. Das, and S. Droege (2018) 'Beat Protectionism and Emissions by a Stroke', Policy Contributions 07/2018, Nature, www.nature.com/articles/d41586-018-05708-7

Midttun, A., and K. Gautesen (2007) 'Feed in or Certificates, Competition or Complementarity? Combining a Static Efficiency and a Dynamic Innovation Perspective on the Greening of the Energy Industry', *Energy Policy*, 35, 1419–22, www.sciencedirect.com/science/article/pii/S0301421506001856

Noland, M., and H. Pack (2003) *Industrial Policy in an Era of Globalization: Lessons from Asia* (Washington, DC, Peterson Institute for International Economics).

Rodrik, D. (2014) 'Green Industrial Policy', *Oxford Review of Economic Policy*, 30:3, 469–91, https://drodrik.scholar.harvard.edu/files/dani-rodrik/files/green_industrial_policy.pdf

Schumpeter, J. A. (1942) 'Capitalism, Socialism, and Democracy', University of Illinois at Urbana Champaign's Academy for Entrepreneurial Leadership Historical Research Reference in Entrepreneurship, https://ssrn.com/abstract=1496200

Volpin, C. (2020) 'Sustainability as a Quality Dimension of Competition: Protecting Our Future (Selves)', *CPI Antitrust Chronicle*, July, pp. 9–18.

World Bank (2021) 'State and Trends of Carbon Pricing 2021', https://openknowledge.worldbank.org/handle/10986/35620

6 Mobilising the Financial System for Decarbonisation

As stated in Article 2 of the Paris Agreement, effectively tackling climate change requires 'making finance flows consistent with a pathway towards low greenhouse gas emissions and climate-resilient development' (UNFCC, 2016: 4). This implies two major reallocations of capital: capital needs to flow into mitigation and adaptation activities, while it also needs to flow out of emitting activities.

However, this reallocation process has barely started. The slow progress has resulted in a persistent funding gap, which needs to be overcome to meet climate investment needs. The funding gap refers to the difference between the magnitude of the financial flows currently going into decarbonisation and the magnitude of the flows that would be necessary to achieve targeted emissions reductions. Table 4.1 in Chapter 4 provides an estimate of the size of this gap at the global level. Estimates range between 1 per cent and 2.6 per cent of global gross domestic product (GDP) per year. Furthermore, the size of the funding gap differs between developed and developing countries, with the latter having larger funding gaps than the former (IPCC, 2022). Despite the uncertainty around these numbers, the need to significantly increase the size of financial flows going into decarbonisation is clear.

Attracting finance for investments aimed at achieving climate objectives is crucial. But contrary forces, if not reduced, can make the efforts to achieve such objectives even harder. For instance, during the 2010s, fossil fuel subsidies were still higher than global climate finance flows (Climate Policy Initiative, 2022). Ensuring policy coherence, for example by eliminating fiscal support to fossil fuels, is crucial to ensure credibility and reduce uncertainty. Policymakers need to provide clear signals of their commitments in order to guide investors in their decisions to mobilise finance towards where it is most needed.

As covered in Chapter 4, investment into the transition will have to be a joint effort from both the private and public sectors. Even though the split between private and public efforts varies across countries, mobilising private investors everywhere will be crucial to making the transition happen.

The first part of this chapter will discuss the factors hindering the allocation of capital to green activities. Even if carbon prices send the correct signals to product and financial markets, the allocation of capital would remain hindered by several market frictions. The frictions we cover are incomplete information, a mismatch between funding instruments and funding needs, a 'home bias' in international capital flows, the mispricing of risk and differences in the cost of capital. Renewable projects are a typical example where these market frictions apply. They are characterised by long time horizons, high levels of risk and high capital intensity, which make them more difficult to fund commercially than conventional fossil fuel projects.

The second main challenge of reallocating financial flows to decarbonisation arises from the potentially destabilising effects of scaling down emitting activities. A mismanaged transition could lead to a sharp devaluation of the assets underlying these activities. This could, in turn, potentially trigger instability in the financial system, spilling over into the economy. The second part of this chapter delves into the risks that the transition could pose to financial stability, explaining the transmission mechanisms and covering the topic of stranded assets.

The last part will discuss policy options to address or minimise the barriers to the efficient allocation of capital to the transition. In particular, regulation fostering sustainable finance can offer a second- or third-best solution when adequate and comprehensive carbon pricing is absent.

6.1.1 A Primer on the Financial System

The financial system is a 'platform' that connects investors, seeking returns on their savings, and borrowers, looking for funds to carry out projects. One of its essential functions is to support efficient capital allocation decisions. The various actors on the financial system differ in three related dimensions: (i) their ability to collect information, (ii) the types of instruments they supply to or demand from the market and (iii) the regulatory constraints they face.

Figure 6.1 offers a simplified scheme of the financial system. Efficiently matching the two groups of actors in the financial system requires solving an inherent information asymmetry between borrowers, who have better information on the quality of their projects,

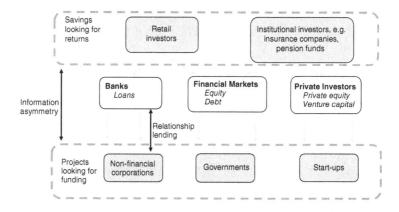

Legend:
Light grey arrows: indicate the direction of flow of funds
Black arrows: information between borrower and lender
Italic: types of funding instruments

FIGURE 6.1 Flow of funds in the financial system – a simplified scheme
Notes: Light grey – direction of flow of funds, black – information, *italic* – types of funding instruments.
Source: Authors.

notably the risk–return profile, and investors, who need to acquire this information. The match can be done by two main categories of actors: banks and financial markets. Other actors, such as private investors or digital platforms (crowdsourcing), can also fill certain niches.

Banks mostly supply funding to economic actors by issuing loans and are characterised by a close relationship with borrowers. This allows them to complement the 'hard information' contained in financial statements with 'soft information' concerning other more personal characteristics of borrowers. The close contact between the bank and the borrower in the lending process is a particular characteristic of banks that allows them to have a superior information collection capacity. This is typically called 'relationship lending'.

Players in the financial markets, on the other hand, do not have the screening capacity of banks and need to base their investment decisions on publicly available information – typically the financial statements of the firms. They rely on timely and accurate disclosure from companies, without which investors may incorrectly price or value assets, leading to a misallocation of capital. This is bureaucratically costly, and hence, bigger firms are the ones with more capacity to produce this kind of information regularly and resort to the financial markets to obtain funding.

In financial markets, firms can choose to issue debt, for example in the form of bonds, or seek an equity type of financing, in which shareholders are given ownership of a part of the firm through shares. There are important differences between these two types of financing. With debt financing the firm has an obligation to repay the loan on a regular schedule but does not give up on ownership. With equity financing the opposite is true: the firm has no formal obligation of repayment, but ownership of all or part of the business is given up. This also implies that in case the firm goes bankrupt, debtors have the priority in claiming back their money, while shareholders take a higher risk of not seeing their investment returned.

Debt financing is attractive when the company expects to perform well and has a good track record in terms of creditworthiness, since the cost of financing would be relatively small. Firms that do not want to be constrained by the obligation to repay debt or for which debt financing would be hard or very costly to obtain typically tend to go for equity financing. This is the case of start-ups or projects at an initial stage of development, which tend to rely on venture capital or public equity markets, when they can access them through initial public offerings.

These differences are important because they imply different risk–return profiles and distinguish the types of lenders and borrowers. Investors differ in their risk aversion and investment strategies. Some of these characteristics are shaped or strongly affected by regulatory constraints. For example, banks are subject to a strict regulatory regime, especially after the 2008 Global Financial Crisis, which curtails their ability to take risks.

Achieving decarbonisation will require scaling up financing significantly and involve all actors of the financial system. Hence, while carbon pricing is a necessary policy to spur the reallocation of capital into decarbonisation activities, it interacts in complex ways with the existing informational and regulatory constraints that characterise the financial system.

6.2   ALLOCATING INVESTMENT TO THE DECARBONISATION OF THE ECONOMY

Four frictions specific to the climate agenda are likely to slow down the process of capital reallocation. First, the climate information architecture is still underdeveloped, raising the risk of greenwashing (as defined later in the section). Second, complexities in matching the supply and demand of financing lead to biases in the types of projects that are funded and where these are located. Third, the important share of capital expenditure in the total costs of decarbonisation projects makes them highly sensitive to factors that affect the cost of capital. Finally, difficulties in measuring and pricing climate risk delay the reallocation out of activities exposed to these risks, raising the likelihood of a disorderly transition.

6.2.1 Underdeveloped Information Architecture

Allocating capital to transition-aligned investments requires knowing which projects fall within this scope. Hence, clarity on how to identify and classify activities and projects is critical to ensuring that funding flows to where it is needed.

At the most fundamental level, an underdeveloped information infrastructure means that the firms themselves might have incomplete information as to the sustainable character of their own projects. But even when project holders can correctly identify their projects as 'green', there remains an information asymmetry with investors if data is not disclosed fully and transparently. As long as there is scope for interpretation in the definition of a green project, there is a risk of greenwashing.

Greenwashing is an umbrella term, covering 'a variety of misleading communications and practices that intentionally or not, induce false positive perceptions of an organisation's environmental performance. It can be conducted by companies, governments, politicians, research organisations, international organisations, banks and NGOs too and it can range from slight exaggeration to full fabrication, thus there are different shades of greenwashing.' This definition is provided by Nemes et al. (2022), who have reviewed the multiplicity of definitions of greenwashing, found in both academic and non-academic sources.

Greenwashing can materialise in several ways. For example, a firm can announce a single green project, while the remaining investment portfolio is biased towards emitting projects, with no prospects of reducing emissions. A firm could thus take advantage of the positive signal sent to the market, for instance when issuing a green bond or when joining a sustainability initiative, even though its overall activities remain mostly brown. A biased selection of which information is transmitted to the public, and particularly to investors, omitting the proportion of green and brown projects can, therefore, create a distorted perception of 'greenness'. Investors would need to invest in monitoring to ensure that their investment is indeed going into the 'green' parts of the portfolio and that it is having a positive impact on the transition.

Greenwashing results in capital misallocation, but it also erodes trust in sustainable finance, thus further slowing down capital reallocation. Therefore, efforts to develop robust definitions and appropriate metrics are crucial to prevent greenwashing, foster trust in sustainable finance and improve capital allocation towards decarbonisation.

6.2.2 Allocation Mismatches

6.2.2.1 Matching Funding Sources to Funding Needs

Mobilising finance for the green transition will require efforts from both public and private investors. Each investor type has different preferences in terms of risk–return profile, time horizon and scale and, thus, preferred types of financing instruments and of projects. On the demand side, projects or technologies that need funding can be at distinct stages of development or maturity – from early stages of research to prototyping or later in the deployment phase. This will necessarily imply different levels of risk, with earlier stages being riskier.

Funding the transition will require matching investor preferences to project needs, which is not a trivial task. Understanding the appropriate financing mix for different technologies and at different stages of development is essential to coordinate efforts among the various types of investors and achieve transition goals (Polzin et al., 2021). The existing mismatch between funding sources and needs is an important contributor to the funding gap.

Polzin and Sanders (2020) describe extensively the various funding sources available, their characteristics and the technologies that best fit those characteristics. Figure 6.2 shows different types of investors, grouped by risk preference and size of investment,

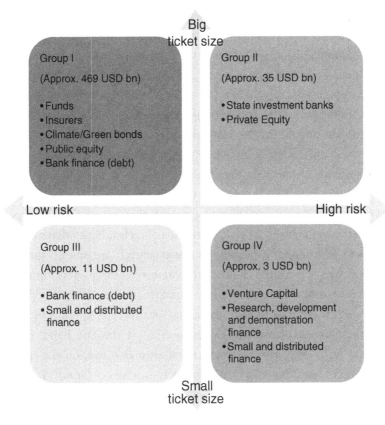

FIGURE 6.2 Sources of financing for the energy transition by size and risk
Source: Authors, based on Polzin and Sanders (2020).

indicating the average supply of financing for the energy transition in Europe.

Group I represents investments that are usually large in total amount and that have low risks and stable cashflows. Examples of technologies funded with these instruments are wind farms, wind and solar component manufacturers, and transmission and distribution infrastructure. These are particularly aligned with the preferences of institutional investors. Given the large-scale and well-established nature of these projects and of the firms that carry them, these would also be able to obtain financing via bond issuance or equity financing.

Capital markets have the potential to channel large amounts of financing towards climate-friendly projects. However, underdeveloped standards create the potential for greenwashing, for example with green bond issuance. Also, in the specific case of green bonds, as a 'use-of-proceeds' type of bond (see Box 6.2 in Section 6.4.1), financing is not restricted to future projects, but firms have flexibility to also use the funds for past expenditures. Therefore, it remains difficult to ensure additionality (namely, the funding of projects that would not have otherwise happened).

Group IV in Figure 6.2 represents funding instruments that are diametrically opposed to those in *Group I*: they are small-scale projects that carry significant risk. Examples of technologies that attract this sort of funding, especially venture capital, are energy storage and electric drivetrains. Public support for research, development and demonstration and small distributed finance (e.g. crowdfunding) have also emerged as financing sources for this type of projects.

In between these two extremes are, on the one hand, large projects with high associated risks – *Group II* – and, on the other hand, small-scale projects with relatively low risk – *Group III*. The former are best suited for public development banks (PDBs), who also have the capacity to mobilise private funding via co-investments. Examples of such projects are offshore wind farms and first commercial plants of new technologies. The latter mainly obtain financing from banks and small distributed finance. Projects aimed at improving the energy efficiency of buildings are a good example.

According to the estimates of Polzin and Sanders (2020), there is no shortage in the quantity of funds available in Europe to invest in various green technologies. The challenge lies in matching the supply and demand. For instance, while there is a huge pool of funds potentially available to invest, regulatory constraints, lack of standards and intermediation deficiencies are preventing institutional investors from redirecting those funds to sustainable projects that match their risk–return profile.

On the other end of the spectrum, small-scale projects struggle to obtain the necessary funding. One explanation for this is the fact that large investors do not look to fund projects of this scale. For the early stages of small risky projects there is still a shortage of investment, which deters exploration of new technologies. For small low-risk projects it would be valuable to scale up crowdfunding type of platforms to provide a complementary alternative to bank lending.

The mismatch between funding sources and needs also implies that certain investors may be playing a relatively smaller role and others a relatively larger role in fostering transition-aligned technologies. This matters because the type of funding affects the direction of innovation (Mazzucato & Semieniuk, 2018). Investors differ in their degree of patience and their ability and willingness to bear risk, and thus align their investment strategies to these preferences. When specific investors have unbalanced portfolios towards specific technologies, this may create a disproportionate influence and, unintentionally, drive the direction of innovation and deployment of technologies.

Understanding the characteristics and heterogeneity among financial players is, therefore, important for informed policymaking. More than simply attracting funding indiscriminately for the transition, being aware of the impact of financing flows from different sources on the development of the various technologies can help policymakers balance technology-specific policies and steer the direction of innovation and the wider deployment of sustainable technologies.

6.2.2.2 *International Allocation of Capital*

The efficient allocation of capital for decarbonisation requires prioritising the mobilisation of capital towards countries with the lowest abatement costs (i.e. cost of deploying technologies that lower emissions for a given level of output). However, this is hindered by the many barriers to cross-border capital flows. Reducing these barriers would lead to socially optimal efficiency improvements given the borderless nature of climate change and, hence, of mitigation impact.

The widely documented 'home bias', whereby investors prioritise projects in their own countries or regions (IPCC, 2022), creates an imbalance between developing and developed countries. The latter have more resources available to invest but these tend to stay within that group of countries. The weak financial system in most developing countries is an important driver of domestic funding gaps in these countries. Challenges around the international mobilisation of capital make it hard to reduce these gaps.

The 'home bias' originates from factors such as differences in regulatory standards and policy support, exchange rate risk and difficulty in obtaining information to support financial decisions. There are also political and governance risks that are specially heightened for developing countries, where the institutional quality is weaker than in advanced economies. Institutional quality plays an important role in a country's ability to attract international capital flows.

Fostering a more investment-enabling environment in emerging markets and developing economies would help attract funds from advanced economies. For example, continued fossil fuel subsidies create a negative carbon price that generates a competitive disadvantage for low-carbon technologies (IMF, 2022). Also, strengthening institutional capacity and regulatory frameworks, such as contract enforcement, property rights and data collection, would reduce barriers currently impeding long-term sustainable investments. However, the time necessary to implement these structural reforms is difficult to reconcile with the urgency of the climate challenge.

6.2.3   Cost of Capital

The cost of capital is a fundamental part of any investment decision since it helps determine if an investment is worth pursuing or not. In simple terms, the cost of capital indicates the minimum return that would pay off the costs of the investment. Financially, an investment gets approved only if it is expected to generate a return higher than the costs undertaken to carry out the project.

In the power generation sector, the contrast between low-carbon and carbon-intensive technologies is particularly stark. As seen in Figure 6.3, low-carbon power generation technologies are capital intensive and characterised by high initial fixed investments

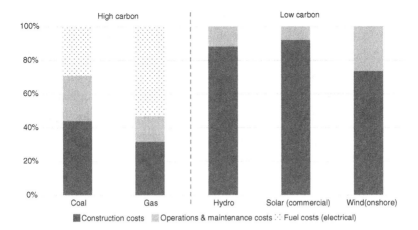

FIGURE 6.3 Cost composition of different power generation
technologies
Notes: Data for the United States of America. Plant types: coal
pulverised (650 MW), gas (CCGT) (727 MW), hydro run of river (>= 5
MW) (median case) (44.7 MW), solar photovoltaic (commercial) (median
case) (0.30 MW), wind onshore (>= 1 MW) (median case) (100 MW).
Source: Authors, based on IEA Levelised Cost of Electricity Calculator
(2020).

and relatively low variable costs. Carbon-intensive energy sources
have the opposite cost profile. The high proportion of initial capital expenditures makes low-carbon power generation technologies
more sensitive to the level and to the volatility of capital costs. Low
capital costs are favourable and enabling to the deployment of these
technologies.

Hirth and Steckel (2016) estimate that, on average, an increase
in the cost of capital by one percentage point increases the levelised electricity costs of wind power by $4 per megawatt hour,[1] of

---

[1] In the power industry, the levelised energy cost (LEC) is the discounted lifetime cost
per unit of output:

$$LEC = \frac{\sum_1^T C_t \left(1+r\right)^{-t}}{\sum_1^T G_t \left(1+r\right)^{-t}}$$

where C_t is the yearly cost, G_t is the yearly output and r is the discount rate or
weighted average cost of capital.

coal-fired power plants by $3 per megawatt hour and of natural gas-fired plants by $1 per megawatt hour. More recently, Schmidt et al. (2019) document the impact of rising interest rates on the levelised cost of energy and find that increases in interest rates could reverse the trend of decreasing cost for renewable energies, potentially raising concerns for the viability of investments in these technologies.

The disproportionate sensitivity of transition-aligned projects to the cost of capital is effectively a barrier that makes such investments relatively unattractive in regions with high capital costs, high macroeconomic uncertainty and low policy support. This could threaten the transition to sustainable energy technologies in many regions.

The cost of capital varies considerably across countries, with the difference being particularly pronounced between advanced and less developed countries (see Figure 3.4 in Chapter 3). This is relevant for cross-country investment allocation and means that underlying determinants of the cost of capital matter. An underdeveloped financial system paired with weak institutions and high investment risks contributes to the high capital costs in developing economies. Hence, even though many developing countries have geographical and climate endowments that favour the deployment of renewable energy, the high cost of capital in those countries ultimately determines the final investment decision (Ameli et al., 2021).

The overall macroeconomic context and monetary policy also play an important role in driving the cost of capital. For instance, a sudden tightening of monetary policy could rapidly lead to increases in the cost of capital via interest rate increases. Given that interest rates vary dynamically over time, the less uncertainty there is about the macroeconomic situation in a country and the more predictable is monetary policy, the easier it is for investors to assess the viability of projects.

Policy support to reduce capital costs in emerging markets or to safeguard against increases in interest rates could reduce the exposure of capital-intensive sustainable projects to the aforementioned hindering factors or to fluctuations in capital costs. Export guarantees for foreign investors or technology-specific feed-in tariffs (that guarantee a price over long periods for renewable energy production) are policy solutions that can reduce the cost of capital in emerging economies. So-called 'thermostatic' policies, which automatically adjust according to market conditions, could be well suited to hedge firms against interest rate surges. A policy mix combining carbon pricing and support to reduce capital costs would yield the greatest abatement of emissions (Hirth & Steckel, 2016).

6.2.4 Climate Risk Assessment

In addition to the aforementioned factors, an important driver of the cost of capital, and hence of the ability of projects to attract financing, is the pricing of risk. Climate considerations create new types of risks to economic activity and to the financial system. There are two main types of climate risks: physical risks, which are driven by the impact of climate change, and transition risks, which derive from the structural changes necessary to reach a low-carbon economy (see Box 6.1 for more details). To the extent that these risks are incorrectly measured and priced, capital will be misallocated.

Measuring and pricing these risks are not easy tasks and require data that is still not widely available. The main challenge for the measurement of climate risks is the incomplete information architecture around data disclosure and reporting. This is particularly important to better understand economic agents' exposure to these risks and how they plan to decarbonise.

Furthermore, standard financial valuation models, such as Value-at-Risk models, are not entirely appropriate to price climate-related risks (Demekas & Grippa, 2021). Limitations of these models include the use of historical records to determine expected value and risk of losses and the assumption that climate risk is exogenous.

The endogeneity of climate-related financial risk refers to the fact that 'the perception of the risk changes the risk itself, unlike most contexts of financial risk' (IPCC, 2022), and is particularly difficult

BOX 6.1 **Different types of climate risks**

TYPES OF CLIMATE RISKS

The term 'climate risk' usually encompasses two types of risk: physical risk and transition risk. The former refers to the risks created by the consequences of climate change, while the latter refers to the risks resulting from climate change mitigation (IPCC, 2022).

More specifically, *physical risk* refers to the component of financial risk that corresponds to losses in the financial value of assets (such as industrial plants or real estate) resulting from the 'interaction of climate-related hazards (including hazardous events and trends) with the vulnerability of exposure of human and natural systems' (D'Orazio & Popoyan, 2019). Many of the impacts of climate-related hazards, such as extreme weather events, sea level rise or increased temperatures, on human systems are documented in Box 1.1 in Chapter 1. In turn, these losses affect the value of financial assets of exposed companies and sovereign entities and have direct negative impacts for insurance companies.

Transition risk refers to the component of financial risk associated with negative adjustments in the value of assets resulting directly or indirectly from the transition to a low-carbon economy. The transition can symmetrically lead to positive adjustments in the value of certain assets, thus also presenting transition opportunities.

Assessing these two types of risks depends on apprehending two very different sources of uncertainty. Physical risk is highly dependent on the ability of climate models to predict global temperature increases and the local climate consequences. These are subject to vast uncertainty given the existence of non-linearities and potential threshold effects. The source of uncertainty underlying transition risk stems mostly from the societal response to the climate challenge. In particular, the timing (now or later), speed (rapid or slow), predictability and the breadth of policy action are still being debated. Hence, under certain policy scenarios (timely, predictable, broad action), the materialisation of losses could be very small, while in others (delayed and disorderly action), risks could materialise in the form of huge losses – for example, stranding of large-scale assets. The wide set of variables to take into consideration under transition risks makes it particularly challenging to quantify.

Finally, other types of risks could arise, such as liability risks, which refer to 'the impacts that could arise tomorrow if parties who have suffered loss or damage from the effects of climate change seek compensation from those they hold responsible' (Carney, 2015).

DRIVERS OF TRANSITION RISK

It is quite straightforward to understand what drives physical risks. But this is often not the case for transition risks. Semieniuk et al. (2021) identify three drivers of transition risks: changes in climate policy and in regulation, technological developments, and adjustments in market and consumer preferences. These can prompt reassessments of prices and quantities in the economy and in the financial sector.

The central argument for *public climate policy* is internalising the carbon externality. The most immediate tool for this is carbon pricing. But governments also use a large array of policy tools to speed up the transition process, for instance establishing timelines to discontinue certain carbon-intensive activities or new regulatory frameworks. To the extent that such policies force firms to reorganise their production processes in unexpected ways, these can be highly disruptive and imply high compliance costs for some industries.

Technological developments can make existing brown technologies comparatively less attractive, not only via increased efficiency but also via reduced costs (financial and regulatory costs) of competing green technologies. Therefore, unless firms relying on or selling exclusively brown technologies adapt or change the business model to more sustainable technologies, they will become less competitive and eventually obsolete.

Shifts in behaviour resulting from increased awareness of climate change can drive demand and prices. Certain changes in consumer preferences are likely to result from an increased willingness to contribute to a more climate-friendly society. For example, such behavioural changes might drive an increase in demand for electric vehicles, to the detriment of internal combustion engines, or to a shift of investor preferences towards environmental, social and governance bonds instead of bonds issued by the oil industry. These behavioural shifts can also have spillover effects on other economic actors. For example, firms could look for ways to make their production processes more sustainable, banks could try to diversify their portfolio towards greener assets or rating agencies could increasingly take into account climate risks in their rating classifications. Agents failing to adapt could face higher funding costs and less demand for their products, resulting is decreased profitability and increased credit risk assessment.

to apprehend. Risks arising from the transition depend on the actions of economic agents – importantly, governments and firms – to move to a low-carbon economy, but, in turn, these actions depend on how these agents perceive the risks from a missed transition.

Adding another layer of complexity is the fact that there is not a single transition path, and the end point may differ from country to country, so there are various courses of action that can be undertaken. This translates into a multiplicity of scenarios that must be considered when assessing transition risks and for which the likelihood of occurring may not be easy to evaluate.

The challenge also applies to physical risks, as climate change, resulting extreme weather events and their impacts on economic activity are influenced by the extent of climate change mitigation (transition to a low-carbon economy) to keep the temperature from increasing above certain thresholds.

The uncertainty around the measurement of climate risks means that investors' perceptions of risk have an important influence on investment allocation choices and, thus, the transition to a low-carbon economy (Battiston et al., 2021). Investor perceptions can have an *enabling role* for the transition if investors realise that a missed transition would create large losses whereas a successful transition would create numerous opportunities. Conversely, investors can play a *hampering role* if they see little opportunities from a successful transition and, hence, do not have much incentive to reallocate capital to low-carbon projects. In the first case, the transition would likely go smoothly. In the second case, there would be a disorderly transition, with late and abrupt repricing and reallocation of capital.

Battiston et al. (2021) illustrate the influence that investors' risk assessment and subsequent choices can have on the transition path: 'If investors assess a higher risk for high-carbon firms, they demand higher interest rates on loans, and higher yields for bonds, to provide funding. They may also divest from some high-carbon firms to reinvest in low-carbon firms in order to balance their portfolio risk.'

The efforts that are underway to tackle the challenges inherent to the evaluation of climate-related risks, such as disclosure standards and climate stress tests, will be discussed more thoroughly in Section 6.4.

6.3 RISKS TO FINANCIAL STABILITY

One of the questions that has been explored in the theoretical literature is to what extent the transition to a greener economy would pose risks to financial stability. Financial stability concerns would be particularly valid if the transition happened in a mismanaged and disorderly manner. In this section we recap the transmission mechanism through which the transition could create instability, next shift the focus to empirical research and stranded assets and finally explore how the current regulatory framework might be setting wrong incentives.

6.3.1 Transmission of Climate Risk Drivers to the Financial System

As discussed in Section 6.2, the mismeasurement and mispricing of climate risks (both physical and transition risks) contribute to the misallocation of capital, slowing down the reallocation of capital out of brown activities to green activities. The presence of climate risks creates an additional societal challenge: the materialisation of these risks, namely sudden asset devaluations, can propagate through the financial system, creating financial instability and ultimately leading to an economic downturn. The transmission of these risks to financial stability operates through a microeconomic channel and a macroeconomic channel (Basel Committee on Banking Supervision, 2021).

The microeconomic transmission channel is driven by the exposure of individual banks and other investors in financial markets to counterparties vulnerable to transition risk (e.g. engaged in carbon-intensive activities) or to physical risk (e.g. with assets exposed to extreme weather events). These counterparties face the risk of a sudden devaluation of their assets.

Drivers of transition risk are also likely to negatively impact the business model and profitability of companies in carbon-intensive markets. By affecting their ability to repay debt, this creates credit risks for the creditors of these companies. If this debt is in the form of a bank loan, banks exposed to such counterparties would see an increase in credit risk and perhaps even a materialisation of this risk via a default in the repayment of the credit. If this debt is in the form of an obligation to bondholders, and the firms face difficulties paying coupons, or even the principle, this could have an impact on investors in financial markets.

Either way, financial actors could incur losses that, if sizable and unexpected, could create instability in the financial system, especially given the interconnections and links among participants in the financial markets. These connections also create the potential for market risk.

The macroeconomic transmission channel captures the aggregate effects of climate risk. Notably, if the introduction of climate policy, in the form of carbon pricing, leads to a drop in economic activity, aggregate income and consumption, this would create widespread credit risk for banks, as the ability of many economic actors to service their debt would be affected. Chapter 2 discusses the mechanisms through which climate policy can affect economic activity. In addition to the negative supply shock implied by carbon pricing and higher energy costs, banks can amplify the economic downturn through the so-called financial accelerator. This refers to the situation whereby banks exposed to brown assets see a decrease in the size of their balance sheets, as brown assets depreciate. This subsequently limits the ability of banks to extend credit to the rest of the economic actors, thereby further depressing economic activity.

These transmission channels are exacerbated in the case of a disorderly transition, in which economic agents have not taken preventive steps to prepare for the transition. Examples of such preventive measures are the diversification of portfolios or a reduction in the exposure to carbon-intensive assets or suppliers. The systemic nature of climate risk could be reinforced by the possible presence of moral hazard (IPCC, 2022). If a majority of financial actors downplays climate-related financial risks, the systemic risk for the financial system would build up and be amplified, and in the event it materialises, the impacts would be significant.

6.3.2 Stranded Assets

The concept of stranded assets, as specific materialisation of transition risk, is central to the discussion of financial instability risks arising from the transition. The abrupt devaluation of certain assets in a scenario of a disorderly transition could lead to a sequence of devaluations that could in an extreme scenario have systemic consequences for the economy and, particularly, the financial system.

A stranded asset is an 'asset which loses significant economic value well ahead of its anticipated useful life, as a result of changes in legislation, regulation, market forces, disruptive innovation, societal norms, or environmental shocks' (van der Ploeg & Rezai, 2020). Therefore, an asset that gets stranded no longer earns the initial expected return due to an announced change, with the new expected return being revised at a significantly lower value. In the case of the transition to a decarbonised economy, the assets that are likely to get stranded are those whose underlying value is linked to carbon-intensive industries or processes, since those are the business activities that need to be discontinued or considerably reduced.

For an asset to get stranded two conditions need to be met. First, there must be an unanticipated change in conditions affecting the profitability of fossil fuel assets. Second, it must be near impossible to shift the underlying capital stock in the carbon-intensive industries to productive use elsewhere after the energy transition. The irreversibility of these investments is a crucial element in determining the extent to which an asset loses its value.

An important aspect to consider is that there is a sequence of devaluations along a chain of interlinked assets from physical to financial. To better understand this, let us consider the example of a fossil fuel extraction company faced with a policy announcement putting an end to the use of fossil fuels:

1. The policy announcement implies that its fossil fuel reserves will have to stay underground and not be extracted. This is the concept of 'unburnable carbon'. These reserves are a physical asset that will lose their economic value.
2. The infrastructure used to extract fossil fuels from the ground and distribute them will also become stranded if it cannot be reconverted to an activity aligned with transition goals. This infrastructure is also a physical asset that gets stranded. However, in the case of infrastructure, the entirety of the asset might not be stranded, if it can be reconverted, albeit at a cost. An example would be the reconversion of pipelines used for the transport of the natural gas into infrastructure for the transport of a greener gas, such as hydrogen.
3. The company operating the extraction will incur large losses on its balance sheet as its activity will be impaired. If the company is not diversified enough and this is its only business activity, it will eventually have to close, a step that has implications for the value of financial assets.
4. In the case of a large listed company, the value of its equity shares in the stock market will suffer an abrupt devaluation. This would have

implications for the owners of these shares and potentially pose risks for financial stability. For instance, if individual investors are the holders of these shares and they suddenly see their investment shrink, they could struggle to repay their bank loans and, hence, contribute to a deterioration in banks' balance sheets. In case the holders of such shares are, for example, funds with a considerable proportion of the portfolio invested in these shares, the ultimate investors on these funds would also suffer losses. A tight interconnection between various financial institutions would imply a wider propagation of these losses. These mechanisms all contribute to the stranding of financial assets.

5. Finally, companies that depend on fossil fuels to conduct their activity would also be affected. These companies would need to change their physical capital to adapt to the use of other sources of energy or, alternatively, close their activity. In this case, the stranded assets would be a mixture of physical and financial assets.

A study by Semieniuk et al. (2022) estimates the present value of stranded assets taking into account this cascading link between assets, from physical reserves to the ultimate owners of equity shares. Losses from unburned carbon and exploration sites will fall mostly on non-OECD (Organisation for Economic Co-operation and Development) countries. At the other end of the chain, the stranded financial assets will fall mostly on OECD-based investors. Also, investment funds seem to be considerably exposed to asset stranding risk, while ultimately the bearers of the losses are private individuals. Pension funds have considerable assets under management that could be at risk of getting stranded if the commitments made under the Paris Agreement are respected (Rempel & Gupta, 2020).

Estimates of the overall impact of asset stranding on the economy vary greatly and are highly sensitive to the scenarios considered. A complete assessment of the economic consequences of stranded assets requires considering both the first-order effects – direct losses from exposure to brown sectors – and the subsequent second-order effects – indirect losses arising from the decline of brown industries, such as unemployment or lower consumption due to a decline in economic activity.

One point of consensus is that the likelihood of abrupt revaluation of assets is heightened in the case of a late and disorderly transition, where financial agents have not fully anticipated the necessary adjustments that the transition entails. On the contrary, with sufficient anticipation, unavoidable losses could be better spread over time, reducing the systemic effects on the financial system.

As suggested by traditional financial principles, an important adjustment that economic actors can make to anticipate the transition is the diversification of both business activity and financial portfolios. Additionally, investments in reconversion of infrastructure or preparedness to do so would also mitigate the risk of asset stranding.

Finally, the answer of market actors and the resulting changes in asset values depends on the credibility of policy announcements. If markets do not perceive those announcements as credible or do not expect immediate action on those commitments, continued operation of carbon-intensive industries remains a rational response. This could explain why past policy announcements and commitments to carbon neutrality have not had a dramatic effect on the valuation of carbon-intensive assets, nor led to a slowdown of investment in fossil fuel extraction.

The empirical study of Sen and von Schickfus (2020) tests the extent to which investors price asset stranding risk following policy announcements and concludes that significant market repricing happens only when compensation mechanisms are ruled out. Prior experience with policymakers announcing concrete action to the detriment of a brown technology alongside mechanisms to compensate those firms for closing early has led investors to expect compensation also in the future. Hence, even though investors are aware of stranding risk, the expectation of compensation for eventual losses limits the sharp repricing of the value of these assets. Only the challenge to compensation leads to a change in their beliefs and subsequent repricing.

Work understanding the repercussions of policy announcements on the value of carbon-intensive assets is important to inform policymakers and help them adapt their actions according to the intended outcomes.

6.3.3 Financial Regulation as a Response to Financial Instability

Concerns regarding financial instability have led to the development of a sophisticated regulatory framework of prudential policies. These aim to contain the build-up of financial imbalances and ensure that the financial system can be resilient to shocks. The ex ante prudential nature of these policies is especially well adapted to the net zero transition by incentivising the anticipation of shocks rather that managing them in an ex post reactive manner.

The global financial regulation, which was developed in the aftermath of the 2008 Global Financial Crisis, aims at strengthening the banking system by implementing a series of requirements to make banks more robust to shocks.

For example, liquidity requirements are imposed with the objective of aligning the maturity of the assets with the maturity of the liabilities, preventing situations of liquidity distress. Specifically, the Liquidity Coverage Ratio favours holding high-quality liquid assets, such as cash or sovereign bonds, to meet short-term needs. These liquidity requirements reinforce the low-risk behaviour in banks' decisions. Likewise, the Net Stable Funding Ratio incentivises banks to hold stable funding – with maturities longer than one year – to cover for their long-term assets. However, given the less attractive nature of long-term funding, as it is more expensive and less liquid, banks will have the tendency to reduce the maturity of their asset portfolios.

Overall, financial regulation serves the important purpose of addressing risks that could trigger instability in the financial system. One such risk is asset stranding. Theoretical work finds that imposing capital requirements successfully mitigates the propagation of fossil asset devaluations through the financial system, illustrating the stabilising potential of prudential policy (Diluiso et al., 2021).

However, these ratios disincentive lending to long-term projects. The issue is that green projects typically have long time horizon and high risk (D'Orazio & Popoyan, 2019). For financial regulation to continue to play its crucial role in keeping the financial sector stable and avoiding liquidity crises, one option is to resort to non-bank funding instruments for green projects that are more suited to their long-term and risky nature, as discussed in Section 6.2.2.

6.4 FINANCIAL POLICIES TO ACHIEVE DECARBONISATION

In the previous sections, we identified various barriers that hinder the efficient allocation of capital to sustainable projects, explaining the presence of a funding gap for the green transition. Additionally, we discussed the new risks created by the transition and their transmission to the financial system and the economy more broadly. In this section, we discuss policy solutions to address the identified barriers and create a more climate-friendly regulatory framework.

6.4.1 Designing a Strong Climate Information Architecture

Throughout previous sections, the lack of reliable and complete data was raised as a barrier to informed decision-making. Over the past two decades, advancements in measurement and classification frameworks, accompanied by increased data collection efforts, have contributed to enrich the climate information infrastructure. However, these efforts need to be stepped up.

A starting point of this climate information architecture is the collection of data on greenhouse gas (GHG) emissions. The Greenhouse Gas Protocol has played an important role in defining standards and providing tools to help firms and countries measure their GHG emissions. GHG emissions are typically divided into three categories: direct emissions from production (scope 1), indirect emissions from consumption of energy (scope 2) and all other indirect emissions, ranging from emissions across the value chain to those associated with waste disposal or wastewater treatment (scope 3). Scope 1 and 2 emissions are the easiest to measure and for which data is the most widely available. Yet, even this limited data availability suggests that scope 3 emissions represent a large share of overall emissions (Lloyd et al., 2022).

6.4.1.1 Taxonomies

At the foundation of a solid climate information architecture is an overarching set of classifications defining which activities and technologies are aligned with the net zero transition and which are not. These classifications are commonly called taxonomies. They help guide investors and firms in their decision-making process by establishing some rules on what is a sustainable economic activity or a green technology.

Ideally, well-defined and internationally harmonised taxonomies would serve as a benchmark for developing standards, certifications and products. This would be especially relevant for the efficient allocation of capital across countries. The easier it is for investors to screen information of foreign companies, the more likely it is for capital to flow across borders to where it is needed. Credible climate information would also help firms obtain investment from capital markets, as a complement to other forms of financing.

The main front runners in the development of taxonomies and classifications of sustainable activities are the European Union, China, and the members of ASEAN.[2] These initial steps have also prompted other countries across the globe to start developing their own taxonomies.

Governments have been designing their own taxonomies to align with their transition goals and give guidance to their economies. The rationale for country-specific taxonomies is to take into account the industrial make-up and stage of technological development of various countries. Different economies are at different levels of development, have different energy endowments and infrastructure, and therefore different optimal transition plans, which could be

---

[2] Association of Southeast Asian nations (ASEAN) member states: Brunei Darussalam, Cambodia, Indonesia, Lao People's Democratic Republic, Malaysia, Myanmar, Philippines, Singapore, Thailand and Vietnam.

reflected in tailored taxonomies. For example, the weight of coal in a country's electricity generation can influence whether natural gas could be considered as a 'transition' technology, as it improves emissions compared to the status quo.

However, if taxonomies vary considerably across countries, international investors will find it difficult to operate cross-borders. International fora are crucial in this regard. The International Platform on Sustainable Finance has been an important forum to discuss the mapping of criteria across different taxonomies, particularly between the European Union and China, and led to the Common Ground Taxonomy Report.[3]

Progress on taxonomies has been valuable, but existing initiatives suffer from a number of shortcomings. In particular, mandatory taxonomies tend to be backward looking and static, limiting their ability to take into consideration rapid technological developments or to consider different types of investment. In addition, while the inclusion of activities into the taxonomy should be driven by scientific criteria, it remains vulnerable to industry lobbying (Demekas & Grippa, 2021). Finally, taxonomies have been focusing on classifying what is 'green' or aligned with the transition but have not clearly defined what is 'brown'. This makes it harder to assess exposure of economic activities to transition risk, which is closely linked to 'brown' activities. To address this flaw, academics developed the Climate Policy Relevant Sectors classification, which provides a classification of activities based on how their revenues could be affected by the transition, positively (i.e. green activities) or negatively (i.e. brown activities) (Battiston et al., 2017).

6.4.1.2   *Standards*

Standards are important to set a layer of rules and ensure some level of harmonisation in the way certain data is disclosed or labels are

---

[3] The report and other initiatives of the International Platform on Sustainable Finance can be found here: https://finance.ec.europa.eu/sustainable-finance/international-platform-sustainable-finance_en

used. Two important sets of standards are disclosure standards and standards on financial instruments.

Disclosure standards provide a framework dictating what type of data should be reported and how this data should be presented. International initiatives have developed standards on climate reporting, providing global baseline guiding principles to help countries establish their own frameworks. Following such guidelines would ensure that climate disclosures are comparable and consistent across jurisdictions. The International Sustainability Standards Board and Global Reporting Initiative lead such harmonisation initiatives at the global level.[4]

The adoption of international disclosure standards remains voluntary, and some regions have developed their own disclosure framework. This is the case of the European Union, where disclosure is mandatory, with the Sustainable Finance Disclosure Regulation, which is targeted at financial institutions, and the Corporate Sustainability Reporting Directive (CSRD), which applies more widely to firms and financial actors. The latter requires companies to digitally 'tag' reported information, which will then feed into a digital single access point. In the case of the European Union, reporting will be mandatory. This is crucial to foster wide information disclosure and contribute to increasing the quantity and quality of climate data. In addition, the CSRD also makes use of digital technology to facilitate access to reported information. Companies are required to digitally 'tag' reported information, which will then feed into a digital single access point.

Evidence shows that the quality of data disclosures, not just environmental performance, is valued by investors (Alessi et al., 2021) and helps direct investments away from carbon-intensive activities (Mésonnier & Nguyen, 2021).

Standards on financial instruments set ground rules for the definition of new financial instruments to fund transition-aligned

---

[4] Disclosure standards developed by the International Sustainability Standards Board: www.sasb.org/standards/; disclosure standards developed by the Global Reporting Initiative: www.globalreporting.org/standards

investments, such as green or sustainability-linked bonds (see Box 6.2). Initially, there were no clear rules and classification of activities as green or sustainable was mostly self-reported. The lack of external verification and data availability to screen these financial instruments raised important concerns about greenwashing, leading to distrust among investors.

BOX 6.2   **New financial instruments to fund transition-aligned activities**

There is a range of new financial instruments to fund transition-aligned activities, but bonds represent the most important development in this sphere. There are two main types of bonds, which differ in how the funds raised from their issuance are used: use-of-proceeds bonds and performance-linked bonds.

USE-OF-PROCEEDS BONDS

Use-of-proceeds bonds are aimed at raising capital to invest on specific projects. The selection of eligible projects is done according to criteria defined prior to issuance and that end up determining the label of the bond. For instance, a 'green bond' should fund projects with environmental benefits, while proceeds from 'social bonds' should be allocated to projects with positive social outcomes. 'Sustainable bonds' combine the two previous categories and should therefore serve to invest in both 'green' and 'social' projects.

Prior to the issuance of the bond, the issuer specifies criteria determining eligible expenditure, how these proceeds will be managed – for instance, the timeframe within which these proceeds can be allocated – and how the information on the use of the funds will be reported. While there is no universal framework that establishes the ground rules for the different types of bonds, there are some widely adopted standards – for example The Principles developed by ICMA.[1]

---

[1] The Principles: www.icmagroup.org/sustainable-finance/the-principles-guidelines-and-handbooks

PERFORMANCE-LINKED BONDS

Performance-linked bonds are aimed not at funding projects that fall under pre-defined eligible categories but rather at funding the overall activity of an issuer that has the ambition to achieve a certain performance. The contractual terms are linked to pre-established performance targets measured by key performance indicators. An example of such bonds is the 'sustainability-linked bonds'. These are typically linked to performance targets relating to the reduction in GHG emissions.

Performance-linked bonds work in the following manner. If the issuer achieves the target(s), it could benefit from paying lower coupons (step-down). If it misses the target(s), it could be penalised by an increase in the coupon (step-up) paid to the bondholders. Therefore, the issuer has the incentive to work towards the goal to obtain more attractive financing conditions. The choice of benefit or penalisation is determined by the issuer and varies widely. The higher the benefit and penalisation, the bigger the incentive to achieve the targets. However, the target should be ambitious for investors to accept large discounts.

In this context, the development of standards clearly defining the criteria that make certain instruments eligible as green or sustainable has been important to increase trust among investors and establish ground rules in financial markets. Private initiatives have been taking the lead on the development of the existing standards on climate bonds, for instance the International Capital Market Association (ICMA) and the Climate Bonds Initiative. But there are also attempts to create standards on the public sphere, like the European Green Bond Standard, which builds on the EU Sustainable Taxonomy.

These financial instruments are still at an early stage of development and a lot remains to be understood. The discussion about the pros and cons of different instruments is ongoing. There are calls to improve consistency of labels (Boffo & Patalano, 2020). Research is underway to determine which instruments are more appropriate for different issuers given their characteristics (Cheng et al., 2022). Finally, there is limited evidence on how sustainable investing translates into actual climate impact (Kölbel et al., 2020). As standards evolve and the issues get clarified, the market for these new financial instruments will expand.

6.4.2 Role of PDBs in Crowding in Private Investment

As mentioned in Section 6.2, more than a general scarcity of funds, the main barrier to capital reallocation into green activities is allocation frictions that create a mismatch between funding instruments and needs and another across countries. In this context, public actors emerge as pivotal entities with the capacity to minimise some of those frictions and to crowd in private investment.

Among public entities, PDBs have characteristics that allow them to fulfil a number of roles that can foster green investments (Geddes et al., 2018).

First and foremost, they are important providers of capital to technologies perceived as risky. This means that they frequently take the role of first movers into new technological areas where other financial players are unwilling to invest. Higher risk tolerance and support for projects in an early phase are crucial to allow for the exploration of various avenues out of which innovative technologies can emerge. PDBs can use various financial instruments, such as credit guarantees (that reduce the risk associated with certain investments) and concessional loans (loans with favourable conditions), that bring in private investors who would otherwise not tolerate the full risks.

Second, their experience with a variety of projects in diverse areas has allowed them to gain expertise in terms of technology risk assessment, which investors see as an important asset. PDBs can transmit this knowledge to investors, helping them become more familiar with the characteristics of different technologies. Finally, they play an important signalling role, by increasing the confidence of investors towards projects with PDBs support.

However, the involvement of PDBs in mobilising finance for climate objectives needs to be aligned with their given mandate (Geddes et al., 2018). While PDBs are independent institutions, their performance and the fulfilment of their mandate are closely monitored by their respective governments. Hence, they need to be transparent in their criteria, using tailored metrics to support the selection of projects according to their goals, and in their disclosures. As with all financial agents, the assessment of projects and choice of metrics are still very dependent on data availability and should follow taxonomies classifying sustainable investments. In countries that wish to set up 'green' PDBs, particular attention needs to be given to the definition of the mandate, for example regarding the technology focus areas or the performance criteria for de-risking instruments.

From an international perspective, PDBs, especially multilateral ones, could also play an important role in emerging economies (Ameli et al., 2021; IMF, 2022). By de-risking investments, they can reduce the cost of capital for private investors, making investments in these areas more attractive and contributing to deepening financial markets. Also, stepping up equity financing relative to debt financing could give a boost to private funding. PDBs could also act as a platform to connect financial players and facilitate the flow of funding to small-scale projects with high risk.

6.4.3 Measuring Climate-Related Risks

Risk perceptions are important determinants of investment decisions. The more the process of repricing of risk is delayed, the more sudden and disorderly the transition will be, with potentially large implications for financial stability. Beyond recognising the importance of these mechanisms, accurately pricing climate risk requires developing appropriate tools and methods to overcome measurement challenges. This is necessary to quantify the exposure of the financial system to losses associated with the transition and to correct relative prices, eventually leading to investment reallocations in favour of low-carbon technologies.

Climate risks have different underlying characteristics relative to traditional financial risks (such as credit or liquidity risk). These are the lack of historical precedent, uncertainty associated with multiple possible transition pathways, inherent endogeneity and incomplete data availability due to poor disclosure. This means that well-established risk management tools in the financial industry (like Value-at-Risk models), which use historical record to determine expected value and risk of losses, are not suited to measure climate-related financial risks (IPCC, 2022).

New risk assessment methods are emerging to cater to the specificity of measuring climate-related risks. In particular, the computation of these risk depends on the parameters of specific transition scenarios. These scenarios necessarily rely on assumptions about how the transition will occur, making risk estimates very sensitive to the transition paths considered. This approach is based on conducting exploratory scenario-based impact assessments that enable the quantification of exposure of individual financial institutions and, more broadly, of the financial system to climate-related risks.

Alongside advances on the methodology front, progress on the data and standardisation front also needs to be ensured. Financial institutions need granular data from non-financial corporations regarding their emissions and their future transition plans in order to assess their climate exposure and understand how the value of assets will be affected under different transition scenarios. Additionally, harmonised formats of data disclosure would facilitate the processing of data to be used as input in the models.

The sensitivity of scenario-based models to the scenarios selected increases the likelihood of systematically underestimating risk. This can hamper a reallocation of capital towards low-carbon projects. Given the importance of scenario choices, the Network of Central Banks and Supervisors for Greening the Financial System (NGFS), comprising over a hundred central banks and supervisory authorities, co-developed a range of plausible scenarios that can be used as a common reference point.[5]

The NGFS climate scenarios are being used as a reference for 'climate stress tests' conducted by central banks and supervisory authorities. These 'stress tests' aim at assessing the exposure of the financial institutions under their remit to certain types of shocks by analysing the reaction of the value of assets in their balance sheets. In the case of climate, the assessment considers disruptions introduced by climate change (physical risks) and the transition (transition risks). Initial reports on climate stress tests conducted by various central banks show that there has been progress on climate risk management frameworks among financial institutions but this has yet to translate into appropriate management of exposure to climate risks (Bank of England, 2022; European Central Bank, 2021).

The recognition of the importance of climate risks and their appropriate management from regulatory authorities has been critical to drive efforts on better disclosures, provide guidance on how to account for these risks in risk management frameworks and push the financial sector to align with climate mitigation efforts.

The developments on climate risk assessment tools have motivated empirical studies trying to quantify exposure to transition risk and to understand if financial agents are already pricing these risks. Overall, the exposure of financial institutions to transition risks remains high, despite increased investments in green projects (Alessi & Battiston, 2022). As for the pricing of these risks, there is evidence that banks are increasing the cost of loans for borrowers exposed to physical risk (Javadi & Masum, 2021) and transition risk (Delis et al., 2019). For financial markets, tentative evidence indicates an increasing trend in the pricing of climate risks (Venturini, 2022). Interestingly, it seems that investors value not only environmental performance, but also good data disclosures (Alessi et al., 2021).

---

[5] NGFS Scenarios portal: www.ngfs.net/ngfs-scenarios-portal

6.4.4 Aligning Prudential Regulation and Green Investment

Section 6.3.3 discussed the trade-off between financial stability and the funding needs of green projects. A number of proposals have been made to change financial regulation, such as capital requirements, to foster green lending and discourage brown lending. However, the challenge with these proposals is to preserve the safeguards for financial stability.

Regarding capital requirements, aimed at guaranteeing an adequate level of capital to cover unexpected losses, proposals have been put forward to introduce a 'green supporting factor' to promote lending to green sectors. A green supporting factor would entail a reduction of the risk attributed to green loans. While this might create the right incentives, it would also misrepresent green projects as less risky than they actually are, which could end up posing serious threats to the stability of the banking sector (Monasterolo et al., 2022).

A more risk-sensible proposal is the introduction of a 'brown-penalising factor'. This measure would entail attributing higher risk to brown assets instead of alleviating the risk assigned to green assets. This would, in fact, correctly reflect transition and asset stranding risks and lead to a reallocation away from the assets that will be most affected by the transition (Diluiso et al., 2021). As such, there would be no relaxation of requirements while changing incentives in the intended direction.

Furthermore, to address the disincentivising effect embedded in the Net Stable Funding Ratio (see Section 6.3.3), there have been suggestions to introduce a lower required stable funding factor for green long-term funding, which would reduce the discouragement of holding long-term assets.

There is a variety of other proposals on how to climate-enhance the existing regulatory framework. D'Orazio and Popoyan (2019) present an overview of some options that have been studied by researchers. For example, a sectoral leverage ratio could limit an overleveraged position for a specific group of assets, in this case, assets of carbon-intensive sectors. Alternatively, credit limits could be introduced to constrain lending to certain types of assets or limit lending to certain counterparts. While the primary purpose would be to establish restrictions to lending to brown sectors, these limits would also act in the direction of safeguarding financial stability, by limiting banks' exposure to assets likely to get stranded.

Solutions to address the identified 'carbon bias' in prudential regulation exist and can play a role in mobilising banks for the transition by penalising brown assets and eliminating some barriers to green lending, without compromising financial stability objectives. The ex ante prudential nature of these policies is especially fit to guide the way and foster an early transition, preventing ex post reactive measures to address negative outcomes that materialise.

6.5   KEY TAKEAWAYS

6.5.1   *Allocating Investment to the Decarbonisation of the Economy*

- For the decarbonisation of the economy to happen, two major reallocations of capital are needed: capital needs to flow into mitigation and adaptation activities, and it needs to flow out of emitting activities. Green finance is still not sufficient to cover all investment needs, creating a massive funding gap.
- While carbon pricing is a necessary policy to spur the reallocation of capital into decarbonisation activities, it interacts in complex ways with the existing informational and regulatory constraints that characterise the financial system.
- The lack of perfect and complete climate-related information is a factor impeding the flow of funds into green projects. The absence of clear frameworks that help classify and screen information leads to high monitoring costs for investors. The risk of misuse of funds – greenwashing – intensifies distrust, further preventing the flow of investments to green activities.
- Allocation mismatches can emerge from (i) the differences between the available funding instruments and the needs of borrowers in terms of time horizon, risk profile and size and (ii) the existence of a home bias,

which limits the international flow of capital reducing the environmental efficiency of capital allocation.

- Green projects are typically more capital intensive and hence more sensitive to the cost of capital. Changes in the macroeconomic situation or monetary policy can thus disproportionally affect investment into green projects. Factors affecting the cost of capital, especially in developing countries, are an issue for investment into the low-carbon projects.

- Climate risk encompasses physical risk and transition risk. The challenges to the measurement and pricing of climate-related financial risks stem from characteristics such as endogeneity and the multiplicity of scenarios. They are an impediment to setting the right incentives.

6.5.2   Risks to Financial Stability

- The transition to a low-carbon economy will necessarily imply the discontinuation of many activities in carbon-intensive industries. A delayed and disorderly transition – in which brown assets suffer from an abrupt and sudden devaluation, leading to asset stranding – can pose a threat to financial stability. An early and predictable transition – where divesting and diversification of portfolios take place – can lessen this risk by reducing exposure to stranded assets.

- There is currently an implicit 'carbon bias' in macro-prudential regulation, which creates a trade-off between financial stability and green investment. The framework could be enhanced to correctly reflect stranded asset risk and reduce the penalisation on long-term climate investments.

6.5.3   Financial Policies to Achieve Decarbonisation

- The design of a strong climate information architecture is key to improving the clarity and understanding of climate-related information in the financial system. The creation of taxonomies that clearly classify activities that are or not aligned with the transition is the foundation of this information infrastructure. Standards on how to disclose information or that set ground rules for financial instruments facilitate data harmonisation and screening.

- Public development banks have extensive experience funding green projects, contributing to de-risking (by providing guarantees) and to reducing the cost of capital (through the provision of concessional loans). They play a crucial role in crowding in private investment and scaling up climate projects. The creation or increased capitalisation of PDBs with green mandates is an important policy tool to mobilise private finance for decarbonisation.

- To improve the pricing of climate-related risks, adequate climate risk assessment methods will need to be used. Exploratory scenario-based impact assessments have emerged as a new method and are currently widely used in climate stress tests. Central banks and supervisory authorities are playing a central role in the use of these methods and contributing to an overall better understanding with regard to the pricing of climate-related risks.

- To reduce the carbon bias implicit in macro-prudential regulatory frameworks and minimise the apparent trade-off between financial stability and green investment, adjustments could be made. The introduction of a brown-penalising factor or counterparty lending limits for brown firms could help reduce banks' exposure to carbon-intensive assets and foster a rerouting of funds to green projects.

REFERENCES

Alessi, L., and S. Battiston (2022) 'Two Sides of the Same Coin: Green Taxonomy Alignment versus Transition Risk in Financial Portfolios', *International Review of Financial Analysis*, 84, 102319, https://doi.org/10.1016/j.irfa.2022.102319

Alessi, L., E. Ossola, and R. Panzica (2021) 'What Greenium Matters in the Stock Market? The Role of Greenhouse Gas Emissions and Environmental Disclosures', *Journal of Financial Stability*, 54, 100869, https://doi.org/10.1016/j.jfs.2021.100869

Ameli, N., O. Dessens, M. Winning, J. Cronin, H. Chenet, P. Drummond, et al. (2021) 'Higher Cost of Finance Exacerbates a Climate Investment Trap in Developing Economies', *Nature Communications*, 12, Article 4046, https://doi.org/10.1038/s41467-021-24305-3

Bank of England (2022) *Results of the 2021 Climate Biennial Exploratory Scenario (CBES)* (London: Bank of England), www.bankofengland.co.uk/stress-testing/2022/results-of-the-2021-climate-biennial-exploratory-scenario

Basel Committee on Banking Supervision (2021) 'Climate-Related Risk Drivers and Their Transmission Channels', BIS, www.bis.org/bcbs/publ/d517.pdf

Battiston, S., A. Mandel, I. Monasterolo, F. Schütze, and G. Visentin (2017) 'A Climate Stress-Test of the Financial System', *Nature Climate Change*, 7:4, Article 4, https://doi.org/10.1038/nclimate3255

Battiston, S., I. Monasterolo, K. Riahi, and B. J. van Ruijven (2021) 'Accounting for Finance Is Key for Climate Mitigation Pathways', *Science*, 372:6545, 918–20, https://doi.org/10.1126/science.abf3877

Boffo, R., and R. Patalano (2020) *ESG Investing: Practices, Progress and Challenges* (Paris: OECD), www.oecd.org/finance/ESG-Investing-Practices-Progress-Challenges.pdf

Carney, M. (2015) 'Breaking the Tragedy of the Horizon – Climate Change and Financial Stability', Speech given at Lloyd's of London, London, 29 September, www.bankofengland.co.uk/speech/2015/breaking-the-tragedy-of-the-horizon-climate-change-and-financial-stability

Cheng, G., T. Ehlers, and F. Packer (2022) 'Sovereigns and Sustainable Bonds: Challenges and New Options', BIS Quarterly Review, Bank for International Settlements, www.bis.org/publ/qtrpdf/r_qt2209d.pdf

Climate Policy Initiative (2022) 'Global Landscape of Climate Finance: A Decade of Data', Climate Policy Initiative, www.climatepolicyinitiative.org/publication/global-landscape-of-climate-finance-a-decade-of-data/

Delis, M. D., K. de Greiff, and S. Ongena (2019) 'Being Stranded with Fossil Fuel Reserves? Climate Policy Risk and the Pricing of Bank Loans', EBRD Working Paper No. 231, European Bank for Reconstruction and Development, www.ebrd.com/publications/working-papers/fossil-fuel-reserves

Demekas, D., and P. Grippa (2021) 'Financial Regulation, Climate Change, and the Transition to a Low-Carbon Economy: A Survey of the Issues' (IMF Working paper No. 2021/296), www.imf.org/en/Publications/WP/Issues/2021/12/17/Financial-Regulation-Climate-Change-and-the-Transition-to-a-Low-Carbon-Economy-A-Survey-of-510974.

Diluiso, F., B. Annicchiarico, M. Kalkuhl, and J. C. Minx (2021) 'Climate Actions and Macro-Financial Stability: The Role of Central Banks', *Journal of Environmental Economics and Management*, 110, 102548, https://doi.org/10.1016/j.jeem.2021.102548

D'Orazio, P., and L. Popoyan (2019) 'Fostering Green Investments and Tackling Climate-Related Financial Risks: Which Role for Macroprudential Policies?', *Ecological Economics*, 160, 25–37, https://doi.org/10.1016/j.ecolecon.2019.01.029

European Central Bank (2021) *The State of Climate and Environmental Risk Management in the Banking Sector: Report on the Supervisory Review of Banks' Approaches to Manage Climate and Environmental Risks*

(Frankfurt: European Central Bank), www.bankingsupervision.europa.eu/
ecb/pub/pdf/ssm.202111guideonclimate-relatedandenvironmentalrisks
~4b25454055.en.pdf

Geddes, A., T. S. Schmidt, and B. Steffen (2018) 'The Multiple Roles of State
Investment Banks in Low-Carbon Energy Finance: An Analysis of
Australia, the UK and Germany', *Energy Policy*, 115, 158–70, https://doi
.org/10.1016/j.enpol.2018.01.009

Hirth, L., and J. C. Steckel (2016) 'The Role of Capital Costs in Decarbonizing
the Electricity Sector', *Environmental Research Letters*, 11:11, 114010,
https://doi.org/10.1088/1748-9326/11/11/114010

IEA Levelised Cost of Energy Calculator (2020), www.iea.org/data-and-statistics/
data-tools/levelised-cost-of-electricity-calculator

IMF (2022) *Global Financial Stability Report* (Washington, DC: International
Monetary Fund), www.imf.org/en/Publications/GFSR/Issues/2022/10/11/
global-financial-stability-report-october-2022

IPCC (2022) *IPCC AR6 WGIII Chapter 15: Investment and Finance* (Sixth report),
www.ipcc.ch/report/ar6/wg3/downloads/

Javadi, S., and A.-A. Masum (2021) 'The Impact of Climate Change on the Cost
of Bank Loans', *Journal of Corporate Finance*, 69, 102019, https://doi
.org/10.1016/j.jcorpfin.2021.102019

Kölbel, J. F., F. Heeb, F. Paetzold, and T. Busch (2020) 'Can Sustainable Investing Save
the World? Reviewing the Mechanisms of Investor Impact', *Organization
& Environment*, 33:4, 554–74, https://doi.org/10.1177/1086026620
919202

Lloyd, S. M., M. Hadziosmanovic, K. Rahimi, and P. Bhatia (2022) 'Trends Show
Companies Are Ready for Scope 3 Reporting with US Climate Disclosure
Rule', www.wri.org/update/trends-show-companies-are-ready-scope-3-re
porting-us-climate-disclosure-rule

Mazzucato, M., and G. Semieniuk (2018) 'Financing Renewable Energy: Who Is
Financing What and Why It Matters', *Technological Forecasting and Social
Change*, 127, 8–22, https://doi.org/10.1016/j.techfore.2017.05.021

Mésonnier, J.-S., and B. Nguyen (2021) 'Showing Off Cleaner Hands: Mandatory
Climate-Related Disclosure by Financial Institutions and the Financing of
Fossil Energy', Working Paper Series No. 800, Banque de France, https://
publications.banque-france.fr/en/showing-cleaner-hands-mandatory-
climate-related-disclosure-financial-institutions-and-financing

Monasterolo, I., A. Mandel, S. Battiston, A. Mazzocchetti, K. Oppermann, J.
Coony, et al. (2022) 'The Role of Green Financial Sector Initiatives in the
Low-Carbon Transition: A Theory of Change', Policy Research Working

Paper No. 10181, World Bank, https://openknowledge.worldbank.org/handle/10986/38028

Nemes, N., S. J. Scanlan, P. Smith, T. Smith, M. Aronczyk, S. Hill, et al. (2022) 'An Integrated Framework to Assess Greenwashing'. *Sustainability*, 14:8, Article 8, https://doi.org/10.3390/su14084431

Polzin, F., and M. Sanders (2020) 'How to Finance the Transition to Low-Carbon Energy in Europe?', *Energy Policy*, 147, 111863, https://doi.org/10.1016/j.enpol.2020.111863

Polzin, F., M. Sanders, and A. Serebriakova (2021) 'Finance in Global Transition Scenarios: Mapping Investments by Technology into Finance Needs by Source', *Energy Economics*, 99, 105281, https://doi.org/10.1016/j.eneco.2021.105281

Rempel, A., and J. Gupta (2020) 'Conflicting Commitments? Examining Pension Funds, Fossil Fuel Assets and Climate Policy in the Organisation for Economic Co-operation and Development (OECD)', *Energy Research & Social Science*, 69, 101736, https://doi.org/10.1016/j.erss.2020.101736

Schmidt, T. S., B. Steffen, F. Egli, M. Pahle, O. Tietjen, and O. Edenhofer (2019) 'Adverse Effects of Rising Interest Rates on Sustainable Energy Transitions', *Nature Sustainability*, 2:9, Article 9, https://doi.org/10.1038/s41893-019-0375-2

Semieniuk, G., E. Campiglio, J. Mercure, U. Volz, and N. R. Edwards (2021) 'Low-Carbon Transition Risks for Finance', *WIREs Climate Change*, 12:1, https://doi.org/10.1002/wcc.678

Semieniuk, G., P. B. Holden, J.-F. Mercure, P. Salas, H. Pollitt, K. Jobson, et al. (2022) 'Stranded Fossil-Fuel Assets Translate to Major Losses for Investors in Advanced Economies', *Nature Climate Change*, 12, 532–38, https://doi.org/10.1038/s41558-022-01356-y

Sen, S., and M.-T. von Schickfus (2020) 'Climate Policy, Stranded Assets, and Investors' Expectations', *Journal of Environmental Economics and Management*, 100, 102277, https://doi.org/10.1016/j.jeem.2019.102277

UNFCC (2016) 'The Paris Agreement', United Nations Framework Convention on Climate Change, FCCC/CP/2015/10/Add.1, https://unfccc.int/documents/184656

van der Ploeg, F., and A. Rezai (2020) 'Stranded Assets in the Transition to a Carbon-Free Economy', *Annual Review of Resource Economics*, 12:1, 281–98, https://doi.org/10.1146/annurev-resource-110519-040938

Venturini, A. (2022) 'Climate Change, Risk Factors and Stock Returns: A Review of the Literature', *International Review of Financial Analysis*, 79, 101934, https://doi.org/10.1016/j.irfa.2021.101934

7 Decarbonisation and Labour Markets

Different political interests have portrayed the green transition as either a great job destroyer or a great job creator. Those fearing large job losses point to specific activities and jobs that are incompatible with net zero objectives and would have to disappear. On the other end of the political spectrum, the green agenda has been promoted as a strategy for creating jobs, because it will require many new activities that have yet to be invented. These extreme interpretations tend to focus on one side of the coin.

Market economies have demonstrated their ability to adjust to large structural transformations. The sectoral composition of modern economies is always in flux, being affected by underlying secular trends such as digitalisation, globalisation and demographic change. All these have reshuffled labour markets, leading to the disappearance of obsolete activities and the emergence of new ones. These transitions have always created fears that the gross job losses would not be compensated and lead to mass unemployment. Instead, over sufficiently long periods of time, these changes have underpinned sustained productivity growth, increased living standards and maintained levels of employment. Nevertheless, the burden of such transitions tends to be concentrated on particular communities and professions, for whom the damages can be long-lasting.

The decarbonisation challenge will imply a reshuffling of economic activity of comparable nature to other macro-trends such as globalisation and digitalisation. It will create similar challenges in terms of balancing the interests of winners and losers. However, the net zero transition differs from digitalisation and globalisation because it is the result of a deliberate policy choice, with the clear objective of decoupling modern economies from fossil fuel use. Burden sharing is a prerequisite of the social and political acceptability of the climate agenda and is thus a necessary element of its success.

As presented in Section 7.2, existing evidence suggests that decarbonisation will have a small net positive effect on total employment. However, this hides many important mechanisms taking place at greater levels of disaggregation, notably across and within sectors, occupations and firms. First, there are large gross effects on employment, with important downscaling of some sectors coexisting with significant job creation in other, possibly unrelated, parts of the economy. Second, dimensions of employment other than jobs are also relevant, such as the task composition of jobs and the evolution of earnings.

Sections 7.3 and 7.4 discuss in detail the employment consequences of the decline of emitting activities and the growth of mitigation activities, respectively. These have been approached from different perspectives, leading to conceptual differences in the definition and measurement of 'brown' and 'green' jobs. The former approaches brown jobs from the industry perspective, relying on information on emissions. The latter approaches green jobs from the task perspective, identifying green jobs as those consisting in performing certain tasks that preserve or protect the environment. The comparison between the evolution of brown and green jobs is therefore not straightforward.

Many market failures hamper the smooth transition of workers between occupations and sectors. Section 7.5 will focus on the skills mismatch and the need for reskilling and upskilling. Section 7.6 will discuss the factors hindering occupational and geographic mobility of workers.

Finally, Section 7.7 will discuss policy solutions to manage the transition in a fair and efficient manner. Labour market policies need to be attuned to the needs of local communities. The choice of climate policy, for example between a carbon price or regulation, can have differing employment consequences, which need to be taken into account.

7.2 NET EFFECTS ON EMPLOYMENT

7.2.1 *Theoretical Mechanisms*

The introduction of climate policy leads to higher costs for firms, either directly through higher energy prices from the introduction of carbon prices or indirectly through higher compliance costs of regulation. The way firms respond to these higher costs depends on the time horizon and on external factors such as employment protection legislation, market structure, the relative prices of energy and labour, capital investments and demand conditions.

Over a sufficiently long time horizon, firms can adjust their production inputs. They can choose a new combination of energy, labour and capital adapted to the new economic conditions. The response of employment will thus depend on the degree to which this input can substitute for energy and how capital can be adapted.

The climate economy models discussed in Chapter 1 rely on this paradigm, where employment is assumed to adjust smoothly to ensure equilibrium. The overall effect on employment follows directly from the evolution of total economic activity, and in practice the deviation from the baseline scenario is quite small. For example, the impact assessment of the 'Fit-for-55' package, which compares reducing emissions in 2030 by 55 per cent of the 1990 level instead of reducing them by 50 per cent, predicts that total employment in the European Union will differ between –0.3 per cent and 0.5 per cent with the stricter target (European Commission, 2020). Whether the net effect is positive or negative depends on other policy choices, especially how revenues from carbon pricing are returned to the economy.

This predicted response of employment is excessively smooth because the models abstract away from frictions hindering the adjustment of labour. However, the presence of frictions will affect the reallocation of resources not only across sectors but also across firms within sectors, implying a higher overall welfare cost of the transition (Guivarch et al., 2011).

At the sectoral level, Integrated Assessment Models (IAMs) assume a smooth transition across sectors, as the emission-intensive sectors (fossil fuel energy, carbon-intensive manufacturing) wind down and the emission-free sectors (renewable energy, clean manufacturing) emerge. However, the nature of economic activity and the tasks workers are asked to perform can differ greatly across sectors. Hence, this reallocation process will not happen as efficiently as predicted and is likely to lead to unemployment.

In addition, in the short run, firms are going to face frictions that hinder their ability to reorganise their use of inputs. This ranges from the time lag necessary for capital investments to become productive, difficulties in finding workers with the desired skills and wage stickiness to difficulties in adjusting the prices at which firms can sell their output. These frictions mean that firms respond to changes in market conditions by adjusting the scale of production, known as the scale effect. Therefore, in the adjustment period, higher energy prices are going to lead to lower output and possibly to decreases in employment, through either reduced hours (intensive margin) or worker lay-offs (extensive margin).

7.2.2   Empirical Estimates of Employment Response to Environmental Policies

Empirical studies are important to understand how firms will respond to higher carbon pricing, new regulation and new investments in green infrastructure. In general, empirical research has looked at the response of employment to various environmental regulations (e.g. the American Clean Air Act) or to changes in energy prices, whether driven by regulation (such as the European Union's Emissions Trading System or British Columbia's carbon tax) or not.

In sectors directly affected by climate policy, namely the manufacturing sector or pollution-intensive sectors, employment effects have been found to be negative or insignificant.[1] Conversely, the deployment of renewable energy leads to significant direct and indirect job creation.[2]

However, this narrow focus on sectors directly affected by energy prices misses the general equilibrium effects and leads to underestimating the change of employment in the whole economy. In particular, sectoral studies do not consider what happens to the displaced workers, whether they succeed in finding jobs in other sectors of the economy. Furthermore, they do not explore what happens to firms in other sectors that are not directly concerned by climate policies.

Studies that look at effects across sectors have in general found positive results. For example, Yamazaki (2017) finds that the carbon tax introduced in British Columbia led to a small but statistically significant annual increase in total employment of 0.74 per cent over the 2007–13 period. Similarly, Fragkos and Paroussos (2018) find that the deployment of renewable energy in the European Union would lead to an increase in total employment of 1.5 per cent by 2050.

However, Stavropoulos and Burger (2020) raise a word of caution regarding estimates of these macroeconomic employment effects, which include so-called induced employment. This refers to second-order effects on all firms in the economy from decreasing investments in fossil energy plants, changes in electricity prices, higher competition for capital, changes in labour wages and changes in household income. Stavropoulos and Burger explore the literature for estimates of these induced effects and find little consensus on the direction and size of such effects.

---

[1] Hille and Möbius (2019) provide an extensive summary of these empirical studies.

[2] Direct employment effects are the jobs created due to the increased capacity of renewable energy, while indirect employment effects are related to the jobs that are created in the industries that support the expansion of the renewable energy sector. See Wei et al. (2010) for an analysis of the United States and Fragkos and Paroussos (2018) for an analysis of the European Union.

Finally, an important caveat of these analyses of the employment effect is that they generally do not take into account the cost of inaction. However, the increasing evidence of the potential damages that climate change might cause to productive systems implies that labour markets and working conditions will be negatively affected (Vandeplas et al., 2022). If the inaction scenario implies large job losses, then climate policies that lead to maintaining employment are good news.

7.2.3 Empirical Estimates of the Elasticity of Substitution between Labour and Energy

A number of studies have sought to produce consistent estimates of the ease with which firms can switch between inputs, the so-called elasticity of substitution. This parameter measures how firms move away from fossil fuels and from energy to other inputs. The values of the elasticities of substitution between capital, labour and energy are a key parameter of IAMs that drives the employment response and determines the costs of simulated climate policy scenarios.

In the short run, before firms adjust their capital stock, energy and labour display some degree of complementarity. This means that higher energy prices lead to lower energy use but also lower employment, as these two inputs need to be used together (Bretschger & Jo, 2022). However, this average effect hides differences across firms. Some firms are able to substitute energy and labour, so they increase their labour demand following higher energy prices. Other firms are unable to make this substitution and hence will decrease the scale of production and labour employed. The aggregate effect is thus driven by the shares of these different types of firms, which can vary within industries.

Unfortunately, once the response of capital is considered, existing data and empirical techniques cannot disentangle the effects of the three factors of production (Henningsen et al., 2019). This means that estimated values of the elasticities of substitution are not generalisable across industries or over longer periods of time.

7.3 DECLINE OF EMITTING ACTIVITIES AND DEFINITION OF BROWN JOBS

Estimating the gross job losses resulting from the transition is a complex task for three reasons. First, it is difficult to pinpoint which jobs are directly responsible for emissions and hence which activities will have to be fully terminated. Second, in many industries the process responsible for emissions can be adapted, leading to a transformation of jobs, especially within firms, rather than their destruction. Finally, it is difficult to disentangle the effects of decarbonisation from other structural changes, such as technological change, which will also significantly impact labour markets in the coming years. For example, digitalisation will transform production processes of firms and affect workers, but its interaction with decarbonisation, especially as an enabling factor, is difficult to predict.

7.3.1 The Definition of Brown Jobs

Intuitively, brown jobs are those whose performance results in emissions. These can result either from the production process itself (e.g. electricity generation, steel, cement, transport) or from the use of the goods produced (e.g. coal, cars).

Emissions from the production process are easier to measure than emissions resulting from the use of goods. Data collected by national statistical offices measures emissions at the industry level, as shown in Figure 7.1. The most emitting sectors are the coke and petroleum industry, the generation of electricity and heat, transport (especially maritime and air transport), manufacturing of non-metal products, which covers cement, manufacturing of metals, especially steel and aluminium, mining and finally agriculture.

Measuring the jobs associated with the production goods responsible for large emissions is much more complex. It requires measuring the emissions resulting from goods. But more importantly, it requires linking their production to jobs across the whole supply chain. However, as Figure 7.1 suggests, the production process

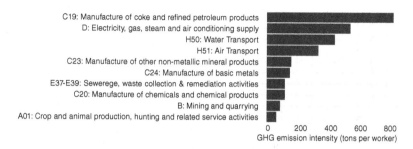

FIGURE 7.1 Ten industries with the highest greenhouse gas emissions per worker in EU27 as of 2019
Source: Authors' calculations based on Eurostat (2019).

(e.g. mining) of a polluting good (e.g. coal) is not necessarily the stage at which most emissions happen. In the case of coal, the emissions arrive further down the supply chain, in the production of electricity and heat (see the discussion of the coal mining industry in Box 7.1). Input–Output Tables offer the potential to have a more precise understanding on where emissions emerge in supply chains.[3] They have been used to calculate the carbon content embedded in final products (Guilhoto et al., 2022).

The definition and measurement of brown jobs rely on this sectoral analysis and take into account all employment in industries considered brown. However, this ignores the occupational make-up of employment and has implications for the reallocation of workers across industries. For example, some functions, such as management or accounting, are easily transferable across industries, a fortiori from emitting industries to others. On the contrary, some activities in brown industries are central to that industry's activity and might not be easily transferable. The 'closeness' of brown jobs to other jobs will be discussed in more detail in Section 7.5.

Furthermore, jobs are likely to disappear in industries that produce goods whose use results in high emissions, even if the production process of these goods emits little. The successful decarbonisation of

---

[3] Input–Output Tables nevertheless suffer from limited international coverage.

BOX 7.1   Coal mining as a case study of a declining industry

The coal mining industry is emblematic of an industry destined to disappear during the green transition. While its link to decarbonisation has been overblown, it does showcase the long-lasting damages resulting from the disappearance of a region's main economic activity.

In the United States and in Europe, employment in coal mining has been on a steady decline over multiple decades. Figure B7.1.1 shows that the American coal mining industry saw the largest employment losses in the 1950s and 1960s, and the remaining employment in this industry in 2020 is around 50,000. This drop is driven by several secular trends, notably the decline in the use of coal in energy generation, productivity improvements resulting from technological change and increased imports enabled by trade liberalisation.

The important characteristic of this trend is that it is highly concentrated at the regional level. For example, across the European Union coal mining represented 185,000 direct and 215,000 indirect

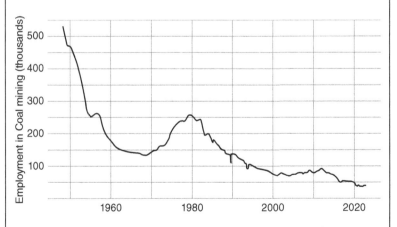

FIGURE B7.1.1 Employment in coal mining in the United States, 1946–2022
Source: Authors' calculations based on US Bureau of Labor Statistics (n.d.).

jobs in 2018 (Cameron et al., 2020). On a country level, Poland faces the greatest risk for job losses, followed by Germany, Romania, Bulgaria and Spain, in this order. On a regional level, the highest proportion of employment in these sectors is found in Silesia (Poland) and in SudVest Oltenia (Romania). Silesia could lose up to 40,000 jobs, which is about half of total employment in the region. Three other regions located in the Czech Republic, Romania and Bulgaria could each lose more than 10,000 jobs in the transition, roughly a third of total employment in each case.

These concentrated job losses create severe economic hardship in their respective communities. Regenerating economic activity in an entire region has historically proven a daunting task. As evidence from the United States suggests, even if displaced workers manage to return to employment, they can experience large drops in earnings. In particular, Walker (2013) finds that workers in sectors affected by the 1990 Clean Air Act lost around 5 per cent of their earnings each year for around three years after the regulation was imposed. This amounts to 20 per cent of their pre-regulatory lifetime earnings, with most of the burden falling upon displaced workers. Coal mining regions like the Ruhr region in Germany tend to feel the economic consequences of phasing out coal and steel for decades.

the economy requires the sale of these goods to decline. A typical example is internal combustion engine (ICE) cars. For example, an EU regulation prohibits the sale of ICE cars from 2035, with a few exceptions. As electric cars and other cars based on new technologies will replace combustion engine cars, their production will likely require a different set of skills and competencies, requiring different workers, and possibly result in shorter value chains thus requiring fewer workers overall. This means that many workers will have to change the nature of their work, shifting across different functions at the same firm, across firms in the same industry or even to different sectors, as explained in more detail in Box 7.2.

Therefore, within the set of brown jobs, there are some that are unambiguously destined to disappear, being incompatible with

BOX 7.2 **Car manufacturing as a case study of a transforming industry**

The automotive industry will be one of the sectors most heavily affected by the transition, given the significant changes its production must go through to meet climate objectives. Switching from ICE vehicles to electric vehicles (EVs) will require significant transformation of the production processes and important reconfigurations of supply chains. While the nature and quality of jobs are likely to change dramatically, they are unlikely to disappear altogether.

Lefeuvre and Galgoczi (2019) estimate that in the European Union total employment in the automobile industry will be stable, or even see small net gains. However, this will be conditional on the Union's capacity to become a net exporter of EVs and to develop local production of key green technologies, especially batteries. Strong forward planning and major investments will be needed to achieve this, as will support for workers who need to be reskilled or relocated to keep their jobs.

While this is fairly encouraging, regional distributional effects should not be overlooked. In fourteen European regions, the share of automotive employment in the manufacturing sector is above 20 per cent. Five of the regions are in Germany. The rest are in the Czech Republic, Italy, Hungary, Romania, Slovakia and Sweden. This puts these regions more at risk of losing a portion of these jobs, especially considering that battery production plants might not be located in the same regions as the ICE production plants that are shut down. The map of Figure B7.2.1 shows regional shares of employment in the automobile industry and the location of ICE manufacturing plants in the European Union. These plants will have to either change their production or be shut down, as the ICE has no future in a carbon-neutral European Union. This leaves regions with an ICE plant more at risk of significant job losses.

For activities that are going to transform rather than disappear, the issue of geographic concentration is less pressing. The main challenge in this case is enabling the transformation of activity.

This will happen through a mix of firms managing their employees' transformation using internal labour markets and an effective reallocation of workers across firms. In particular, firms with innovative green processes should be allowed to grow and increase green employment. Policymakers should be conscious of how various regulatory measures constrain this process.

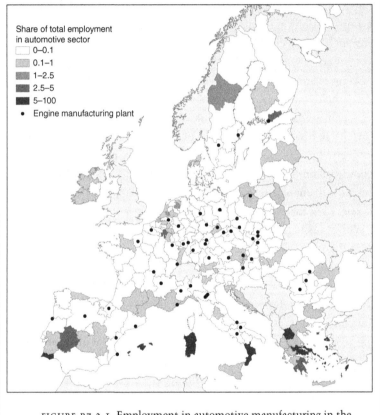

FIGURE B7.2.1 Employment in automotive manufacturing in the European Union
Source: Authors' calculations based on European Commission (2018b) and Eurostat.

net zero emissions, while others are likely to transform. The former tend to be those associated with specific emitting goods, especially the extraction of fossil fuels. The latter is a much broader

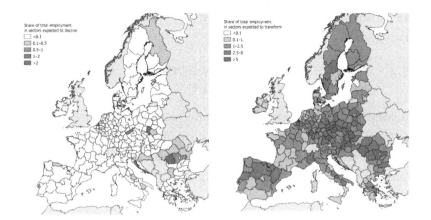

FIGURE 7.2 Location of 'at-risk' jobs in the European Union; share of employment in sectors expected to decline (LHS) and expected to transform (RHS)
Notes: As defined by the European Commission (2018b), the sectors expected to decline are (i) mining and coal and lignite, (ii) extraction of crude petroleum and (iii) natural gas, and the sectors expected to transform are (i) the manufacture of chemicals and chemical products, (ii) the manufacture of other non-metallic mineral products, (iii) the manufacture of basic metals and (iv) the manufacture of motor vehicles, trailers and semi-trailers.
Source: Authors' calculations based on European Commission (2018b) and Eurostat.

category, covering jobs in industries that currently emit but where production process can be altered to meet the net zero targets. Figure 7.2 shows estimates of these two types for the European Union. The left panel shows the distribution of jobs expected to decline, and the right panel shows the distribution of jobs expected to transform.

Sectors expected to decline employ a much smaller number of workers than those expected to transform (Cameron et al., 2020). For example, in the European Union, sectors expected to decline accounted for around 338,000 jobs in 2018, or 0.15 per cent of total employment. The vast majority of jobs in these industries will disappear during the transition, putting workers at a high risk of unemployment. Sectors expected to transform employed around

19 million (8.47 per cent of total employment) workers across the European Union in 2018.

7.4   GROWTH OF MITIGATION ACTIVITIES AND THE DEFINITION OF GREEN JOBS

Achieving decarbonisation will require performing a vast array of mitigation activities, each requiring the input of workers, in one shape or the other – be it installing renewable capacity, renovating buildings to improve their energy efficiency, designing and manufacturing new products, adapting business processes and so on. Hence, 'green jobs', namely the jobs associated with this collection of activities, is a nebulous concept to define.

A starting point is the definition of the United Nations Environment Programme (UNEP) proposed in 2018:

> Green jobs are work in agricultural, manufacturing, research and development (R&D), administrative, and service activities that contribute substantially to preserving or restoring environmental quality. Specifically, but not exclusively, this includes jobs that help to protect ecosystems and biodiversity; reduce energy, materials, and water consumption through high efficiency strategies; decarbonize the economy; and minimize or altogether avoid generation of all forms of waste and pollution. (UNEP, 2018)[4]

Several approaches have been used to operationalise this definition and measure green jobs. Many studies looking at job creation from decarbonisation have focused on the narrow and easy to define the energy sector. For a broader definition of green jobs, two main perspectives have been used: a top-down approach identifying 'green' industries (beyond energy) and counting employment in these industries; and a bottom-up approach looking at the content of jobs and counting jobs that perform 'green' tasks.

---

[4] Additionally, this definition encompasses the need for these jobs to be 'decent', namely to pay fair wages, to ensure gender equality in the workplace and to provide the freedom to organise and participate in the decision-making of the firm.

7.4.1 Jobs in the Energy Sector

One consistent finding is that the energy transition out of fossil fuels towards renewable sources of energy will lead to employment creation in the energy sector. This is because renewable energy is more labour intensive than fossil fuels. Wei et al. (2010) document that in the United States non-fossil-fuel activities (renewable energy, energy efficiency, carbon capture and storage, and nuclear power) create more jobs per unit energy than coal and natural gas. Fragkos and Paroussos (2018) confirm this result for the European Union. They find that renewable energy technologies are on average more labour intensive and have a higher domestic job content relative to fossil fuels. The low-carbon transition will therefore lead to the net creation of 200,000 direct jobs in the energy sector, representing 1 per cent of the EU workforce by 2050.

This trend also holds at the global level (IEA, 2022). According to the International Energy Agency's (IEA) projections, employment in the energy sector is set to grow and will outweigh declines in fossil fuel jobs. By 2030, fourteen million new clean energy jobs will be created worldwide, with another sixteen million workers shifting to new roles related to clean energy.

7.4.2 The Definition of Green Jobs

7.4.2.1 Industry and Product-Based Definitions of Green Jobs

Akin to the definition of brown jobs, green jobs can be defined from an industry perspective, for example jobs in industries that preserve and protect the environment, and from the perspective of goods that preserve the environment.

The sectoral definition of green jobs relies on measuring employment in a narrow list of industries providing environmental services.[5] This backward-looking definition produces very small estimates of

---

[5] For example, in NACE's (Nomenclature of Economic Activities') industrial classification 'A02' corresponds to forestry and logging and 'N81' corresponds to services to buildings and landscape activities, both of which are 'green'.

the share of green jobs in the economy. In the few countries that apply this methodology, a consistent share of around 2 per cent of total employment is found to work in green jobs (Elliott & Lindley, 2017). One important caveat of this definition is that it is unable to give an indication of the new jobs that are going to be created.

The product-based definition of green jobs is also problematic. It suffers from the same problem as the analogous definition of brown jobs, in the sense that it requires an understanding of the whole supply chain. But it also suffers from an additional difficulty, which is to determine whether a good preserves the environment. Whereas brown goods are those that are responsible for emissions, green goods are those responsible for avoided emissions. This depends entirely on the counterfactual.

Car manufacturing represents a useful illustrative example. EVs are responsible for emissions, at the production stage and depending on the energy mix of electricity production. Hence, the extent to which EVs are a 'green' product is heavily dependent on the goods they replace. In this case, it is assumed that the counterfactual is the widespread sale and use of ICEs. But alternative counterfactuals with even fewer emissions, such as the widespread deployment of public transport, car-sharing and cycling, are also possible and would lead to a different assessment of how green EVs are.

7.4.2.2   Task-Based Definition of Green Jobs
Another operational definition of green jobs has approached the question from a task perspective, looking at what workers do on the job (Vona et al., 2018, 2019). In practice, this definition heavily relies on the O*NET (Occupational Information Network) database. This database, maintained by the US Department of Labor, collects information on the skills needed and the tasks performed in each of the 912 different occupations of the US labour market.[6]

---

[6] The information in the O*NET database is collected from two primary sources: a sample of incumbent workers and occupational analysts. Workers are asked about their tasks and work activities. Occupational analysts provide a rating of skills and

In particular, researchers use a special section of O*NET dedicated to the Green Economy Program. Green jobs are measured in two ways: using binary categories and using a continuous measure of the share of green tasks in a job.

The binary indicator is provided by O*NET experts who identify three groups of occupations:

1. New and emerging green occupations: this is the narrowest definition of green occupations, exclusively dedicated to green tasks.
2. Green occupations with enhanced skill requirements: these are occupations that will experience substantial changes in their task composition or skills required.
3. Increased demand occupations: these are occupations whose task profile will not change significantly but whose demand will increase.

The continuous indicator is an extension of the binary classification, which creates a continuous variable measuring the share of green tasks for each occupation. Green tasks are identified as those tasks that are unique to the first two categories in the list. As for all occupations, these perform a range of other tasks, some of which are very general and performed by many other occupations. The index measures the share of green tasks in the total list of tasks performed by these occupations. Table 7.1 provides a few examples of occupations with differing levels of greenness identified in the O*NET database. Using this spectrum of 'greenness' of an occupation, it transpires that few occupations are entirely green (Bowen et al., 2018).

This task-based methodology links intuitively to an analysis of skill requirements of green jobs, in comparison to brown and neutral jobs. Anticipating the discussion of Section 7.5, transitioning from a non-green occupation to one with low greenness will be all the easier, as fewer tasks will need to be added to a worker's job description, implying limited needs for reskilling.

abilities required for a job based on the job descriptions they receive. O*NET argues that analysts know the skill side better, but workers are the best source of information about day-to-day activities.

Table 7.1 *Examples of green occupations by level of greenness*

	Greenness = 1	Greenness between .5 and .3	Greenness < .3
Green enhanced occupations	Environmental engineers, environmental science technicians, hazardous material removers	Aerospace engineers, atmospheric and space scientists, automotive speciality technicians, roofers	Construction workers, maintenance and repair workers, inspectors, marketing managers
New and emerging occupations	Wind energy engineers, fuel cell technicians, recycling coordinators	Electrical engineering occupations, biochemical engineers, supply chain managers, precision agriculture technicians	Traditional engineering occupations, transportations planners, compliance managers

Source: Authors' calculations based on Vona et al. (2018).

7.4.2.3   Vacancy-Based Definition of Green Jobs

Finally, researchers are exploring other methodologies to measure green jobs. The use of job vacancies has gained favour with some researchers (Curtis & Marinescu, 2022; Saussay et al., 2022) because vacancies offer the most up-to-date information on the needs of employers. This methodology is particularly useful to identify emerging trends, especially in the task composition and skill requirements of green jobs.

7.4.3   Estimates of Green Employment

Given these differing definitions, it is difficult to establish a coherent picture of the number of green jobs that currently exist in the economy and to obtain reliable predictions of the future number of green jobs.

Industry-based measures suggest that around 2 per cent of employment is in green jobs, in both the United States and the European Union.

The task-based definition suggest that in 2014 19.4 per cent of jobs in the United States could be classified as green, with 1.2 per cent working in new and emerging green occupations, 9.1 per cent in green occupations with enhanced skills,[7] and a further 9.1 per cent in increased demand occupations (Bowen et al., 2018). Applying a similar methodology to the European Union suggests that in 2016 total green employment was 40 per cent, with 17.4 per cent working in the narrowly defined new and emerging green occupations (Bowen & Hancké, 2019).

The methodology based on job vacancies tends to be much narrower, focusing on specific activities. For example, Curtis and Marinescu (2022) focus on vacancies in the solar and wind installation industries and find that in the United States in 2019 these represented 52,500 and 13,500 jobs respectively. Using a similar method, Saussay et al. (2022) find that around 1.3 per cent of vacancies in the United States concerned 'low-carbon' jobs.

7.4.4 Neutral Jobs

An important consideration of this discussion is that most jobs in the economy can be considered 'neutral'. These are jobs that are not responsible for high emissions and do not require the performance of green tasks (IMF, 2022). They represent the majority of jobs in advanced economies, and the pool from which workers for green jobs are likely to come and into which workers leaving brown jobs are likely to go.

As Figure 7.3 illustrates, in the European Union, activities such as electricity production, transport, manufacturing, agriculture and

---

[7] These two categories together represent direct green jobs, amounting to 10.3 per cent of US employment, in 2014.

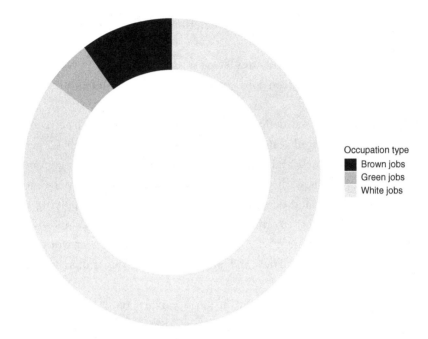

FIGURE 7.3 Differential impact of the green transition on the labour market
Source: Authors' calculations based on Bowen et al. (2018) and Vandeplas et al. (2022).

mining sectors together produce about 90 per cent of all CO_2 emissions but account for less than 25 per cent of employment (IMF, 2022). Conversely, construction, wholesale, retail and other services together employ more than 75 per cent of the workforce while generating less than 12 per cent of CO_2 emissions (European Commission, 2018a).

7.4.5 Characteristics of Green Jobs

One important takeaway from the existing research on green jobs is that these are associated with desirable characteristics. For example, green jobs tend to be held by workers who earn higher income, are more skilled, are less subject to automation (Consoli et al., 2016) and live in urban areas (IMF, 2022). However, this research merely highlights the selection into green jobs, rather than identify specific mechanisms that would explain these correlations.

Nevertheless, one result that seems to have gathered rather robust evidence is the fact that green jobs earn a premium, especially compared to brown jobs. This seems to be robust to controlling for the characteristics listed earlier. For example, the International Monetary Fund (IMF, 2022) finds that even after controlling for worker characteristics, workers in green occupations have around 7 per cent higher earnings. Curtis and Marinescu (2022) find that occupations in the solar and wind industries in the United States earn 15 per cent and 5.5 per cent more than similar occupations, also controlling for worker characteristics.

Given these characteristics of green jobs, especially the persistent wage premium, one important policy objective is to ensure that there are no labour shortages hindering the fast deployment of green technologies, to ensure the transition happens on time and cost efficiently.

7.5 MANAGING TRANSITIONS

The green transition will make thousands of workers redundant while at the same time creating many opportunities. Ensuring a rapid, efficient and fair transition requires finding opportunities for displaced workers, in green or non-green activities, and finding workers for firms involved in mitigation activities. Managing transitions between these activities requires overcoming barriers to occupational and geographic mobility.

7.5.1 The Skills Mismatch

This section discusses what are the skills needed in green jobs and what are the skills of current workers in brown occupations at risk of being displaced. This helps us to understand to what extent the green transition will require investments to increase the general skill level and to change the composition of skills.

7.5.1.1 Vertical Matching of Skills

A strong consensus emerges that green occupations are high-skilled occupations, namely managers, business and finance executives, computer and mathematics specialists, architects and engineers, and life, physical and social scientists.[8] Consequently, they are occupied by workers with higher levels of education and more experience. This is consistent with the wage premium documented in Section 4.4. In particular, Vona et al. (2018) find that stricter environmental regulations have been skill-biased, leading to higher demand for high-skilled workers and decreased demand for low-skilled workers.

This skill bias can be due to the relative infancy of many green technologies and business models (Vona et al., 2018). The skill-bias technical change hypothesis postulates that at the onset of a new wave of technological change the demand for high-skilled workers initially increases but subsequently dissipates inasmuch as codification facilitates the use of new technologies by more workers (Aghion et al., 2002; Vona & Consoli, 2015).[9] By analogy, the early stage of development of most green technologies can explain this observed demand for highly skilled workers.

Many occupations in brown activities, especially in fossil fuel energy, are also better skilled than average. For example, the IEA documents that the share of high-skilled workers in the energy sector is 45 per cent, compared to 25 per cent in the rest of the economy. Within this already high-skilled sector, green energy is attracting many researchers to develop new energy technologies (IEA, 2022).

Hence, in the initial phase of the green transition, economies will need many workers with high qualifications, of the type provided in the education system rather than on the job. One important policy implication is thus that education systems need to anticipate the need for skills. Furthermore, displaced workers from brown sectors have a skill level that places them closer to the needs of green jobs than the average worker in the economy.

---

[8] These correspond to occupational groups 11, 13, 15, 17 and 19 in the US classification of industries.

[9] However, as this hypothesis suggests, empirical evidence derived from observing the current state of deployment of green technologies might not be reflective of trends as the transition advances.

7.5.1.2 Horizontal Matching of Skills

Managing the transition of workers across brown and green activities also requires a horizontal match in the composition of skills and tasks, between green, brown and neutral occupations. Evidence suggests that on average, within skills groups, the composition of tasks performed in green, brown and neutral occupations displays important overlap, with green and brown jobs being closer to each other than to neutral jobs (Bowen et al., 2018; Vona et al., 2018).

In particular, using the 'greenness' index described earlier, Vona et al. (2018) identify the general (i.e. not green-specific) tasks performed by occupations with a high green index. They find that the most prominent general tasks of green occupations are engineering and technical skills, operations management, monitoring and science, in order of importance.[10] These are general skills already prevalent in the labour market, suggesting that adding certain green tasks to existing occupations in other sectors of the economy is manageable.

For example, IEA (2022) reports that workers in coal and other fossil fuels have many of the skills needed to fill positions in growing clean energy sectors and that employment in these industries represents thirty-two million jobs globally today. Companies have an important role to play in managing this transition, because they have an incentive to retain talent. They are best placed to transfer their workers to the low-carbon segments of their business, as needs arise.

Although all this evidence appears rather encouraging, the IEA warns that this is not an option in all industries and all companies. The coal mining industry stands out as an area requiring attention from policymakers to ensure a just transition for affected workers.

---

[10] Engineering-related skills are needed to supply and maintain renewable energy devices and energy-efficient products. Climate-friendly operation management is important in increasing energy efficiency of firms (Martin et al., 2012) and implementing other environmentally friendly measures at the firm's level. Monitoring of compliance with regulatory standards will be increasingly needed to ensure that firms act accordingly with environmental goals set by policymakers. Lastly, application of general science is needed to accelerate green research and development.

The task-based analysis of Vona et al. (2018) also identifies extraction workers, as well as construction workers, as worthy of further scrutiny. Among the group of low-skilled occupations, these particular exceptions display a large skill gap between brown and green jobs, suggesting that workers displaced by environmental regulation in these jobs may face particular challenges finding new employment.

7.5.2 Funding Reskilling and Upskilling

Decarbonisation will require a general increase in the skill level of the workforce and a shift in the skill composition of particular target groups. The question that arises is thus to what extent will firms and workers have enough private incentives to invest in these skills and whether public efforts will be needed.

As discussed in Box 7.3, economic theory predicts that firms and workers will invest in training to the extent that they can appropriate the rents created by the productivity gains. Hence, the extent to which firms will be involved in re- and upskilling programmes

---

BOX 7.3   Funding of general and firm-specific skills

Labour economists distinguish between two types of skills: general and firm-specific skills. Acquiring general skills improves a worker's productivity across all firms, whereas acquiring a firm-specific skill improves productivity only in a given firm (Becker, 1964).

The question of who, of the worker and of the firm, has an incentive to fund the training costs depends on the respective bargaining positions of the two actors and how they will split the surplus created by the additional training. The easier it is for a worker to transfer their skills to other firms, especially to competitors, the less inclined an employer will be to cover the costs of training. Hence, in a perfectly competitive market, firms have little incentive to provide general training. But they will have some incentive to provide firm-specific training, depending again on the ease with which workers can find alternative opportunities. In the presence of monopsony power, which increases their bargaining power, firms will have an incentive to fund general skills (Acemoglu & Pischke, 1999).

Firms can have an incentive to participate in training costs irrespective of the type of skills in the following circumstances:

1. Transaction costs in search and matching in the labour market increase the market power of employers.
2. Asymmetric information between the current employer and other employers in the market limits the outside options of workers.
3. Effort monitoring costs, which reduce wages, also induce firms to invest in training.
4. The interaction between specific and general skills might lead to even higher productivity gains.
5. Labour market policies such as minimum wages and institutions (e.g. labour unions) can increase the incentives of firms to engage in training.

depends on how transferable green skills are across firms. One can expect heavier involvement of firms in the specific skills identified earlier compared to the green general skills.

Additionally, the incentives that workers have to invest in training also matter and will be determined by factors such as the perceived likelihood of finding employment in new occupations, geographic mobility, credit constraints and cultural norms.

Finally, the argument for public provision of training rests on the presence of social externalities from workers acquiring green skills. This is not a discussion limited to the context of the green transition, and the case for the public provision of education and training has already been made. The global positive externality from achieving decarbonisation and mitigating climate change only reinforces these arguments.

7.6 BARRIERS TO MOBILITY

7.6.1 Barriers to Occupational Mobility

Bachmann et al. (2020) document that the baseline rate of occupational mobility in Europe is 3 per cent, that is 3 per cent of workers change occupations every year. This tends to be associated with job changes: in around 50 per cent of the times workers change jobs, they also change their occupations. However, this average masks very different work histories. Across the European Union, around 50 per cent of occupation changes are voluntary and tend to be associated with wage gains. But around 35 per cent of occupation changes are involuntary and accompanied by a fall in earnings.

It remains unclear whether the green transition will require that workers change jobs at a faster rate and whether the proportions of voluntary and involuntary occupational changes will stay stable. What is clear is that the green transition will require many workers to change what they are doing, and hence factors that slow down occupational mobility will be detrimental to achieving the climate objectives.

Bachmann et al. (2020) further explore the factors that predict occupational mobility. At the individual level, age and education explain occupational mobility. But across countries, labour market institutions, especially the stringency of Employment Protection Laws (EPL), explain differences in occupational mobility. However, employment protection seems to have an indirect impact on occupational mobility – that is, the negative correlation between occupational mobility and employment protection is driven by the probability to make a job change with an associated occupational change, rather than by the probability to make an occupational change given a job change.

By dampening the rate of job turnover, and thereby the rate of occupational changes, high EPL will hinder the ability of countries to adapt to structural transformations that require occupational changes, such as the green transition.

7.6.2 Barriers to Geographic Mobility

Geography plays an important role. The geographic distribution of economic activity is determined both by exogenous factors such as the availability of natural resources and endogenous factors such as the availability of economic resources, strongly driven by agglomeration effects.

The location of electricity generation, be it brown or green, is to a large extent determined by resource availability, both fossil fuels and renewable sources (wind, solar, hydro). Hence, the switch out of fossil fuels to renewable electricity will imply a relocation of activity across space.

However, the decarbonisation of other economic activities, such as industrial activity or transport services, will be linked to the existing presence of economic activity. The geographical reallocation is thus much more difficult to predict, as it will depend on the presence of physical and human capital. Nevertheless, it is expected that certain areas will see a sharp decline in activity while others see booms, implying some amount of geographic reallocation of resources.

The extent of co-location of declining fossil fuel activities and growing green activities is an empirical question, one that has not been resolved conclusively. On the one hand, evidence for the United States finds a positive correlation between these two activities, suggesting that geographic mobility will not be an important barrier (Curtis & Marinescu, 2022). On the other, this pattern might be specific to the United States, driven by the presence of both oil and solar industries in Texas. Looking across the Organisation for Economic Co-operation and Development (OECD), Botta (2019) confirms that the employment effect of the low-carbon transition is likely to be geographically concentrated, as carbon-intensive sectors like coal mining are centralised and clustered. He also finds that the jobs created by the transition will not be located in these same regions. As such, labour mobility packages are crucial to helping transfer workers towards new employment opportunities.

Capital can be relatively easily shifted as typical amortisation of existing capital stocks require new investments every ten to twenty years. Workers face many barriers when it comes to relocation, even across small distances, let alone across countries, including family and social ties and access to housing. Evidence for the United States and Europe suggest that the number of workers who change their region of residence ranges between 1 per cent and 3 per cent. Mobility in the United States is estimated to be higher than in Europe.

7.7   POLICY DISCUSSION

In 2015, the International Labour Organisation set out 'Guidelines for a Just Transition towards Environmentally Sustainable Economies and Societies for All', in which it called for active labour market policies to 'help enterprises and workers in the anticipation of changing labour market demands in the context of the transition' and social protection policies to increase 'resilience and [safeguard] populations against the impacts of economic and environmental vulnerabilities and shocks' (ILO, 2015: 16, 17). Having effective and well-targeted labour and welfare policies that are mutually reinforcing is the cornerstone of any just transition; the challenge is calibrating them so they adequately support workers and do not reproduce or create any inequalities.

An example of this is the task force on the just transition for Canadian Coal Power Workers and Communities, one of the first of its kind, mandated by the government of Canada in April 2018. This task force visited fifteen different communities across Alberta, Saskatchewan, New Brunswick and Nova Scotia, toured mines and plants, met with workers and held public engagement sessions. The list of recommendations emerging from this local consultation includes a pension bridging programme for workers close to retirement, income support for transitioning workers until they find another job, the availability of education and skills building services, and aid for re-employment and mobility.

7.7.1   Meeting the Skill Needs of the Green Transition

Effective skills policies are essential to meeting both social objectives of the green transition: managing the reconversion of displaced workers and avoiding a skills shortage in green activities.

Based on a review of worker training programmes, Sartor (2018) recommends that worker transfer programmes and on-the-job training be favoured over retraining programmes and that when the latter need to be used they target workers who are considered most likely to succeed – that is generally younger workers or those with some form of secondary education (Sartor, 2018). Additionally, workers should not just receive income compensation while they retrain and/ or look for another job; it is also important that they are able to keep their health and pension benefits (Barrett, 2001). All of these policies provide workers with a strong social safety net, giving them the tools and the backing needed to transition away from their previous employment, into new and potentially greener industries.

7.7.2 *How Effective Are Reskilling Policies?*

A systematic review of retraining programmes globally by Kluve et al. (2019) estimates that only about one third of reskilling programmes have a positive impact on labour market outcomes, in terms of both employment rates and earnings. This low rate of success could be explained by a lack of employment opportunities, a mismatch between the skills being given and the skills needed by local employers, inadequate monitoring and revising of the training programmes, and the absence of complementary job-search services like career counselling and employer–employee matching (Sartor, 2018). There is some evidence that the most effective retraining programmes are those that are periodically reviewed and revised (Kluve et al., 2019), that target specific workers considered most likely to succeed and that respond to specific job offers and skill mismatches in the local labour market (Sartor, 2018).

7.7.3 *Meeting the Needs of the Labour Markets*

To respond to the skill bias of green activities, strong labour and welfare policies should go hand in hand with publicly available and up-to-date labour data in all transitioning areas and their neighbouring regions. By having a clear picture of exactly what skills are needed, local retraining programmes and regional mobility packages can be better targeted.

Scotland's Partnership for Continuing Employment is a good example of this type of targeted retraining. The programme was established to help reskill and train workers affected by oil and gas facility closures and gave them two training options: the 'individual route' and the 'procured route'. The 'individual route' allowed workers to receive funding for any training they chose, on the condition that they proactively contact potential future employers to verify that the training would give them in-demand skills; the 'procured route' funded training for workers based on pre-assessed opportunities and an evaluation of the needs of the local labour market. This type of policy requires investments to build local authorities' capacity for data collection and dissemination as well as collaboration with the private sector, which needs to disclose in-depth data on employment needs and skill requirements.

7.7.4 Importance of Locality

One of the central messages of the preceding discussion is that the consequences of the transition will be very localised, affecting particular communities much more strongly than others. Hence, policymakers should engage with local stakeholders before and all throughout the transition process. Not only does this allow for the creation of tailor-made policies that take local drivers into consideration, but it is also a way to build trust between the different actors of the transition. As such, local or regional authorities should generally be favoured to develop just transition policies, in close collaboration with affected workers and communities.

Interactions between local issues and the challenges of a just transition make understanding local conditions crucial, in particular with respect to the age, gender and health dimensions.

7.7.4.1 Age

A study by the OECD (2012) found that the share of older workers is generally larger in polluting industries than other industries, making it more of a challenge for these workers to transition to other jobs and underlining the need for pension bridging programmes.

7.7.4.2 Gender

One of the important dimensions to take into account is the gender of workers in the affected industries. For instance, 90 per cent of the workers laid off during coal mine shutdowns in the United Kingdom in the 1960s and 1970s were men. Reports seem to indicate that this led to a secondary effect on women's labour markets, which suffered from a crowding out effect as a result of these mass lay-offs (Botta, 2019). Some local mining regions still disproportionately employ men. In Silesian mining industry (the biggest mining industry in the European Union), more than 90 per cent of the workers employed in 2019 were men. Overall, the gender dimension might be more or less problematic depending on the composition of labour markets of the affected areas and should be taken into consideration when shaping just transition policies.

7.7.4.3 Health

As the example of Appalachia, one of the regions most affected by the coal phase-out in the United States, shows, economic transformations have ramifications across all areas of social welfare, especially health. This region is plagued by an opioid epidemic, with a high correlation between areas historically dependent on coal and areas where the epidemic is the most hard-hitting. The Appalachian Regional Commission is the authority in charge of the just transition for coal workers and communities in this region. In its 2018 report, the issue of transitioning and developing the region's workforce included discussions not only on the coal phase-out and welfare aid for workers in transition and retraining programmes but also on health challenges and ways to tackle opioid addiction on a systemic level (Appalachian Regional Commission, 2018). These issues are indissociable in Appalachia, and the just transition is at their very intersection.

7.7.5 Local Transition Centres: A Tool to Achieve a Bottom-Up Approach

Given the weight of local determinants in the just transition process, how can policymakers ensure they have a truly bottom-up approach?

During the policymaking process, this is usually done by creating a commission or a task force whose mandate is to meet with affected communities to hear their concerns, better understand the local situation and establish a relationship between them and the agency in charge of the transition.

Beyond this initial stock-taking, the dialogue between policymakers and local stakeholders should be continually reaffirmed and strengthened. As described in IDDRI's report on implementing coal transitions (Sartor, 2018), the government needs to be able to answer all the questions workers may have about their future, including how it will be ensured that they can find an alternative job or a bridge to retirement, how their livelihood will be guaranteed during the transition, who will pay for these programmes and how and, most importantly, why should they trust the transition authority? One way to provide answers to these questions and accompany workers and communities in the transition is to establish local transition centres, equipped with adequate resources and staffed with qualified personnel that understands local conditions. The Canadian just transition task force found that in Alberta, where such centres have existed since 2017, they are highly valued by the communities they operate in. They work as an information platform between potential employers and workers, providing the latter with individualised career counselling and training for job searching.

In Canada, transition centres are generally funded by public authorities but staffed by people either from the local community or from the industry being impacted (e.g. coal). They provide a central point of information for workers already under stress due to a possible job loss, providing them with support to access government programmes for social support, to find ways of retraining/reskilling and to look for other employment opportunities. It is preferable for these centres to open before severe labour market disruptions happen. On average, they stay open for three to five years, or until there is no longer a need for them (Task Force on Just Transition for Canadian Coal Power Workers and Communities, 2018).

BOX 7.4 **Case study: Enel**

An interesting case when discussing the availability of labour data is that of Enel, Italy's largest company in the electric sector and a European leader in terms of installed capacity. The company has clearly stated its aim of becoming a world leader in the field of renewable energy and has even committed itself to being climate neutral by 2050 (Enel, 2020). It also has a history of engaging with social partners and trade unions during periods of organisational change to ensure transitions are not only economically beneficial but also socially just. Enel developed the Futur-e project in 2015, which aimed at managing the closure and conversion of twenty-three thermoelectric plants and one mining site. The strategy was to involve local stakeholders to identify unique, sustainable development opportunities for each individual site, re-use the existing infrastructure as much as possible and retrain and redeploy all employees of the former plant/mine, either to a different unit on the same site or to another location. As of 2019, all workers from the affected sites had been relocated on a voluntary basis (Galgoczi, 2019). This outcome was made possible by two factors. First, the company has built a solid system of industrial relations with its highly unionised workforce through regular consultation and negotiation as well as historically non-conflictual relations; second, the retraining and redeployment were successful in large part because the company has open access to extensive information on its workers' skills and characteristics, as well as on its own production needs and employment opportunities. This allowed it to develop a well-functioning internal labour market to respond to the needs of its different units, aided by retraining opportunities and the relocation of some of its workers.

The case of Enel illustrates the significant role that companies play in this process. Their position and characteristics give them unique ways to facilitate the transition. Beyond what Enel has shown to be possible in terms of internal worker compensation, retraining and redeployment, companies can also implement preferential hiring policies for displaced workers and give out formal certifications to workers they cannot avoid laying off so they have an easier time finding training or their next employment opportunity.

Other policies may of course be implemented to foster cooperation between just transition authorities and local communities, provided they lay the ground for 'adequate, informed and ongoing consultation ... with all relevant stakeholders' (ILO, 2015) as well as create opportunities for workers and communities to make the transition their own, as the Enel case study shows (Box 7.4).

7.7.6 Acknowledging the Differential Effects of Climate Policies

Different climate policies have different labour market impacts, for example by affecting the speed at which the reallocation happens or whether firms have more or less incentives to substitute labour. Policymakers should be aware of these trade-offs when choosing between different climate policy tools, given the importance of ensuring the social and political acceptability of the climate agenda.

Climate policies cover a range of interventions, *from* taxes to internalise harmful environmental externalities *to* subsidies to promote positive externalities, the provision of infrastructure and other public goods providing environmental benefits, and other measures designed to correct market failures affecting the environment, including direct regulations where the theoretically appropriate taxes and subsidies are difficult to calculate or apply in practice.

Hafstead and Williams (2018) compare the carbon pricing with emissions standards, which work as a constraint on emissions per unit of output. An emissions standard is equivalent to a tax on emissions combined with a subsidy on the output. This implies that the price of polluting goods will increase less under a performance standard than under an equivalent emissions tax. This leads to a much lower shift in employment (both the job losses in the polluting sector and gains in the non-polluting sector) from two mechanisms. First, because the final price of polluting goods does not increase as much, consumer demand does not decrease as much. Second, because fewer workers are displaced out of polluting activities, the labour market remains tighter for green activities, so green firms do not gain as much from easier hiring. This suggests that, to the extent that policymakers want to minimise sectoral shifts in employment, performance standards (and related intensity-standard policies) may be attractive, even though they are less efficient overall than emissions taxes that finance other tax reductions.

7.8 KEY TAKEAWAYS

7.8.1 Introduction

- The green transition will represent a structural transformation of labour markets happening alongside other structural shifts, such as digitalisation and globalisation.

7.8.2 Net Effects on Employment

- The net effect of decarbonisation on employment will be small, and most likely positive. However, this hides potentially large reallocations across industries, regions, occupations and firms.

7.8.3 Decline of Emitting Activities and Definition of Brown Jobs

- As the most emitting activities wind down, jobs in these sectors will be destroyed. These jobs destructions will be concentrated not only in specific industries, notably fossil fuel extraction, but also in specific regions. Past experiences show that replacing a declining economic activity of a region or local labour market can take up to a generation.
- Many emission-intensive industries will have to be restructured rather than entirely phased out. Reallocation of activity will also happen within industries, between emitting and low-carbon firms. The nature of jobs in these transforming industries will change considerably, with implications for the mix of skills demanded by employers.

7.8.4 Growth of Mitigation Activities and the Definition of Green Jobs

- At the same time, the growth of mitigation activities will require the creation of green jobs spanning numerous sectors of the economy. Green jobs will be created in sectors that are directly linked to mitigation, such as the renewable energy sector and the construction sector. As firms change their processes to improve energy efficiency and develop green products, the demand for green jobs will permeate the economy.

- Green occupations are higher skilled and filled by workers with higher levels of qualification than non-green jobs. Education systems should anticipate this need by increasing the supply of skilled workers in the economy.

- Many workers that used to work in brown sectors will have to acquire new skills to move to other industries. In specific cases, there is a large overlap in the skill requirement of occupations in certain brown industries and certain green industries. This suggests that workers will be able to transition smoothly between these two types of activities.

7.8.5 Managing Transitions

- Green jobs will require a number of activity-specific skills. Many workers already have skills that may be considered green. However, the demand for green engineering, technical and architectural skills will increase significantly, and to the extent that training will not be provided by firms on the job, the acquisition of these skills should be promoted explicitly.

7.8.6 Barriers to Mobility

- The green transition will require many workers to change what they are doing. Therefore, factors that slow down occupational mobility, such as restrictive Employment Protection Laws, will be detrimental to achieving the climate objectives.

- A mismatch in the geographic distribution of declining brown jobs and emerging green jobs does represent a friction that can hamper the green transition. Policymakers need to observe whether job creation happens in places where job destruction is problematic and implement measures to help with geographic mobility.

7.8.7 Policy Discussion

- The success of the green transition will require locally tailored labour market responses. These can be based on local transition centres that connect the workers to employers and promote on-the-job training and internal labour markets.

REFERENCES

Acemoglu, D., and J.-S. Pischke (1999) 'Beyond Becker: Training in Imperfect Labour Markets', *The Economic Journal*, 109:453, 112–42, https://doi.org/10.1111/1468-0297.00405

Aghion, P., P. Howitt, and G. Violante (2002) 'General Purpose Technology and Wage Inequality', *Journal of Economic Growth*, 7:4, 315–45.

Appalachian Regional Commission (2018) Performance and Accountability Report: Fiscal Year 2018, www.arc.gov/wp-content/uploads/2019/02/FY2018PerformanceandAccountabilityReport-1.pdf

Bachmann, R., P. Bechara, and C. Vonnahme (2020) 'Occupational Mobility in Europe: Extent, Determinants and Consequences', *De Economist*, 168:1, 79–108, https://doi.org/10.1007/s10645-019-09355-9

Barrett, J. (2001) 'Worker Transition & Global Climate Change', Center for Climate and Energy Solutions, www.c2es.org/document/worker-transition-global-climate-change/

Becker, G. S. (1964) 'Human Capital: A Theoretical and Empirical Analysis with Special Reference to Education, First Edition', National Bureau of Economic Research, www.nber.org/books-and-chapters/human-capital-theoretical-and-empirical-analysis-special-reference-education-first-edition

Botta, E. (2019) 'A Review of "Transition Management" Strategies: Lessons for Advancing the Green Low-Carbon Transition', OECD Green Growth Papers, https://ideas.repec.org//p/oec/envddd/2019-04-en.html

Bowen, A., and B. Hancké (2019) *The Social Dimensions of 'Greening the Economy': Developing a Taxonomy of Labour Market Effects Related to the Shift toward Environmentally Sustainable Economic Activities* (Luxembourg: Publications Office of the European Union).

Bowen, A., K. Kuralbayeva, and E. L. Tipoe (2018) 'Characterising Green Employment: The Impacts of "Greening" on Workforce Composition', *Energy Economics*, 72, 263–75, https://doi.org/10.1016/j.eneco.2018.03.015

Bretschger, L., and A. Jo (2022) 'Complementarity between Labor and Energy: A Firm-Level Analysis', unpublished manuscript, https://doi.org/10.2139/ssrn.4236136

Cameron, A., G. Claeys, C. Midoes, and S. Tagliapietra (2020) 'A Just Transition Fund – How the EU Budget Can Best Assist in the Necessary Transition from Fossil Fuels to Sustainable Energy', www.europarl.europa.eu/thinktank/en/document/IPOL_STU(2020)651444

Consoli, D., G. Marin, A. Marzucchi, and F. Vona (2016) 'Do Green Jobs Differ from Non-green Jobs in Terms of Skills and Human Capital?', *Research Policy*, 45:5, 1046–60, https://doi.org/10.1016/j.respol.2016.02.007

Curtis, E. M., and I. Marinescu (2022) 'Green Energy Jobs in the US: What Are They, and Where Are They?', National Bureau of Economic Research, https://doi.org/10.3386/w30332

Elliott, R., and J. Lindley (2017) 'Environmental Jobs and Growth in the United States', *Ecological Economics*, 132:C, 232–44.

Enel (2020) 'Corporate Vision', www.enel.com/company/about-us/vision

European Commission (2018a) *Employment and Social Developments in Europe 2019: Sustainable Growth for All: Choices for the Future of Social Europe* (Luxembourg: Publications Office of the European Union), https://data.europa.eu/doi/10.2767/305832

(2018b) 'In-Depth Analysis in Support on the COM(2018) 773', https://knowledge4policy.ec.europa.eu/publication/depth-analysis-support-com2018-773-clean-planet-all-european-strategic-long-term-vision_en

(2020) *Stepping up Europe's 2030 Climate Ambition: Investing in a Climate-Neutral Future for the Benefit of Our People* (Brussels: European Commission).

Eurostat (2019) Air Emissions Accounts by NACE Rev 2 Activity, https://ec.europa.eu/eurostat/databrowser/view/ENV_AC_AINAH_R2/default/table?lang=en&category=env.env_air.env_air_aa

Fragkos, P., and L. Paroussos (2018) 'Employment Creation in EU Related to Renewables Expansion', *Applied Energy*, 230, 935–45, https://doi.org/10.1016/j.apenergy.2018.09.032

Galgoczi, B. (2019) 'Phasing out Coal – A Just Transition Approach', ETUI Research Paper – Working Paper 2019.04, https://doi.org/10.2139/ssrn.3402876

Guilhoto, J. M., C. Webb, and N. Yamano (2022) *Guide to OECD TiVA Indicators, 2021 Edition* (Paris: OECD), https://doi.org/10.1787/58aa22b1-en

Guivarch, C., R. Crassous, O. Sassi, and S. Hallegatte (2011) 'The Costs of Climate Policies in a Second-Best World with Labour Market Imperfections', *Climate Policy*, 11:1, 768–88, https://doi.org/10.3763/cpol.2009.0012

Hafstead, M. A. C., and R. C. Williams (2018) 'Unemployment and Environmental Regulation in General Equilibrium', *Journal of Public Economics*, 160, 50–65, https://doi.org/10.1016/j.jpubeco.2018.01.013

Henningsen, A., G. Henningsen, and E. van der Werf (2019) 'Capital-Labour-Energy Substitution in a Nested CES Framework: A Replication and Update of Kemfert (1998)', *Energy Economics, Replication in Energy Economics*, 82, 16–25, https://doi.org/10.1016/j.eneco.2017.12.019

Hille, E. and P. Möbius (2019) 'Do Energy Prices Affect Employment? Decomposed International Evidence', *Journal of Environmental Economics and Management*, 96, 1–21, https://doi.org/10.1016/j.jeem.2019.04.002

IEA (2022) 'World Energy Employment – Analysis – IEA', www.iea.org/reports/world-energy-employment

ILO (2015) *Guidelines for a Just Transition towards Environmentally Sustainable Economies and Societies for All* (Geneva: ILO), www.ilo.org/wcmsp5/groups/public/@ed_emp/@emp_ent/documents/publication/wcms_432859.pdf

IMF (2022) 'A Greener Labor Market: Employment, Policies, and Economic Transformation', *World Economic Outlook*, New York: International Monetary Fund, https://doi.org/10.5089/9781616359423.081.CH003

Kluve, J., S. Puerto, D. Robalino, J. M. Romero, F. Rother, J. Stöterau, et al. (2019) 'Do Youth Employment Programs Improve Labor Market Outcomes? A Quantitative Review', *World Development*, 114, 237–53, https://doi.org/10.1016/j.worlddev.2018.10.004

Martin, R., M. Muûls, L. de Preux, and U. Wagner (2012), 'Anatomy of a Paradox: Management Practices, Organizational Structure and Energy Efficiency', *Journal of Environmental Economics and Management*, 63:2, 208–23, https://doi.org/10.1016/j.jeem.2011.08.003

OECD (2012), 'The Jobs Potential of a Shift Towards a Low-Carbon Economy', OECD Green Growth Papers, No. 2012/01 (Paris: OECD Publishing), http://dx.doi.org/10.1787/5k9h3630320v-en.

Sartor, O. (2018) 'Implementing Coal Transition – Insights from Case Studies of Major Coal-Consuming Economies', IDDRI, www.iddri.org/en/publications-and-events/report/implementing-coal-transition-insights-case-studies-major-coal

Saussay, A., M. Sato, F. Vona, and L. O'Kane (2022) 'Who's Fit for the Low-Carbon Transition?: Emerging Skills and Wage Gaps in Job and Data', Fondazione Eni Enrico Mattei (FEEM), www.jstor.org/stable/resrep44011

Stavropoulos, S., and M. J. Burger (2020) 'Modelling Strategy and Net Employment Effects of Renewable Energy and Energy Efficiency: A Meta-Regression', *Energy Policy*, 136, 111047, https://doi.org/10.1016/j.enpol.2019.111047

Task Force on Just Transition for Canadian Coal Power Workers and Communities (2018) 'A Just and Fair Transition for Canadian Coal Power Workers and Communities' Government of Canada, www.canada.ca/en/environment-climate-change/services/climate-change/task-force-just-transition/final-report-complete.html

UNEP (2018) 'Green Jobs: Towards Decent Work in a Sustainable, Low-carbon World', UNEP/ILO/IOE/ITUC, www.unep.org/civil_society/Publications/index.asp

US Bureau of Labor Statistics (n.d.), All Employees, Coal Mining [CES1021210001], FRED, Federal Reserve Bank of St. Louis, https://fred.stlouisfed.org/series/CES1021210001

Vandeplas, A., I. Vanyalos, M. Vigani, and L. Vogel (2022) 'The Possible Implications of the Green Transition for the EU Labour Market', https://economy-finance.ec.europa.eu/publications/possible-implications-green-transition-eu-labour-market_en

Vona, F., and D. Consoli (2015) 'Innovation and Skill Dynamics: A Life-Cycle Approach', *Industrial and Corporate Change*, 24:6, 1393–415.

Vona, F., G. Marin, and D. Consoli (2019) 'Measures, Drivers and Effects of Green Employment: Evidence from US Local Labor Markets, 2006–2014', *Journal of Economic Geography*, 19:5, 1021–48, https://doi.org/10.1093/jeg/lby038

Vona, F., G. Marin, D. Consoli, and D. Popp (2018) 'Environmental Regulation and Green Skills: An Empirical Exploration', *Journal of the Association of Environmental and Resource Economists*, 5:4, 713–53, https://doi.org/10.1086/698859

Walker, W. R. (2013) 'The Transitional Costs of Sectoral Reallocation: Evidence from the Clean Air Act and the Workforce*', *The Quarterly Journal of Economics*, 128:4, 1787–835, https://doi.org/10.1093/qje/qjt022

Wei, M., S. Patadia, and D. M. Kammen (2010) 'Putting Renewables and Energy Efficiency to Work: How Many Jobs Can the Clean Energy Industry Generate in the US?', *Energy Policy*, 38:2, 919–31, https://doi.org/10.1016/j.enpol.2009.10.044

Yamazaki, A. (2017) 'Jobs and Climate Policy: Evidence from British Columbia's Revenue-Neutral Carbon Tax', *Journal of Environmental Economics and Management*, 83, 197–216, https://doi.org/10.1016/j.jeem.2017.03.003

8 Greening Central Banks

The fight against climate change should be the top priority of policy-makers in the coming years to avoid an environmental catastrophe. All public policies must be mobilised and coordinated to ensure the objective of net zero by 2050 is reached. As we have seen in particular in Chapters 4 and 6, financing socially desirable decarbonised activities that are underfunded needs to be a crucial part of the governments' strategy.

Central banks play a key role in the financial system, and in the banking sector in particular. The numerous tools at their disposal can influence investments and decisions about the allocation of resources in the economy. Some scholars and even central bankers have therefore suggested that monetary policy should play a significant role in the decarbonisation process. In this chapter we explore whether and how monetary policy can and should contribute to achieving climate goals.

But, first, what do we mean by monetary policy here? In general, monetary policy is defined narrowly as the policy implemented by monetary authorities to achieve macroeconomic goals, which is typically defined as price stability alone or price stability and full employment. In this chapter, we will discuss about the possible implications for, and the possible role of central banks in, the decarbonisation process more generally. Indeed, central banks have been delegated additional tasks over the years. Many central banks are, for instance, responsible for ensuring financial stability. This can be pursued partly with traditional monetary policy instruments, but also with other, more specific, tools, in particular if the central bank is also the financial supervisor of the banking sector. These different responsibilities will be affected and could also play an important role during the transition to a net zero economy.

Two main questions are discussed in this chapter: How decarbonisation and climate policies could impact the practice of central banking? And how central banks could (and should) contribute to the decarbonisation process?

As we will see, given the special role that most central banks currently play in the economy, this chapter will discuss economic issues, but it will also examine crucial questions about the legitimacy of such public institutions, which have been given a high degree of independence in pursuing a narrowly defined mandate, and how to build the right institutional framework to face new challenges such as climate change.

8.2 IMPLICATIONS OF DECARBONISATION FOR THE CONDUCT OF MONETARY POLICY

8.2.1 Impact on the Main Macroeconomics Variables Relevant for Monetary Policy

Like all other public policies, monetary policy will be affected by the radical transformation that the decarbonisation of our economies will entail. Indeed, both climate change and climate mitigation policies should have a meaningful impact on the main macroeconomics variables relevant for monetary policy: inflation, output, employment, credit growth and so on (as discussed at length in previous chapters). Decarbonisation will impact their levels but also probably their volatility as the frequency of macroeconomic shocks might increase. Will this affect the transmission of monetary policy to the economy and possibly reduce its effectiveness, making the job of central banks more difficult during this period? This is what we will discuss in this first section.

The main mandate of most central banks today is to achieve low and stable inflation, and it is likely that the transition to net zero will have some impact on their main variable of interest. There could indeed be inflationary pressures coming from three main drivers (Schnabel, 2022). The first is from climate change itself: more frequent natural disasters and extreme weather events, such as draughts and floods, will have an impact on agricultural production, which will lead to spikes, and more generally to volatility, in food prices. Given the sizeable weight of food prices in consumer price indices (e.g. around 15 per cent in the euro area), this could be an important driver of inflation. However, this will be much more relevant if climate change is not kept in check than in the scenario in which net zero is achieved by 2050.

Second, climate mitigation policies should also exert upward pressures on prices, at least in the short term. Indeed, a steady rise in the carbon price between 2020 and 2050 (as can be seen in the left panel of Figure 4.3) should result in a persistent increase in the price of carbon-intensive goods during that period. However, there are three main offsetting factors. The objective of carbon pricing is to lead to a change in behaviours (e.g. through energy efficiency) that will reduce the consumption, and thus the weight, of carbon-intensive goods in the consumption basket, and thus in the price index. And this effect could also be partially offset by the fall in the price of renewable energy (which is already visible in particular in solar energy). Finally, a carbon tax creates government revenues that can lead to lower taxes elsewhere, thereby reducing price pressure. This stands in contrast to the usual energy price shock, where fossil fuel importers import inflation with associated welfare losses.

And third, the high demand for inputs needed to green the production and the storage of energy (e.g. the metals to build renewable energy powerplants and batteries in sufficient quantity) should increase their prices significantly, especially in the short term as new extraction sites still need to be developed.[1] More generally the massive increase in green investment could lead to inflationary pressures

[1] Lithium prices, for instance, increased by more than 1,000 per cent between January 2020 and March 2022 (Schnabel, 2022).

due to increasing demand, a phenomenon labelled as 'greenflation' by the European Central Bank's (ECB) executive board member Schnabel (2022).

As far as the impact on growth and employment is concerned, as discussed extensively in previous chapters, the implications of the transition on these variables are very difficult to predict and especially to quantify precisely. There exist multiple channels that will impact positively and negatively growth and employment, and in the absence of any certitude on the magnitude of each of these effects, overall effects are characterised by high uncertainty. Nevertheless, as we have seen in Chapter 4 (Figure 4.6), in the models collected by the Intergovernmental Panel on Climate Change at least, the scenarios leading to net zero by 2050 all forecast a sizeable increase in real gross domestic product during the decarbonisation process. The average economic growth in these sixty-six scenarios is at 2.8 per cent per year between 2020 and 2050 (with a relatively low range between 2.4 per cent and 3 per cent if we exclude the top and bottom 5 per cent of the distribution). This is mainly driven by the strong assumption in most of these models that decisive green technological change will materialise and boost productivity growth so much that it will revert its secular decline of the past two decades.

The natural rate of interest rate – that is the equilibrium rate between the demand for and the supply of funds compatible with full employment and price stability – provides an important benchmark to assess the monetary policy stance. This equilibrium rate should be affected through various channels by the transition to net zero. The much-needed green investment boom should put an upward pressure on interest rates during the transition. But other forces, such as a lower labour supply or higher risk aversion, could push the equilibrium interest rate in the other direction. This means that, at this stage, unfortunately, the overall effect is ambiguous.

Finally, the transition should also affect the financial sector, which represents a crucial transmission channel for monetary policy. As discussed at length in Chapter 6, both climate change and climate mitigation policies could result in bank losses, a reduction of collateral value and higher risk from households and companies. This could impair the capacity of banks to provide credit to the economy and affect the way credit responds to changes in monetary policy (in terms of quantity and price). If this transmission channel were impaired, central banks would have to use other channels – such as the exchange rate, expectations or asset price channels – more forcefully and might therefore have to adjust their tools to ensure that monetary policy remains effective. Anyway, central banks will not be simple bystanders and should play a role to ensure that the financial sector remains healthy, given their financial stability mandate and their direct role as financial supervisor in some jurisdictions.

8.2.2 Main Challenges for Monetary Policy

As a result of these broad transformations in economic structures, the conduct of monetary policy could be more challenging during the transition for two main reasons. First, because central banks will have to take into account these changes in their analysis and will need to adjust their models and forecasting tools considerably. Second, and most importantly, because central banks might face more stringent policy dilemmas during the transition (Cœuré, 2018). Most of the time, they have to deal with aggregate demand shocks. These are relatively easy to manage for central banks because they represent a 'divine coincidence' (as put by Blanchard & Galí, 2007) as inflation, growth and employment generally all move in the same direction. This means that there is no difficult trade-off for central banks who do not have to choose between price stability and economic activity. If the economy faces a negative demand shock, central banks reduce their key interest rates to boost output and increase inflation towards the target. If the shock is positive, they increase their key interest rates, which slows down the economy and reduces too high inflation.

However, when the economy faces supply-side shocks, inflation and economic activity can be pushed in opposite directions. There are good reasons to think that supply-side shocks might be more frequent than they used to be during the transition, as carbon pricing and climate disasters could both put an upward pressure on prices while depressing activity, leading potentially to some difficult trade-offs for central bankers. In theory, knowing that their policies only affect the economy with a lag, central banks generally adopt a medium-term perspective and do not react to price increases that are driven by temporary supply-side shocks on which they have little control, especially in the short term.[2] However, despite this medium-term orientation, there is a limit at how much central banks can look through supply-side shocks if there is some chance that they become persistent, as second-round effects materialise and inflation expectations are dis-anchored and feed inflation further (Cœuré, 2018).

Coming back to the three drivers of inflationary pressures during the transition discussed previously, the first two drivers can be identified as adverse supply shocks and could thus be problematic for monetary policy. Fortunately, their impact could be short-lived especially if mitigation is successful. The last one, 'greenflation', on the contrary, would be exacerbated by a successful transition towards a green economy, but it looks more like traditional demand shocks and could thus represent less of a trade-off for central banks (Schnabel, 2022).

8.3   CAN CENTRAL BANKS SUPPORT DECARBONISATION?

As we have seen, the impact of decarbonisation on the conduct of monetary policy could be substantial and central banks will have to take it into account when designing monetary policy in the next decades. However, another essential question is whether they should support governments or participate actively in the fight against climate change and, if the answer to this question is positive, how they could do so in a legitimate way.

---

[2] For instance, when inflation is driven by rising global energy prices, hiking rates in a particular jurisdiction that is not a major energy producer should have no, or little, direct effect on the root of the problem.

8.3.1   Main Tools at the Disposal of Central Banks to Fulfil Their Mandates

Central banks have been given several mandates over the years: price stability, macroeconomic stabilisation, financial stability, well-functioning of the payment system and so on. They are also often supposed to contribute to the general economic welfare of the population, as long as it does not endanger their primary mandates. To achieve these objectives, they have many tools at their disposal.

To fulfil their macroeconomic mandate – which often takes the form of a more precise price stability mandate – one of the most common tools used by central banks is to lend money to financial institutions at a given interest rate against some collateral assets.[3] This is, for instance, how the ECB has implemented monetary policy through its various 'refinancing operations' since it was established in 1999. This influences short-term market rates and in turn the rest of the yield curve. Central banks then modulate the level of their key policy rates to influence the economy and stabilise the business cycle. This was the main monetary policy instrument of central banks in the years preceding the Global Financial Crisis.

However, with the financial crisis and the subsequent economic crisis that led central banks to lower their key interest rate to very low levels (sometimes even slightly negative), central banks had to resort to other tools to make monetary policy even more accommodative. They therefore introduced 'unconventional' monetary policy instruments. The United States, the United Kingdom and Japan rapidly implemented large-scale asset purchases[4] – a policy often referred to as 'quantitative easing' (QE) – buying various type of assets, mainly sovereign bonds or national agencies' bonds but

---

[3] In the United States, 'open market operations' mainly take the form of repurchase agreements (repos). Under a repo, the US Federal Reserve (Fed) buys a security under an agreement to resell it in the future. In practice, a repo is thus equivalent to a collateralised loan by the Fed, in which the difference between the purchase and sale prices reflects the interest rate.

[4] The ECB started its own large-scale asset purchase programme later, in 2015.

also, in some jurisdictions (e.g. the euro area or Japan), private assets, such as corporate bonds or asset-backed securities. The main objective of these purchases was to lower directly the long-term part of the yield curve and relax financing conditions to boost investment and consumption in durable goods, and thus stimulate the economy and bring inflation back towards its target at a time when aggregate demand was too low and deflation risks were mounting.

In addition to these two principal monetary policy tools,[5] central banks make use of other tools to fulfil their other objectives. Indeed, many central banks around the globe are also in charge of ensuring financial stability. In various jurisdictions, such as the euro area, governments have delegated to the central bank the responsibility of supervising the banking sector. This trend has particularly increased after the 2007–10 Global Financial Crisis. The main objective of financial supervision is to ensure that risks are well taken into account by banks both on the asset and on the liability side of their balance sheets. In order to do that, financial supervisors set capital requirements, ensure compliance with prudential rules in force in their jurisdiction, conduct supervisory review and stress tests and can generally impose corrective measures and sanctions, and even withdraw banking licences if necessary.[6]

The main question that interests us here is whether these tools could, and should, be used to green the financial sector and thus, indirectly, the economy (as explained in Chapter 6).

8.3.2   Relatively Uncontroversial Support of Central Banks to the Transition

In the framework of their financial stability mandate, central banks and financial supervisors could actually play a crucial role.

---

[5] Central banks also use other monetary policy tools such as forward guidance but they are less relevant to support the transition.

[6] In addition to micro-prudential tools, to avoid the build-up of aggregate financial risk, in some countries central banks also have macro-prudential tools in their toolboxes, such as higher requirements for banks in the form of counter-cyclical buffers, but again these are less relevant to support the transition.

Indeed, despite the increased frequency of the materialisation of physical risks in recent years (with heat waves, tornadoes, wildfires and floods), climate-related risk is a financial risk that may affect households, firms, banks and insurance companies. The mispricing of these risks could have substantial implications in terms of financial stability if it cuts across a wide range of firms and sectors. Additionally, although desirable from a climate perspective, a rapid increase in carbon pricing and a quick transition to net zero could also have negative consequences by stranding assets in some sectors (e.g. in oil, gas, and in highly carbon-intensive manufacturing). This could lead to significant losses for investors and for banks. Supervisors increasingly ask financial institutions to disclose how exposed they are to climate-related risks and to take them into account as soon as possible.

In the conduct of monetary policy, there is some technical room to take climate change into account and to support the transition without endangering the main mandate of central banks. The decisions to use certain monetary policy tools (such as QE or lending programmes) would still be taken to fulfil their macroeconomic mandates. But once these decisions are taken on these grounds, monetary tools could be tilted to ensure that environmental criteria are taken into account by central banks when designing their operations, as long as it does not reduce their macroeconomic effectiveness.

Indeed, for the moment, whenever central banks use private assets in their operations (in their asset purchase programmes or as collateral), most of them apply a 'market neutrality' criterion. This implies that the portfolio allocation in their asset purchases should mimic the average market allocation and that in their collateral framework the risk assessment is based on the evaluation made by private credit-rating agencies. The reason why central banks aim at 'market neutrality' is that they want to avoid playing an allocating role in the economy that could go beyond their narrowly defined mandate. Indeed, the basis for their independence from direct political influence is the fact that their mandate is narrowly defined.

However, the current market allocation is dominated by brown activities as negative externalities from climate change are not properly taken into account. As a result, the use of private assets by central banks' operations is also biased in that direction. For instance, the allocations of the ECB's corporate asset purchases that took place mainly between 2016 and 2022 have been highly concentrated in brown industries, reflecting that these industries were the ones most able to issue debt during that period (Matikainen et al., 2017).

It is the task of the appropriate climate policy set by governments to ensure that the market allocation moves away from brown to green assets. Central banks could, as public actors with a mandate to support government policy, take into account the market failures that lead to this brown-biased market allocation and correct it in their interventions. For QE, this would mean that, in the future, whenever this tool is used to fulfil their macro mandate, the portfolio of assets purchased could deviate from the 'market neutral' portfolio (as long as the market is brown-biased at least): that is green assets would be over-allocated while brown assets would be under-represented compared to their actual market share. The ECB already announced in July 2022 that it would go in this direction to decarbonise its corporate bond holdings, by tilting its purchases and reinvestments towards issuers with better climate performance. Nevertheless, this step remains controversial as the bank is seen by some as going beyond its narrowly defined mandate.

In their lending operations, central banks could adjust their collateral framework to take into account climate-related risks to decide which assets should be eligible and what haircut should be applied when they are accepted as collateral. They could apply higher haircuts to brown assets than to green assets to properly reflect climate-based risks. This would make brown assets marginally less attractive and less liquid and would thus result in an increase in the cost of investment in brown activities compared to green activities. This could meaningfully alter the banks' loan portfolio towards green activities (Schoenmaker, 2019).

Overall, this would mean that to be eligible as collateral or in asset purchases of central banks, private institutions would be required to disclose climate-related risks comprehensively. This would incentivise issuers to adopt standardised disclosure practices and probably act as a catalyst in financial markets.

Nevertheless, doing so would not be without challenges either, as the boundary between correcting a market failure properly and favouring a particular sector in the economy is not crystal clear. Besides, there exist many market failures in the economy and central banks have not been created to solve market failures. Some guidance from governments or elected representatives would thus be needed to clarify what they expect precisely from central banks in that regard and how supporting them in the transition should be ranked compared to other objectives (see Box 8.1 about the ECB).

8.3.3 A More Active Support from Central Banks to Accelerate the Transition

As we have seen, despite their narrow mandates and independence from elected policymakers, central banks do not necessarily have to stay idle in the fight against climate change and could adjust their operations to take into account climate-related risks properly. But should they play a more active role in the fight against climate change? Those who advocate for a more active role generally envisage two main tools to do so.

First, it has been proposed that central banks finance the transition through 'Green QE'. The maximalist version of Green QE would take the form of the central bank financing directly the investments needed for decarbonisation with monetary creation, no matter what the state of the economy is and what the monetary stance should be. A more measured version would be that the decision to launch QE should be driven by the macro situation but that all assets purchased as part as QE should be green.

However, one first issue with Green QE is that QE is a monetary instrument that is used only when short-term rates are near

BOX 8.1   **How to increase central banks'
legitimacy to support the transition: the case
of the ECB**[1]

The European Treaties confer large powers to the ECB to act on
objectives other than its primary mandate of price stability. Article
127 of the Treaty on the Functioning of the European Union
stipulates that without prejudice to price stability, the ECB shall
support the general economic policies in the Union with a view to
contributing to the achievement of the objectives of the Union as
laid down in Article 3 of the Treaty on European Union.

Over the years, this Treaty provision has often been used by those
who want to push the ECB to act in various directions. For instance,
trade unions traditionally want the ECB to pursue full employment
more forcefully, while non-governmental organisations wish the ECB
would do more to fight climate change or inequality. As a matter
of fact, the scope of objectives mentioned in Article 3 of the Treaty
on European Union – ranging from security, equity and economic
growth to environmental protection, innovation and many other
laudable EU objectives – opens the door to an infinite number of
possible objectives for the ECB.

To some extent, such flexibility is useful as it leaves open the
possibility to address new challenges. But vagueness can also lead
to inaction. Indeed, by cutting through the vagueness and explicitly
justifying its monetary policy stance based on a secondary objective,
the ECB would be perceived as making political decisions, and it
hence prefers to stay away from that.

The neglect of the secondary objectives is understandable when
considering that the ECB mandate is blank on the guidance on
how these secondary objectives should be ranked and attained. The
ECB suffers from 'democratic authorization gaps' (de Boer & van 't
Klooster, 2020), that is the drafters' failure to foresee the situations
the ECB currently finds itself in: having to decide between different

---

[1] This box partly reproduces an op-ed published in *Le Monde* and in other news-
papers by one of the authors with several other co-authors (Berès et al., 2021).

goals that all have far-reaching consequences beyond what the Treaty writers anticipated.

While the ordering is clear between the ECB's primary price stability mandate and its secondary goals, whether and how the ECB should act on these secondary objectives is unclear and subject to difficult trade-offs. Should the ECB favour jobs or climate? Sometimes using different tools to achieve different objectives could be possible but sometimes not. Dealing with such trade-offs is inherently a political task and the ECB should welcome some explicit guidance on which secondary objectives are the most relevant for the European Union in a particular situation. As former ECB board member Benoit Cœuré once said: 'Setting priorities between different objectives is the definition of policy ... and that is what parliaments do' (Assemblée Nationale, 2019, author's translation).

This is why, to add legitimacy for the ECB acting on its secondary objectives, a formal procedure involving the European Council and/ or the European Parliament could be developed in order to specify and prioritise the policy areas where the ECB would be expected to deliver.

In practice, the existing channels of accountability between the European Parliament and the ECB could be used as a conduit for such prioritisation. The Parliament could, for instance, use its annual resolutions on the ECB to vote a ranking of three top secondary objectives, and could choose to refocus the quarterly 'monetary dialogue' hearings with the ECB president to carry out regular checks on the delivery of the thus-interpreted mandate.

In this manner, the ECB could receive renewed legitimacy for an expanded set of goals. It could work efficiently, adjusting its toolkit towards a clear and politically defined set of policy objectives, guided by democratic institutions.

zero and the yield curve needs to be further lowered to face deflation risks. It is therefore essentially a tool that is used temporarily in the downward phase of the cycle. This temporary nature of QE is at odds with the massive and durable needs to finance the transition in the next three decades (see Chapters 4 and 6). Another risk with Green QE is that it could endanger the primary objective of central banks. This is quite obvious in the maximalist permanent version of using QE as the central bank would have to balloon its balance sheet permanently to fund green activities, thereby undermining the achievement of its primary price stability objective. But it could also be problematic in its more moderate version: given the limited size of the green assets' market, at least for the moment, limiting QE purchases to green assets could drastically limit the effectiveness of this tool and make the task of central banks more difficult (especially if they often need to resort to asset purchases as a monetary policy tool, for instance if rates are low for structural reasons).

Second, it has been suggested that central banks could deliberately and radically tilt the sectoral allocation of credit made by commercial banks by using several of their tools. Green activities would get a preferential treatment in credit allocation in terms of quantity available and of price. Financial institutions would be compensated by central banks for lending more and at lower rates to these priority borrowers. This could be done either directly, by having access to dedicated refinancing lines with differentiated rates, or indirectly, through differentiated capital or reserve requirements for instance.

In the euro area, this could take the form of 'Green Targeted Long-Term Refinancing Operations' (TLTROs), in which the ECB would provide liquidity at a cheaper interest rate to commercial banks as long as they fulfil some lending target for green investments and energy efficiency measures (van't Klooster, 2022). The ECB's TLTROs were established in 2014 to stimulate bank lending to the real economy through favourable borrowing conditions for banks. The main mechanism behind TLTROs was that the more loans the banks issued to non-financial corporations and households, the more attractive the interest rate on their TLTRO borrowings would be. The incentive to banks to use TLTROs was reinforced further in 2020 when the ECB decided to cut the TLTRO rate below the deposit rate, meaning that banks fulfilling lending benchmark volumes set by the ECB would be subsidised by the Eurosystem on their borrowing (Claeys, 2020). Green TLTROs' advocates envisage that a similar dual rate system could be put in place to incentivise banks to specifically fund green projects at a cheaper rate. One persuasive argument is that TLTROs already slightly tilt the allocation of credit by banks because the benchmark volumes for loans have explicitly excluded loans to households for house purchases since their creation.

In fact, orientating sectoral allocation would not be new for central banks. They have done so at various occasions. After the Second World War, when many central banks were not yet independent, credit allocation by them was the norm in developed economies. At the time, they were often considered to be the financial arm of the Treasuries and participated fully in the industrial and trade policies implemented by the state, which resulted in some sectors benefiting from a priority treatment from monetary authorities (Monnet, 2018).

This is still standard practice in some countries where the central bank is not independent from the government. For instance, the People's Bank of China (PBoC) uses refinancing lines dedicated to sectoral priorities to ensure that the allocation of credit across sectors follows China's strategic plans. In recent years, the PBoC has therefore focused more and more on low-carbon sectors. It announced in 2021 the launch of a new facility, the carbon emission reduction facility, that provides lending at a preferential rate to commercial banks which themselves make loans to finance clean energy projects, and more generally for projects that lead to emissions reduction, at a lower rate than to their other borrowers (PBoC, 2021).

8.3.4 Mandate and Institutional Setup: Limits to an Active Role

These various cases have one thing in common: they mainly happened in countries or during periods in which central banks were not really independent from their governments.

At this stage it is critical to understand more in depth the institutional setup in which major central banks in the world – the US Federal Reserve, the ECB, the Bank of England and the Bank of Japan – operate. Although institutional details and the degree of autonomy differ meaningfully, one of their common features is that these central banks are supposed to be independent from their governments. This has not always been the case, and central bank independence is a relatively recent phenomenon. But in the wake of widespread inflation in the 1970s and early 1980s, many countries decided to make their monetary authorities operationally independent to insulate them from day-to-day politics and avoid governments possibly using monetary policy to create short-term economic booms for electoral purpose or to defend particular interests, which could be detrimental to price stability in the medium term. Independence is thus a tool well suited to solve the long-term commitment problem to price stability.

The economic and political consensus that emerged at the beginning of the 1990s on the role central banks should play in the economy[7] – and that was formalised in the 'inflation targeting' strategy (Bernanke & Mishkin, 1997) – dictates that central banks should be independent institutions run by non-elected technocrats, that they should be given a narrowly defined mandate by elected officials and that monetary policy should be used solely to stabilise macroeconomic activity, with a particular focus on inflation, because low and stable inflation is considered a precondition for a good and fair functioning of the economy.

In such a framework, favouring specific sectors or activities over others in a deliberate and drastic way (and not only marginally to correct market failures) could be seen as incompatible with the independence of central banks, as these decisions are more akin

---

[7] As far as economic research is concerned, seminal research by Kydland and Prescott (1977), Barro and Gordon (1983) and Rogoff (1985) played a crucial role in pushing governments to delegate the management of monetary policy to individuals who were insulated from the government and averse to inflation.

to industrial policy that should probably not be made by unelected technocrats.

Finally, it is worthwhile pointing out that in some circumstances, pursuing price stability and supporting the transition may be in contradiction. While the last decade was characterised by a period of low rates and low inflation, the next decades may well be characterised by an economy with inflationary tendencies, multiple negative supply shocks and a central bank facing more daunting trade-offs. In such a new economic world, where rates are higher, the scope for central banks to support green goals while pursuing the price stability mandate is more limited.

8.3.5 Does the Monetary Policy Institutional Setup Need to Evolve to Support Decarbonisation?

Central banks' institutional setup limits them from playing a more decisive role in the green transition. Indeed, central bank independence and the discretion given to unelected officials on policy matters that affect the whole society is justified only as long as their mission is well defined. In a democracy, unelected and independent policymakers should not make important value judgements for society as a whole. This framework makes it difficult for central bankers to decide, by themselves, if they should use their tools to actively participate in decarbonisation in a democratically legitimate way.

However, given the crucial nature of the issue at stake, a rethink of the whole institutional framework in which central banks operate – that would combine effective climate action with institutional legitimacy – could be explored if such a change could help decisively in achieving decarbonisation. But before radically reforming the whole macroeconomic policy framework, it is important to know first if this would really help. Would it lead to a more efficient policy mix to achieve net zero? Would the central bank be the best public actor to implement these measures? Or could they be more simply done directly by the governments or by other public institutions?

Coming back to the opportunity to use differentiated rates (e.g. through 'green TLTROs' in the euro area), if we judge that reducing the funding costs of green investment is useful to achieve net zero, does it necessarily have to be done by the central bank? Actually, fiscal policy, with a combination of subsidies and taxes, could provide the exact same incentives to the private sector to fund green projects, with the same cost for the consolidated budget of the state (i.e. which combine the government and the central bank). Indeed, when the central bank offers a lower rate to banks to incentivise them to lend to firms or households – as the ECB did when it decided to put its TLTRO rate below the deposit rate, effectively subsidising banks, to encourage them to increase their lending to the real economy – this reduces the profits that the central bank makes on these refinancing operations. Given that in most countries central banks' profits are eventually redistributed to governments, a reduction of their profits should reduce fiscal revenues by the same amount.

From an economic or budgetary perspective, it would therefore be equivalent if such a measure is executed by the central bank or by fiscal authorities. But in the current institutional setup, using fiscal instruments would have the advantage of being more accountable and thus more legitimate (Goodfriend, 2014). Given this equivalence between fiscal and monetary instruments from an economic perspective, it does not appear particularly useful to delegate this mission to central banks. Indeed, to be legitimate the benefits of delegation must be substantial, which do not seem to be the case in this situation (Tucker, 2018). In light of this, it would probably make even less sense to revise the whole institutional setup only to give the possibility to central banks to put in place these measures in a more legitimate way, because revising fundamentally the way central banks operate, and possibly reducing their independence from governments, could also have unintended consequences for price stability.

Overall, the optimal solution to decarbonise our economies remains a combination of carbon pricing to change incentives (forcing all economic agents to take into account the negative externalities of

CO_2 emissions) and of fiscal measures to accelerate green innovation and the deployment of much needed green investments (as discussed in detail in Chapters 4 and 5). In addition to these central measures, to improve financing conditions of green activities, governments could act either directly by subsidising loans or guaranteeing them or indirectly through their public development banks.

These state-owned banks can provide funding at a subsidised rate for projects that are considered socially desirable and not pursued (or under-pursued) by commercial banks. Compared to central banks, public development banks also have the advantage that they can provide funding to priority sectors on a more permanent basis (and not only when the state of the economy dictates it). Moreover, even though some of these public banks have existed for a long time, for most of them, their mandate can be easily adjusted to transform them into climate banks, or at least more easily than the rulebook governing central banks.[8]

Given what we just discussed, it seems that the only reason left to delegate these measures to central banks is if governments were prevented from implementing the measures themselves for political reasons (or because they do not have a public development bank in place) and the central bank would be the only credible and efficient public actor able to do it. In that case, legitimacy is difficult to achieve as it is political reasons in the first place that prevent proper government action. A potential avenue to make it legitimate, without reforming in depth the whole monetary framework put in place three decades ago, could be to conclude a punctual inter-institutional agreement between the government and the central bank in which the Treasury would directly mandate the central bank to do this lending at a preferential rate for them. In that case, it would also probably be desirable that the cost of this policy would be directly covered by the government, so that the cost is transparent for the taxpayers. Such

---

[8] For instance, the ECB's price stability mandate and independence are enshrined in EU treaties that can be revised only at the unanimity of all the member states of the European Union.

an arrangement would probably be possible in jurisdictions like the United Kingdom in which the Treasury and the Bank of England have a close relationship despite the independence of the central bank, but it might be much more complex, if not legally impossible, in other jurisdictions and in particular in multi-country jurisdictions like the European Union in which the central bank would have to interact with multiple treasuries and in which the autonomy of the central bank is much greater.

More generally, central banks should not be seen as the only game in town. It is important to remember that elected governments are the ones that have pledged to act forcefully at the occasion of the Paris Agreement and in subsequent Conference of the Parties and that they need to fulfil their promises. Hence, relying heavily on central banks to play their part could be detrimental, as it would allow governments to conveniently shift the responsibility – and also potentially the blame in case of failure – to unelected technocrats whenever they consider these actions (however desirable they are) as politically costly.

8.4 KEY TAKEAWAYS

8.4.1 Implications of Decarbonisation Relevant for the Conduct of Monetary Policy

- Both climate change and the economic transformation induced by climate mitigation policies will have an impact on the main macroeconomics variables relevant for monetary policy such as inflation, output, employment and credit growth.
- The transition to net zero will particularly affect the main variable of interest of central banks – inflation – through three main channels: climate change itself, climate mitigation policies and the high demand for products needed to decarbonise should all put upward pressure on the price level.
- Growth, employment and the natural rate of interest rate, which all matter highly for monetary policy, should also be affected. But it is difficult at this stage to know exactly in which direction they will evolve.

- The impact on the financial sector could be substantial and should be monitored carefully by central banks, given that this is a key transmission channel of monetary policy. But central banks will not be bystanders and have a role to play in ensuring the well-functioning of the financial sector, given their financial stability mandate and their direct role as financial supervisors in some jurisdictions. If the financial sector does not transmit monetary policy well, central banks will need to think about other channels and other tools.

8.4.2 Main Challenges for Central Banks during the Transition

- Given the radical transformation of the economy, central banks will need to change their analysis, models and forecasting tools.
- Central banks might face more difficult policy trade-offs during the transition, as supply-side shocks might become much more frequent and their effects more persistent.

8.4.3 Relatively Uncontroversial Adjustments to Central Banks' Tools to Support Decarbonisation

- To correct the market bias towards brown activities, central banks could deviate from market neutrality in their tools and operations.
- When doing QE, the portfolio of assets purchased could be adjusted so that the weight of green assets is increased compared to brown assets.
- In their lending operations, the collateral framework should take into account climate-related risks to decide which assets should be eligible and what haircut should be applied when they are accepted as collateral.
- Such adjustments remain controversial and would not be without challenges either, as the boundary between correcting a market failure properly and favouring a particular sector in the economy is not crystal clear. But the measures could be undertaken without conflict to the central banks' main mandate.

8.4.4 A More Active Role of Central Banks to Accelerate the Transition?

- It has been advocated that central banks could play a more active role in the fight against climate change either through 'Green QE' or by trying to deliberately and significantly tilt the allocation of credit of commercial banks through their other tools.

- However, given the current institutional framework in which major central banks evolve, favouring specific activities over others in a deliberate and drastic way could be seen as incompatible with their independence, as these decisions are more akin to industrial policy, which should probably not be made by unelected technocrats. Moreover, such a role could directly undermine their main mandate to achieve price stability.

8.4.5 Does the Monetary Policy Institutional Setup Need to Evolve to Support Decarbonisation?

- Given the crucial nature of the issue at stake, a rethink of the institutional framework in which central banks operate – that would combine effective climate action with institutional legitimacy – should be explored if such a change could help decisively in achieving decarbonisation.

- However, fiscal policy, with a combination of subsidies and taxes, could provide the exact same incentives to the private sector to fund green projects as the central bank, with the same cost for the consolidated budget of the state, but with the advantage of being more accountable and thus more legitimate. Hence it does not appear necessary to reform the current monetary policy institutional setup.

REFERENCES

Assemblée Nationale (2019) Travaux parlementaires, 15 May, www.assem blee-nationale.fr/dyn/15/comptes-rendus/cion_fin/l15cion_fin18190 74_compte-rendu

Barro, R., and D. Gordon (1983) 'A Positive Theory of Monetary Policy in a Natural-Rate Model', *Journal of Political Economy*, 91:4, 589–610.

Berès, P., G. Claeys, N. de Boer, P. Demetriades, S. Diessner, S. Jourdan, et al. (2021) 'La BCE devrait avoir un mandat politique clair qui expliciterait quels objectifs secondaires sont les plus pertinents pour l'UE', *Le Monde*, 9 April, www.lemonde.fr/idees/article/2021/04/09/la-bce-devrait-avoir-un-mandat-politique-clair-qui-expliciterait-quels-objectifs-secondaires-sont-les-plus-pertinents-pour-l-ue_6076202_3232.html

Bernanke, B., and F. Mishkin (1997) 'Inflation Targeting: A New Framework for Monetary Policy?', *Journal of Economic Perspectives*, 11:2, 97–116.

Blanchard, O., and J. Galí (2007) 'Real Wage Rigidities and the New Keynesian Model', *Journal of Money, Credit and Banking*, 39, 35–65.

Claeys, G. (2020) 'The European Central Bank in the COVID-19 Crisis: Whatever It Takes, within Its Mandate', Policy Contribution 09/2020, Bruegel, www .bruegel.org/sites/default/files/wp_attachments/PC-09-2020-final.pdf

Cœuré, B. (2018) 'Monetary Policy and Climate Change', Speech at the conference on 'Scaling up Green Finance: The Role of Central Banks', organised by the Network for Greening the Financial System, the Deutsche Bundesbank and the Council on Economic Policies, Berlin, 8 November, www.ecb.europa .eu/press/key/date/2018/html/ecb.sp181108.en.html

de Boer, N., and J. van't Klooster (2020) 'The ECB, the Courts and the Issue of Democratic Legitimacy after Weiss', *Common Market Law Review*, 57:6, https://ssrn.com/abstract=3712579

Goodfriend, M. (2014) 'Lessons from a Century of FED Policy: Why Monetary and Credit Policies Need Rules and Boundaries', *Journal of Economic Dynamics and Control*, 49, 112–20.

Kydland, F., and E. Prescott (1977) 'Rules Rather than Discretion: The Inconsistency of Optimal Plans', *Journal of Political Economy*, 85, 473–90.

Matikainen, S., E. Campiglio, and D. Zenghelis (2017) 'The Climate Impact of Quantitative Easing', Policy Paper, Grantham Research Institute on Climate Change and the Environment, May, www.lse.ac.uk/grantha minstitute/wp-content/uploads/2017/05/ClimateImpactQuantEasing_ Matikainen-et-al.pdf

Monnet, E. (2018) *Controlling Credit: Central Banking and the Planned Economy in Post-war France, 1948–1973*, Studies in Macroeconomic History (Cambridge: Cambridge University Press).

PBoC (2021) 'PBOC Officials Answer Press Questions on the Launch of Carbon Emission Reduction Facility', Press release, 9 November, www.pbc.gov.cn/ en/3688110/3688172/4157443/4385447/index.html

Rogoff, K. (1985) 'The Optimal Degree of Commitment to an Intermediate Monetary Target', *Quarterly Journal of Economics*, 100, 1169–89.

Schnabel, I. (2022) 'A New Age of Energy Inflation: Climateflation, Fossilflation and Greenflation', Speech at the panel on 'Monetary Policy and Climate Change' at the ECB and Its Watchers XXII Conference, Frankfurt am Main, 17 March, www.ecb.europa.eu/press/key/date/2022/html/ecb .sp220317_2~dbb3582f0a.en.html

Schoenmaker, D. (2019) 'Greening Monetary Policy', Bruegel Working Paper 19–02, 19 February, www.bruegel.org/sites/default/files/wp_attachments/ Greening-monetary-policy.pdf

Tucker, P. (2018) *Unelected Power: The Quest for Legitimacy in Central Banking and the Regulatory State* (Oxford, UK: Princeton University Press).

van't Klooster, J. (2022) 'The European Central Bank's Strategy, Environmental Policy and the New Inflation: A Case for Interest Rate Differentiation', Policy Insight, Grantham Research Institute on Climate Change and the Environment. July, www.lse.ac.uk/granthaminstitute/wp-content/uploads/2022/07/The-European-Central-Banks-strategy-environmental-policy-and-the-new-inflation.pdf

Conclusions

The Macroeconomics of Decarbonisation – Between Degrowth and Green Growth

We started our journey by illustrating in the Introduction the relationship between economic growth and greenhouse gas (GHG) emissions and by discussing the historical challenge of decoupling them at a sufficient speed to achieve carbon neutrality by mid-century. The subsequent chapters then provided an in-depth analysis of the various macroeconomic implications characterising this process. At this point, we would like to go back to our initial question and ask ourselves: given all the complexities we have analysed, is it realistic to expect the world to be able to decouple economic growth from GHG emissions in time to save the planet, and by avoiding negative repercussions on our economies and societies? To do so, we will first discuss how the economic literature has so far tackled this question – namely presenting degrowth and green growth theories – and we will then conclude by illustrating our view on all of this.[1]

A LOOK AT DEGROWTH THEORIES

Guided by past experience, the basic premise of degrowth theorists is that the world will not be able to sufficiently reduce GHG emissions while global gross domestic product (GDP) grows. Current economic models, which are inherently focussed on accumulation and growth, are therefore inevitably headed towards environmental and climate disaster.

Such pessimistic views about the long-term sustainability of economic growth are not new. They have been around in some form

---

[1] This chapter is partly based on an article published by two of the authors in the peer-reviewed journal *Sustainability* (Lenaerts et al., 2022).

at least since the *Essay on the Principle of Population* by Thomas Malthus (1789). He postulated that famines and economic collapse were inevitable unless birth rates decreased, based on the belief that population growth is exponential and growth of food production merely linear. This argument was echoed throughout the twentieth century in environmentally inspired works by, for example, Osborn (1948) and Vogt (1948) and, most notably, in *The Population Bomb* by Paul Ehrlich (1968). Meadows et al. (1972) predicted in *The Limits to Growth* that global population and economic activity would peak in the early twenty-first century and advocated an economic and demographic 'equilibrium state' to avoid an uncontrolled collapse when humanity's need for resources finally exceeds the earth's capacity.

Like *Limits to Growth*, modern degrowth theories subscribe to the idea that humanity must achieve a lower economic 'steady state' to avoid environmental catastrophe. The term 'degrowth' was probably first used in the writings of French philosopher André Gorz in 1972 and in the work of economist Georgescu-Roegen (1971, 1979), who wrote that economic activity in the long run is limited to a level supported by solar flows due to the laws of thermodynamics. The term was popularised in the 1990s and 2000s by Serge Latouche (e.g. 2009) who criticised economic development as a goal. In the early 2000s 'degrowth' was used as a slogan by social and environmental activists in France, Italy and Spain. Finally, it emerged as an international research area in 2008 at the first Degrowth Conference in Paris (Demaria et al., 2013; Kallis et al., 2018), with many publications being produced particularly in the first half of the 2010s, in the context of the 2008 Global Financial Crisis and the sovereign debt crisis in Europe. Researchers including Giorgos Kallis (e.g. 2011), Jason Hickel (e.g. 2020), Tim Jackson (e.g. 2009) and Kate Raworth (e.g. 2017) are today at the forefront. Several variations of degrowth are advocated under different names, including 'wellbeing economics', 'steady-state economics', 'post-growth economics' and 'doughnut economics'.

Despite the common basic premise, 'degrowth' does not always mean the same in practice. Authors are also not always clear on exactly what should 'degrow'. There are at least five different interpretations: degrowth of GDP, consumption, worktime, the economy's physical size and 'radical' degrowth, referring to a wholesale transformation of the economic system (van den Bergh, 2011). It is perhaps better to say that degrowth covers all these interpretations. Material and energy consumption and the economy's physical size need to degrow, out of a concern for resource depletion and more recently climate change. Worktime degrowth is one tool to do so, GDP degrowth is an inevitable consequence (not an aim per se) and radical degrowth a necessary condition to make a post-growth economy socially sustainable (Kallis, 2011).

Realising the negative social consequences commonly associated with recessions, degrowth scholars indeed set out to define a path to actively 'guide' GDP downward, rather than to passively let the world slip into a depression and to cause widespread suffering. Demaria et al. (2013, p. 209) therefore defined degrowth as a call for 'a democratically led redistributive downscaling of production and consumption in industrialised countries as a means to achieve environmental sustainability, social justice and well-being'. As the definition suggests, the degrowth literature is not limited to the economy–environment nexus but is also concerned with (international) redistribution and equity, political participation, social fairness and 'beyond GDP' conceptions of welfare.

To achieve a managed transition, proponents advance a myriad of policies as part of a systemic change. We will only touch on them superficially. Perhaps the most important and common proposal is to limit the supply of production factors, most notably labour. Reductions in working hours are seen as a way to reduce consumption while increasing social welfare through more free time and achieving high levels of employment. The latter must also be supported by shifting employment towards labour-intensive sectors and steering innovation to increase resource productivity rather than labour productivity, using green taxes and 'cap-and-share' schemes (Kallis, 2011; Kallis et al., 2018). Another element is to reduce aggregate investment by firms to net zero, which does not exclude that some (clean) sectors grow at the expense of other (dirty) sectors (Kallis et al., 2018).

Other ideas found in the literature are the re-localisation of economies to shorten the distance between consumers and producers and the encouragement of the sharing economy (Paech, 2012), as well as new forms of (regional) money and limitations to property rights (Kallis et al., 2012; van Griethuysen, 2012). Some advocate for zero interest rates to avoid the growth imperative created by having to pay back interest (Binswanger, 2013), caps on savings to reduce wealth inequality and doing away with the logic of accumulation by firms and owners of capital. The aim is to arrive at a steady state in which the whole economy is consumed, which would end growth (Loehr, 2012).

Importantly, many of the proposed policies are considered by authors themselves to be incompatible with capitalism and unlikely to be implemented by liberal representative democracies. Kallis et al. (2018) therefore argued that in the absence of democratic degrowth policies a period of involuntary economic stagnation caused by climate change might usher in an authoritarian version of capitalism, unless more democratic alternatives are put forward.

Finally, it should be noted that degrowth proponents, like green growth, devote relatively little attention to limiting population growth, which would theoretically offer another – though contentious – way to reconcile GDP per capita growth and emission reductions. Where it is discussed, most authors view it as undesirable, especially when non-voluntary, and point out that the large and growing populations of the Global South put relatively little stress on the environment (Cosme et al., 2017).

A LOOK AT GREEN GROWTH THEORIES

Whereas degrowth backers believe that the slow decoupling of GDP and emissions thus far is indicative of the future, the green growth narrative is more optimistic. It is often noted that there have not yet been significant climate efforts globally, but that this need not continue. For instance, there has been a drastic decline in the prices of renewable energy technologies during the last decade. Since 2010 the cost of energy from solar panels and wind turbines have declined by 85 per cent and 68 per cent respectively, thus becoming lower than fossil fuel alternatives even without subsidies. This should change the economic incentives of governments and firms and encourage the much higher investments needed in low-carbon energy generation.

Furthermore, green growth proponents argue that suitable policies and price mechanisms can spur technological development in unexpected ways, as they have done in the past. It is therefore incorrect to say that decoupling cannot accelerate. The central role of technology was already highlighted in the earlier literature rejecting degrowth pessimism. Stiglitz (1974) and Kamien and Schwartz (1978) did not yet address GHG emissions but rather examined whether continued consumption growth is possible in a world with exhaustible resources. They found that technology-driven efficiency gains allow the limits set by nature to be pushed forward so that continued expansion is possible. Later works, including Weitzman (1999), Acemoglu et al. (2012) and Aghion et al. (2016), discussed endogenous and directed technical change with more optimistic outlooks.

The 1987 Brundtland report *Our Common Future* is seen as a milestone for green growth with its definition of 'sustainable development' (Jacobs, 2012),[2] since it lay at the basis of global ecological policy thinking of the next few years, such as at the Earth Summit and the Rio Declaration in 1992, which explicitly called for economic growth to address environmental problems. The term 'green growth' only gained popularity in the wake of the Global Financial Crisis of 2008 as an idea for short-term stimulus that incorporated environmental objectives (e.g. OECD, 2009) and was adopted as a policy

---

[2] 'Development that meets the needs of the present without compromising the ability of future generations to meet their own needs' (World Commission on Environment and Development, 1987, p. 41).

objective by international organisations in the subsequent years (Jacobs, 2012). Today it underpins the United Nations' Sustainable Development Goals, and most governments and international organisations have adopted the green growth narrative as part of long-term development policies (e.g. European Commission, 2019; OECD, 2011; UNEP, 2011; World Bank Group, 2012) and post-COVID recovery plans (e.g. White House, 2022).

Like degrowth, the term 'green growth' is not precisely defined. For example, the World Bank, the Organisation for Economic Co-operation and Development (OECD) and the United Nations Environment Programme each define green objectives differently (Hickel & Kallis, 2020). Jacobs (2012) wrote that green GDP growth is understood as either (i) higher growth than in a scenario without strong environmental or climate policies, in both the short and the long run (dubbed the 'strong' version of green growth), or (ii) lower though still positive growth in the short run and higher growth in the long run, as high future costs of climate damages are avoided by incurring manageable costs now (the 'standard' version, as found in the Stern review (2007)).[3]

Whatever the exact interpretation of green growth, publications following this school of thought promise on the one hand environmental benefits in the form of avoided climate damages and short-term co-benefits such as improved air quality (Karlsson et al., 2020) and on the other hand economic benefits resulting from increased investment and innovation. This 'double dividend' forms the heart of the green growth argument. Overall, however, the empirical evidence for a double dividend looks mixed. In fact, some of the reports by official institutions state that an economic dividend can be achieved only if very specific assumptions are made, while in many scenarios,

---

[3] Sometimes adding to the confusion is a lack of clarity about the baseline against which growth is compared: is it a trajectory based on historical average growth rates or a no-action scenario that includes serious damage from climate change in the long run? This is not trivial, as in comparison to an economy wrecked by runaway climate change, an economic scenario that avoids climate disaster yet has sluggish economic growth could still be called 'green growth'.

strong climate action could at least in the short-term lower GDP growth (European Commission, 2020).

Green growth policy plans generally rest on four pillars: (i) subsidies for innovation and investments in renewable energy and energy efficiency that boost GDP; (ii) carbon pricing to further stimulate investments in efficiency and renewables, and to avoid rebound effects, combined with the recycling of tax revenues to cut corporate or labour taxes and boost employment, or to redistribute; (iii) assumptions about innovation to accelerate the decoupling process, notably about the use of negative-emission technologies and (iv) compensation schemes for the poorest households, displaced workers and disadvantaged regions to make the transition politically feasible. The green growth narrative therefore usually still involves substantial government intervention, even if the most bullish proponents of green growth argue it will come about as a result of free markets and does not require anything other than carbon pricing.

A GLOBAL GREEN GROWTH PATHWAY IS POSSIBLE

Given the magnitude of the challenge, it is unsurprising that economists disagree about whether the world can decouple economic growth and GHG emissions at a sufficiently fast pace to avoid dangerous climate change. Degrowers argue that absolute decoupling has never been achieved at a global scale and that even countries that do achieve it progress too slowly. As such they arrive at the conclusion that global GDP must inevitably decline to save the planet.

They are right to highlight the considerable gap that still exists between the current climate mitigation efforts and available tools on the one hand and what is needed on the other hand. They point to the fact that most of the low-emission scenarios envisioned by the Intergovernmental Panel on Climate Change, which assume continued economic growth, rely to varying degrees on technologies such as carbon capture and storage, which is applied to fossil power plants, or bioenergy with carbon capture and storage, which is used to extract GHG from the atmosphere and thus compensate for earlier emissions. These technologies do not yet exist at scale and should not be relied on, they argue, since their economic viability is unproven and they could even create new environmental problems such as excessive land and water use (Keysser & Lenzen, 2021).

Antal and van den Bergh (2016) gathered a few more arguments directed against the prospect of decoupling through green policies. The most common argument is the existence of a rebound effect from investment in energy efficiency and clean energy. This means that as societies invest to reduce emissions, the increased income or savings resulting from those investments will at least partially offset the intended beneficial effects through increased consumption of non-renewable energy in another way. This can happen both at a micro level and at a macro level. An example of the former is that as cars become more energy efficient, consumers are more inclined to buy large SUVs, since driving them becomes cheaper (Cozzi & Petropoulos, 2021). In terms of the Kaya identity, this means that a reduction in the energy intensity of GDP is cancelled out and nothing changes. At the macro level there could be a rebound effect if large energy investments raise GDP *per capita* growth, which in turn necessitates even faster decoupling. Here the terms of the Kaya identity discussed in the Introduction are impacted.

In addition, there is a risk that more stringent policies could see lower compliance because of what the authors call an 'environmental Laffer curve', with economic actors preferring to cheat rather than to respect regulations as the expected cost of being caught and sanctioned is lower than the cost of complying.

A final objection is the possibility of burden-shifting: while not an issue for climate change, other environmental risks could be exacerbated indirectly by emissions reduction efforts, for example soil pollution from mining for minerals used in batteries.

These arguments show that there is indeed considerable uncertainty about the feasibility of rapid decoupling and therefore of green growth, not least because of technological questions. Yet scholars that predicted imminent collapse in the past all proved too pessimistic (at least so far) precisely because they failed to predict the significant advances in agricultural yields, technological innovation and substitution, and declines in population growth rates. Advances in resource efficiency have often been driven by market forces, such as for oil in the 1970s, when scarcity drove up prices, creating incentives for cost-saving innovation. However, technological progress is highly unpredictable, and since the atmosphere as a deposit for CO_2 is a rival but non-excludable good, purely market-driven innovation and substitution will not solve the problem of climate change (Eastin et al., 2011). The other arguments mentioned also do not seem unsurmountable given the right policy responses.

This is why, in any case, strong policies are indeed necessary. But we do not believe degrowth is a valid option. Firstly, it is hard to imagine that a critical mass of the global population will voluntarily agree to it. The level of income per capita to which rich and poor countries would have to converge is difficult to estimate because it depends on the future dynamics of the factors of the Kaya identity (how much further will the global population grow?) and the interactions between them. As average incomes decline in rich countries, will that also reduce the energy intensity of GDP due to a more modest consumption behaviour or might the opposite happen in the absence of incentives for efficiency? Would people revert back to cheaper and more dirty technologies (van den Bergh, 2011)? It is clear that at least ceteris paribus the average global income should be even lower than it is today. This will not offer much solace to poor countries that are still allowed to grow and is very unlikely to find support in wealthy liberal democracies.

Of course, GDP per capita is flawed as a measure of welfare, at least at elevated levels. One can also raise legitimate questions about its normative basis. Yet alternative conceptions proposed by degrowth seem equally flawed for the same reason. Furthermore, declines in GDP will have very real effects on debt sustainability and the affordability of health care systems in the current institutional context. In a connected and presumably non-degrowth world, the external effects of degrowth in a single country therefore remain unclear. To conclude, it is important to outline how degrowth narratives carry their own unpredictability and environmental risks, perhaps even more than green growth. In short, bar coercion, there might just not be many alternatives besides serious attempts at achieving green growth.

REFERENCES

Acemoglu, D., P. Aghion, L. Bursztyn, and D. Hemous (2012) 'The Environment and Directed Technical Change', *American Economic Review*, 102:1, 131–66, available at http://dx.doi=10.1257/aer.102.1.131

Aghion, P., A. Dechezlepretre, D. Hemous, R. Martin, and J. Van Reenen (2016) 'Carbon Taxes, Path Dependency and Directed Technical Change: Evidence from the Auto Industry', *Journal of Political Economy*, 124:1, 1–51, available at https://doi.org/10.1086/684581

Antal, M., and J. van den Bergh (2016) 'Green Growth and Climate Change: Conceptual and Empirical Considerations', *Climate Policy*, 16:2, 165–77, available at https://doi.org/10.1080/14693062.2014.992003

Binswanger, H. (2013) *The Growth Spiral* (Berlin: Springer).

BloombergNEF (2021) 'New Energy Outlook 2021', BloombergNEF, available at https://about.bnef.com/new-energy-outlook/

Cosme, I., R. Santos, and D. O'Neill (2017) 'Assessing the Degrowth Discourse: A Review and Analysis of Academic Degrowth Policy Proposals', *Journal of Cleaner Production*, 149, 321–34, available at https://doi.org/10.1016/j.jclepro.2017.02.016

Cozzi, L., and A. Petropoulos (2021) 'Global SUV Sales Set Another Record in 2021, Setting Back Efforts to Reduce Emissions', International Energy Agency, available at www.iea.org/commentaries/global-suv-sales-set-another-record-in-2021-setting-back-efforts-to-reduce-emissions

Demaria, F., F. Schneider, F. Sekulova, and J. Martinez-Alier (2013) 'What Is Degrowth? From an Activist Slogan to a Social Movement', *Environmental Values*, 22:2, 191–215, available at https://doi.org/10.3197/096327113X13581561725194

Eastin, J., R. Grundman, and A. Prakash (2011) 'The Two Limits Debates: Limits to Growth and Climate Change', *Futures*, 43:1, 16–26, available at https://doi.org/10.1016/j.futures.2010.03.001

Ehrlich, P. (1968) *The Population Bomb* (New York: Sierra Club/Ballantine Books).

European Commission (2019) 'The European Green Deal', COM(2019) 640 final, available at https://ec.europa.eu/info/publications/communication-european-green-deal_en

(2020) 'Impact Assessment Accompanying the Document "Stepping up Europe's 2030 Climate Ambition: Investing in a Climate-Neutral Future for the Benefit of Our People"', SWD(2020) 176 final, available at https://eur-lex.europa.eu/legal-content/EN/TXT/?uri=CELEX:52020SC0176

Georgescu-Roegen, N. (1971) *The Entropy Law and the Economic Process* (Cambridge: Harvard University Press).

(1979) *Demain la décroissance: entropie-écologie-économie* (Lausanne: Pierre-Marcel Favre).

Gorz, A. (1972) *Proceedings from a Public Debate* (Paris: Nouvelle Observateur).

Hickel, J. (2020) *Less Is More: How Degrowth Will Save the World* (London: Cornerstone).

Hickel, J., and G. Kallis (2020) 'Is Green Growth Possible?', *New Political Economy*, 25:4, 469–86, available at https://doi.org/10.1080/13563467.2019.1598964

Jackson, T. (2009) *Prosperity without Growth: Economics for a Finite Planet* (London: Earthscan).

Jacobs, M. (2012) 'Green Growth: Economic Theory and Political Discourse', Grantham Research Institute on Climate Change and the Environment Working Paper No. 92.

Kallis, G. (2011) 'In Defence of Degrowth', *Ecological Economics*, 70:5, 873–80, available at https://doi.org/10.1016/j.ecolecon.2010.12.007

Kallis, G., C. Kerschner, and J. Martinez-Alier (2012) 'The Economics of Degrowth', *Ecological Economics*, 84, 172–80, available at https://doi.org/10.1016/j.ecolecon.2012.08.017

Kallis, G., V. Kostakis, S. Lange, B. Muraca, S. Paulson, and M. Schmelze (2018) 'Research on Degrowth', *Annual Review of Environment and Resources*, 43, 291–316, available at https://doi.org/10.1146/annurev-environ-102017-025941

Kamien, M., and N. Schwartz (1978) 'Optimal Exhaustible Resource Depletion with Endogenous Technical Change', *Review of Economic Studies*, 45:1, 179–96, available at https://doi.org/10.2307/2297093

Karlsson, M., E. Alfredsson, and N. Westling (2020) 'Climate Policy Co-benefits: A Review', *Climate Policy*, 20:3, 292–316, available at https://doi.org/10.1080/14693062.2020.1724070

Keysser, L., and M. Lenzen (2021) '1.5°C Degrowth Scenarios Suggest the Need for New Mitigation Pathways', *Nature Communications*, 12:2676, available at https://doi.org/10.1038/s41467-021-22884-9

Latouche, S. (2009) *Farewell to Growth* (Cambridge: Polity).

Lenaerts, K., S. Tagliapietra, and G. Wolff (2022) 'The Global Quest for Green Growth: An Economic Policy Perspective,' *Sustainability*, 14, 9.

Loehr, D. (2012) 'The Euthanasia of the Rentier – A Way toward a Steady-State Economy?', *Ecological Economics*, 84, 232–39, available at https://doi.org/10.1016/j.ecolecon.2011.11.006

Malthus, T. (1798) *An Essay on the Principle of Population* (London: J. Johnson).

Meadows, D., D. Meadows, J. Randers, and W. Behrens (1972) *The Limits to Growth* (New York: Universe Books).

OECD (2009) 'Declaration on Green Growth', OECD Legal Instruments, Organisation for Economic Cooperation and Development, available at https://legalinstruments.oecd.org/en/instruments/OECD-LEGAL-0374

(2011) *Towards Green Growth* (Paris: Organisation for Economic Cooperation and Development).

Osborn, F. (1948) *Our Plundered Planet* (New York: Little, Brown and Company).

Paech, N. (2012) *Befreiung vom Überfluss: auf dem Weg in die Postwachstumsoekonomie* (Munich: Oekom Verlag).

Raworth, K. (2017) *Doughnut Economics: Seven Ways to Think Like a 21st-Century Economist* (London: Random House).

Stern, N. (2007) *The Stern Review: The Economics of Climate Change* (Cambridge: Cambridge University Press).

Stiglitz, J. (1974) 'Growth with Exhaustible Natural Resources: Efficient and Optimal Growth Paths', *Review of Economic Studies*, 41, 123–37, available at https://doi.org/10.2307/2296377

UNEP (2011) *Towards a Green Economy. Pathways to Sustainable Development and Poverty Eradication* (Nairobi: United Nations Environment Programme).

van den Bergh, J. (2011) 'Environment versus Growth – A Criticism of "Degrowth" and a Plea for "Agrowth"', *Ecological Economics*, 70, 881–90, available at https://doi.org/10.1016/j.ecolecon.2010.09.035

van Griethuysen, P. (2012) '*Bona diagnosis, bona curatio*: How Property Economics Clarifies the Degrowth Debate', *Ecological Economics*, 84, 262–69, available at https://doi.org/10.1016/j.ecolecon.2012.02.018

Vogt, W. (1948) *Road to Survival* (New York: William Sloane Associates).

Weitzman, M. (1999) 'Pricing the Limits to Growth from Minerals Depletion', *Quarterly Journal of Economics*, 114:2, 691–706, available at https://doi .org/10.1162/003355399556025

White House (2022) 'The Build Back Better Framework. President Biden's Plan to Rebuild the Middle Class', available at www.whitehouse.gov/ build-back-better/

World Bank Group (2012) *Inclusive Green Growth. The Pathway to Sustainable Development* (Washington, DC: World Bank Group).

World Commission on Environment and Development (1987) 'Our Common Future', UN Sustainable Development Goals Knowledge Platform, United Nations, available at https://sustainabledevelopment.un.org/resources/ documents

Index

Printed in the United States
by Baker & Taylor Publisher Services